'Everything you wanted to know about teaching and have been constantly asking – you will find it all addressed within this impressive book that will be a landmark text for years to come. Through comprehensive coverage and thorough analysis of the international research on teaching, including their own foundational contributions, Day and Gu masterfully show what it takes to teach, teach well, and keep on teaching well in the face of anything and everything. This is the most expert analysis of teaching we currently have, and the most original discussion of professional resilience in the field.' – **Andy Hargreaves, Thomas More Brennan Chair in Education, Boston College, USA**

'This book is a gem. Day and Gu have drawn on a comprehensive array of studies to convincingly argue that traditional, psychological notions of teacher resilience overlook the complexity of teachers' work and lives. Their renewed analysis points to the vital importance of individual, relational and organisational factors in influencing the ways teachers develop the drive, strength and optimism to "make a difference" to the success of their students. For teachers and their leaders, this book promotes hope and optimism rather than despair, agency rather than resignation, and pro-action rather than reaction, in the face of significant challenges to teachers' resilience. This thoughtful tome is a "must read" for those charged with providing the conditions that ensure that our students have dedicated, skilled, and effective teachers in every classroom.' – **Bruce Johnson, Professor of Education, University of South Australia, Australia**

'In this pioneering study of teacher resilience, Christopher Day and Qing Gu demonstrate again why they are among the world's leading researchers today on the lives and work of teachers.' – **David T. Hansen, Weinberg Professor of the Historical and Philosophical Foundations of Education and Director of the Program in Philosophy and Education, Columbia University, USA**

'This is a landmark book. Drawing on empirical research by the authors and by others, it weaves together a scholarly emphasis on relational versions of resilience with concerns about the quality of education, teacher retention and teachers' well-being. Above all it points to what can be done in schools to nurture and sustain teachers as valued professionals. I am convinced that school leaders, researchers and teachers will keep returning to the evidence presented here.' – **Anne Edwards, Professor of Education, University of Oxford, UK**

'This book makes a significant contribution to our understanding of the complexities of teachers' work and their lives in schools. It examines and develops the concept of teacher resilience and how the complex interplay between education policy, and the social, cultural and intellectual environments in which teachers work shapes how they manage their personal and professional lives. The concept of "everyday resilience" is woven through the book through examples of teachers' personal narratives. These authentic voices of teachers give the book a vitality and authenticity.

Day and Gu demonstrate the significance of community among teachers and the importance of mutual care and support to sustain their passion and commitment for teaching. The development of a shared set of values and moral purpose reinforces teachers' commitment to their role, which the authors argue needs to be nurtured and sustained. The data presented in the book helps us to hear, feel and experience the struggles teachers experience in their multifaceted lives in and outside of classrooms.

This is an important and timely book, it should be read by teachers, policy makers and students.' – **Judyth Sachs, Professor and Deputy Vice Chancellor, Provost, Macquarie University, Australia**

Resilient Teachers, Resilient Schools

This book unpicks the complex, dynamic interaction between the psychological and professional assets, workplace conditions and leadership support, which enable teachers who stay in teaching to continue to make a difference in their careers, regardless of shifts in policy, workplace, professional and personal circumstances.

While much has been written over the years about teacher stress and burnout, there is very little research that reports on the conditions that are essential for teachers to sustain their commitment and effectiveness over their professional lives, in contexts of challenge and change. Drawing upon a range of educational, psychological, socio-cultural and neuro-scientific research, together with vivid accounts from teachers in a variety of primary and secondary schools internationally, and from their own research on teachers' work, lives and identities, the authors discuss the dynamic nature, forms and practices of teacher resilience. They argue that resilience in teachers is not only their ability to bounce back in extremely adverse circumstances but also their capacity for everyday resilience, enabling them to sustain the commitment and effectiveness needed to respond positively to the unavoidable uncertainties inherent in their professional lives.

The authors conclude that resilience in teachers can be nurtured by the intellectual, social and organisational environments in which they work and live, rather than being simply a personal attribute or trait determined by nature or past experience. *Resilient Teachers, Resilient Schools* will be of key interest to policy makers, head teachers, teachers, and training and development organisations who wish to improve quality and standards in schools.

Christopher Day is Professor of Education at the University of Nottingham, UK

Qing Gu is Associate Professor at the Centre for Research in Schools and Communities in the School of Education, University of Nottingham, UK.

Teacher Quality and School Development Series
Series Editors: Christopher Day and Ann Lieberman

Resilient Teachers, Resilient Schools

Building and sustaining quality in testing times

Christopher Day and Qing Gu

Routledge
Taylor & Francis Group
LONDON AND NEW YORK

First published 2014
by Routledge
2 Park Square, Milton Park, Abingdon, Oxon OX14 4RN

and by Routledge
711 Third Avenue, New York, NY 10017

Routledge is an imprint of the Taylor & Francis Group, an informa business.

British Library Cataloguing in Publication Data
A catalogue record for this book is available from the British Library

Library of Congress Cataloging in Publication Data
A catalog record for this book has been requested

ISBN: 978-0-415-81893-3 (hbk)
ISBN: 978-0-415-81895-7 (pbk)
ISBN: 978-0-203-57849-0 (ebk)

Typeset in Galliard
by Saxon Graphics Ltd, Derby

Printed and bound in Great Britain by
TJ International Ltd, Padstow, Cornwall

We dedicate this book to all those teachers whose capacity for everyday resilience throughout their careers enables them, regardless of circumstance, to continue to build on their knowledge of those they teach and the subject they are teaching, in order to apply this knowledge to an appropriate range of classroom practices and make a difference to the learning and achievement of every one of their students ... and to those who seek to understand what helps and what hinders them from doing so.

Contents

Foreword

There is perhaps no greater phrase in education that is as popular and prevalent as the idea that 'teacher quality' is the key to good schools. But how do we define it? What does it mean? What does it look like? How do people become resilient and highly qualified in the face of all the changes that teachers are being asked to make? *Resilient Teachers, Resilient Schools: Building and sustaining quality in testing times* takes on these ideas in a brilliant discussion of the complexity and depth of what it means to be a resilient teacher of quality.

Drawing on international research and many illustrations from practice, Day and Gu engage us in an important discussion of the connections between teachers as individuals, their relationships (both personal and professional), and the organisational conditions in which they work. As we read we build the understanding of how teachers who are resilient over time become teachers of quality.

We first look at the empirical findings of how researchers the world over have looked at resilience and what it means. They found that:

- Many teachers *learn* to have a positive response to adversity.
- Teachers *learn* how to become resilient over time.
- When teachers feel competent and are supported in their workplace, resilience can be built.

The capacity to become resilient comes to many people as they learn to become problem solvers, develop a strong sense of purpose and feel socially competent. But this, we learn, is dependent on individual circumstances influenced by the environment. I found myself constructing my own growth as an elementary teacher even though it was many years ago. As a first-year teacher I had 46 students in the sixth grade. As if that wasn't enough, modern mathematics had just been introduced and it was the beginning of an era of individualised reading. I was in a new school with a new principal in Simi Valley, a new suburb of Los Angeles. Although this may not be typical, our well-being as teachers was clearly because our principal was sensitive, smart and supportive. But equally important was the group of teachers who all drove together the 30 miles to our school. Although I struggled through the first year, I felt supported by peers, principal and family and that, along with the enthusiastic sixth-graders, kept me going. For me the positive influences of the social environment and my own small wins that first year made me confident enough that I was learning to be a teacher!

The authors point out that the pressure to get student results, the rise of external accountability and an increased workload has worked away at teacher's resilience. To teach demands 'everyday resilience' but these current demands pressure teachers' sense of their own professional identity and often change the nature of the school culture. Everyday resilience diminishes as teachers lose their sense of why they became teachers in the first place. As the authors put it: 'External job demands and social mediation interact to build or reduce self-efficacy, job fulfillment and capacity to be resilient.'

A very strong case is made in learning that teachers need nurturance, just like their students, and they need to feel cared for as teaching is so demanding. Although students and their learning are at the centre of a teacher's life, the teacher is very sensitive to policy influences, workplace relationships, and her own sense of moral purpose and sense of agency.

Those who stay in teaching learn to get through tough situations and not take them personally. Those who leave teaching tend to respond more personally to the challenges that the new demands seem to require and it nicks away at their professional sense of self. They become detached from their sense of mission and hence from teaching in general.

But teachers change over time. Again, the authors document what we know from research about teaching over the career. If the culture of the school is supportive and professional learning continues, there is a greater chance that teachers will stay in teaching. But if there are repeated attacks on one's sense of self and teachers feel vulnerable to changing circumstances, rather than supported, resilience declines and teachers lose their motivation and effectiveness.

Like other professions, we learn that career advancement is critical as it enhances the work, ups the ante on increased expectations, and encourages teachers to use their growing understandings about students, subject matter content and learning.

Conditions in one's school are critical for teachers. When teachers feel supported and encouraged by their colleagues, and when there are opportunities to work together, teachers gain the resilience they need to continue learning, stay motivated, and satisfied with their work as teachers.

Leadership is critical to good working conditions, we learn, as it is principals who can set the climate, encourage community, and invest in teachers as individuals. Job fulfillment reduces some of the stress that teachers feel and principals can help in the way they connect to teachers and how they build a collaborative culture. In these school cultures teachers are more positive, come to trust one another and build optimism among their colleagues, despite the demands that are being made that often narrow a view of teaching by teaching to the test.

The authors build a marvelous case for why we must work for resilience in teaching, not just because it is an important thing to do but because it has much to do with supporting teachers of quality. Documenting research and examples from practice, they make a substantial case for resilience because it keeps teachers' commitment to teaching well, supports teachers' professional identity and builds a quality teaching force. That is what it will take to meet the challenges of a changing society!

Ann Lieberman, Senior Scholar at Stanford University

Introduction

We begin this book by considering the learning entitlements of every student in every school in every country of the world. We believe that each one has an entitlement not only to the provision of educational opportunities, but also to be taught by teachers who, as well as being knowledgeable about curriculum and pedagogically adept, are constant and persistent in their commitment to encouraging their students to learn and achieve, regardless of the students' own motivation and existing knowledge or ability; and who are themselves demonstrably passionate about their own learning. In one sense, these are self-evident truths about the core task of every teacher to engage students in learning which will assist them in their personal, social and intellectual development. In another sense, however, the ambitions which are embedded in these truths will not always be easy to achieve consistently over a 30-year career span.

Students are not only entitled to the best teaching. They are also entitled to be taught by teachers who are well led. School leaders, especially principals, play a key role in successfully steering their schools through changing social and policy landscapes; in providing optimal conditions, structures and cultures for learning and teaching; in enabling teachers to respond positively to the unavoidable uncertainties inherent in their everyday professional lives; and through this, to sustain their commitment, well-being and effectiveness in making a difference to the learning, achievement and life chances of children and young people. It is these, together with the nuanced and dynamic interactions between personal, workplace, socio-cultural and policy environments, which support and enable those who stay in teaching to continue to teach to their best and which sustain them in doing so. As students in successful schools have told us, their teachers and principals are not there for the money. They are there because they 'care about us'. It is strong leadership and a collective as well as individual sense of moral purpose and ethic of care that make these schools resilient and effective.

Yet as the social glue of societies and many families begins to thin outside the school, accounts also continue to emerge of the disenchantment and alienation of many students and of tired teachers within schools for whom learning has become a chore and for whom teaching has become 'just a job'. Much research on teachers' work and lives notes with alarming regularity in many countries, the lowering of teacher morale, rises in stress, presenteeism and, in its extreme form, burnout. Themes of 'teacher attrition' and 'stress' continue to dominate the educational research literature and remain a regular feature of surveys on teacher morale and well-being nationally and internationally. Alongside this, the 'knock-on effect' of high teacher turnover and dropout rates on the achievement of pupils, particularly for those in high poverty communities where these tend to be high, has led policy makers and teachers' associations to become increasingly concerned with problems, not only in retaining teachers, but also retaining teachers of commitment and quality.

Policies for retention have been framed predominantly around teachers in their early years of teaching, since this is where most attrition seems to occur. However, at a time when the age profile of teachers in the UK, the USA and many other countries is skewed towards those with more than 20 years' experience and in which they are expected to comply with successive and persistent policy reforms, changing curricula and demographic school environments, there is an urgent need, also, to investigate further the ways in which the resilience of the existing majority of the more experienced teachers may be sustained and renewed so that they are able to fulfil effectively the demands of teaching to their best in the twenty-first century.

Teachers' work is carried out in an era of testing times where the policy focus in many countries has shifted from provision and process to outcomes (OECD, 2012a). The OECD's Programme for International Student Assessment (PISA), for example, is having an unprecedented influence on national policies for improvement and standards across many nation states. The rapidly growing international interest in 'surpassing Shanghai' and outperforming the world's leading systems (Tucker, 2011) has contributed to intensify further national and international emphases upon standards, performativity and accountability. For many schools in many countries, this means that their educational values and practices, particularly in relation to the progress and achievement of their students, are now under increased public scrutiny. At the same time, widespread movement of population in many countries has seen the makeup of the local communities which schools serve become more diversified (OECD, 2010). Coupled with this change in student populations are the broader, more explicitly articulated social and societal responsibilities that schools are expected to have in supporting their communities, other schools and other public services (OECD, 2008). In many countries, also, schools are expected to manage a concurrent movement towards the decentralisation of financial management and quality control functions to schools (Ball, 2000, 2003; Baker and LeTendre, 2005; OECD, 2008, 2010). Thus, to be successful in these testing times, teachers, schools and school leaders need to be forward thinking, outward looking, optimistic, hopeful and above all, resilient.

This book will examine what it is that enables teachers and schools to sustain the quality of their passion and commitment through good times and bad and what might prevent them from doing so. Drawing upon international research and using rich illustrations from practising teachers in different professional life phases in a range of schools, it will examine the complex, individual, relational and organisational conditions and interactions which influence their motivation and ability to be resilient. We will associate resilience with **the persistence of hope and endeavour** among teachers to do their best to reach and engage every student in learning which will benefit them, regardless of the challenges which this may bring. We will do so in the knowledge that resilience is not simply an individual trait, developed or not developed only through the childhood experiences of individuals. Of course, individuals' ability to be resilient will vary at given times and in particular sets of circumstances; and individuals will manage these in different ways. However, the capacity to be resilient is almost certain to fluctuate over the course of a career. The extent to which individual teachers are able to exercise their capacity to be resilient will depend not only upon their individual histories and their inner sense of motivation and commitment, but also upon the influence of the school environment, their colleagues and the quality of their school leadership. We will, therefore, locate our examination of resilience in the **policy, social, cultural and intellectual environments** in which teachers' work and lives are embedded.

The book will synthesise key research in education and other disciplines about resilience. Recent advances in positive psychology and neuroscience, for example, have provided important contributions which have enabled researchers in education to reconceptualise the deficit problems of stress, attrition and presenteeism as a positive need for resilience. They have found that resilience is not a fixed psychological trait but a dynamic capacity which can be influenced by socio-cultural factors, and that the capacity for resilience may grow or become eroded by these. Thus, 'the qualities teachers bring with them to their work are not always enough to ensure better teaching practices' (Kennedy, 2010: 591). Like Kennedy, we make a distinction between *teacher quality* and *teaching quality*, since it is not only who teachers are that counts, but also what they do in the classroom. The chapters in the book will also draw upon empirical research conducted by the authors and their colleagues to provide rich illustrations of different scenarios or sites of struggle in which teachers and leaders in different career phases and in different schools are able to retain their capacity to be resilient.

We will argue in this book that being a resilient teacher goes beyond mere survival on an everyday basis. Teaching to their best across a career span of 30 years or more requires that teachers are able to exercise what we call the '**everyday resilience**' that classroom conditions inherently demand. Resilience in this sense is more than the willingness and capacity to bounce back in adverse circumstances. So far as we are aware, the book will be the first of its kind to provide a comprehensive overview of research and practice-informed new knowledge about the nature of teacher resilience, how it may be nurtured in context and why it matters for the improvement of quality and standards in schools. Despite the likely associations between self-efficacy, well-being, commitment, emotional energy, resilience and standards of teaching and learning, there have been few empirical studies which have focused upon understanding why, for some teachers, teaching becomes just a job whilst for others it remains a passionate calling; and how workplace contexts as well as personal dispositions influence teacher resilience trajectories.

This book is also about school leaders who, often against the odds, manage to meet and overcome the challenges of persistent policy reforms and shifting teaching and learning contexts and who courageously create and build organisational and relational conditions which enable teachers to develop their capacities for their students' achievement and success. It is our hope that its contents will provide an informed and productive approach, not only to issues of attracting, developing and sustaining teacher quality and commitment but also to establishing the kinds of conditions which enable and encourage teachers to teach to their best throughout their careers in changing personal, professional, school, social and policy contexts. Rather than continuing to focus upon stress, we believe that we should seek to understand what schools, teachers themselves and policy organisations can do to build teachers' capacities to be resilient, so that the demands of teaching can be well led and managed and pupils' entitlements to be taught by highly knowledgeable, committed and enthusiastic individuals achieved.

Part I
The nature of teacher resilience

1 The nature of resilience
Interdisciplinary research perspectives

In this chapter, we will report a range of research informed studies which plot the path towards new understandings of the nature of resilience in teachers. Advances in research in psychology, positive psychology, neurology, business and organisational studies and other disciplines will provide important conceptual bases for our discussion on resilience in the workplace as a psychological and socio-cultural phenomenon which is best understood as a dynamic process within a social system of inter-relationships. Recent research in education will contribute further to our nuanced conceptualisation of the dynamic and relational nature of resilience in teachers. The chapter will show that teachers' capacity to be resilient in adverse circumstances and to maintain what we call 'everyday resilience' is influenced by and associated with their psychological, emotional, behavioural and cognitive (academically or professionally) functioning within a range of personal, relational and organisational settings. It is not, therefore, an innate, fixed quality but shaped and cultivated by the social, cultural and intellectual settings in which teachers work and live. The chapter will also show that resilience is not a quality that is reserved for *the heroic few*. Rather, it can be shared by many ordinary teachers who remain extraordinarily committed to serving the learning and achievement of the children on an everyday basis and also over the course of their professional lives.

Resilience: advances in understandings

Advances in understandings of the nature of resilience in other disciplines provide an important conceptual contribution to our analysis of teachers' self-reported perceptions of their resilience. This research generally suggests that resilience itself is an unstable construct (Rutter, 1990; Cicchetti, 1993; Masten *et al.*, 1999) involving psychological, behavioural and cognitive (academically or professionally) functioning as well as emotional regulation (Greenberg, 2006; Luthar and Brown, 2007) within a range of personal, relational and organisational settings.

The notion of resilience originated in the disciplines of psychiatry and developmental psychology as a result of a burgeoning attention to personal characteristics or traits that enabled some children, although having been classified as being at risk of having negative life outcomes, to adapt positively and thrive

(Howard *et al.*, 1999; Waller, 2001). From a chronological perspective, the decade of the 1980s marked a paradigmatic change to the concept of resilience, from one which focused upon understanding the pain, struggle and suffering involved in the adaptation process in the face of adversity, to one which focused more on understanding positive qualities and strengths (Gore and Eckenrode, 1994; Henderson and Milstein, 2003). Over the last two decades, the focus of resilience research in the disciplines of social and behavioural sciences has developed from identifying personal traits and protective factors to investigating underlying protective processes, i.e. how such factors may contribute to positive outcomes (Luthar *et al.*, 2000). However, despite this progress in focus, Howard *et al.* (1999) and Luthar *et al.* (2000) maintain that research in the area of resilience will be seriously constrained if a theoretical basis for resilience continues to be missing from most studies. Since the turn of this century, ground-breaking advances in biology research have provided powerful, additional evidence of the robust effects of early caregiving environments and, thus, promising and compelling arguments for the kinds of interventions which are likely to make a difference to children's life trajectories (Luthar and Brown, 2007; see also Curtis and Cicchetti, 2003; Cicchetti and Valentino, 2006).

Despite this diversity in approaches to researching resilience, a critical overview of empirical findings from different disciplines over time suggests that there are shared core considerations in the way resilience is conceptualised between disciplines. First and foremost, much previous research on resilience presupposes the presence of threat to the status quo, a positive response to conditions of significant adversity (Masten and Garmezy, 1985; Masten *et al.*, 1999; Cicchetti and Garmezy, 1993; Luthar *et al.*, 2000). Secondly, it suggests that resilience is not a quality that is innate or fixed. Rather, it can be learned and acquired (Higgins, 1994). Associated with this is the third consideration that the personal characteristics, competences and positive influences of the social environment in which the individual works and lives, independently and together, interact to contribute to the process of resilience building (Gordon *et al.*, 2000; Rutter, 2006; Zucker, 2006). Indeed, Luthar *et al.* (2000) assert that the term 'resilience' should always be used when referring to a dynamic 'process or phenomenon of competence' which encompasses 'positive adaptation within the context of significant adversity' (2000: 554).

The nature of resilience

1. Resilience as a psychological construct

Fredrickson's recent development of a 'broaden-and-build' theory of positive emotions (2001, 2004) provides a useful psychological conceptual framework. She observes that a subset of positive emotions – joy, interest, contentment and love – promote discovery of novel actions and social bonds, which serve to build individuals' personal resources (Fredrickson, 2004). These personal resources, ranging from physical and intellectual resources to social and psychological resources, 'function as reserves that can be drawn on later to improve the odds of successful coping and survival' (Fredrickson, 2004: 1367). In other words, positive emotions fuel psychological resilience:

> Evidence suggests, then, that positive emotions may fuel individual differences in resilience. Noting that psychological resilience is an enduring personal resource, the broaden-and-build theory makes the bolder prediction that experiences of positive emotions might also, over time, build psychological resilience, not just reflect it. That is, to the extent that positive emotions broaden the scopes of attention and cognition, enabling flexible and creative thinking, they should also augment people's enduring coping resources (Isen, 1990; Aspinwall, 1998, 2001; Fredrickson and Joiner, 2002).
>
> (Fredrickson, 2004: 1372)

Most importantly, she suggests that 'the personal resources accrued during states of positive emotions are durable, (outlasting) the transient emotional states that led to their acquisition', and that 'through experiences of positive emotions ... people transform themselves, becoming more creative, knowledgeable, resilient, socially integrated and healthy individuals' (2004: 1369).

Fredrickson's broaden-and-build theory of positive emotions, from a psychological perspective, provides an important contribution to the establishment of a conceptual basis for understanding the resilient qualities of teachers who are doing a job that is itself not only intellectual but also emotional in nature; and it mirrors the work of a range of educational researchers on the nature of teaching (Palmer, 1998; Nias, 1989, 1999; Fried, 2001). Hargreaves (1998: 835), for example, suggests that emotions are at the heart of teaching:

> Good teaching is charged with positive emotions. It is not just a matter of knowing one's subject, being efficient, having the correct competences, or learning all the right techniques. Good teachers are not just well-oiled machines. They are emotional, passionate beings who connect with their students and fill their work and their classes with pleasure, creativity, challenge and joy.

In her study of American high school teachers Nieto also found that what had kept teachers going in the profession was 'emotional stuff' (2003: 122). She describes teaching as an intellectual endeavour which involves love, anger and depression, and hope and possibility. Nieto (2003) argues that in the contemporary contexts for teaching, a learning community is an important incentive that keeps teachers going (we develop this theme in Chapter 6). In pursuit of learning in 'communities of practice' (Wenger, 1998), teachers will consolidate a sense of belonging and shared responsibility, enhance morale and perceived efficacy, develop aspects of resilient qualities, and thrive and flourish socially and professionally. More importantly, their resilient qualities do not merely serve their positive developmental progression. They also interact with negative influences and constraints and, together with teachers' professional qualities, may develop in strength. Large-scale research into variations in the lives, work and effectiveness of primary and secondary teachers in a range of schools in England (Day *et al.*, 2007a) also observed that in the emotional context of teaching, pupils' progress and growth constantly fuelled teachers' job satisfaction and motivation, but that this was mediated positively or negatively by a number of factors which affected their capacities to rebound from disappointments and adversity and sustain their commitment to the profession, and with this, their effectiveness.

2. Resilience: a multidimensional, socially constructed concept

While the concept of resilience elaborated in the discipline of psychology helps clarify the internal factors and personal characteristics of trait-resilient people, the notion of resilience which takes into account the social and cultural contexts of individuals' work and lives advances a perspective that views resilience as multidimensional and is best understood as a dynamic within a social system of inter-relationships (Walsh, 1998; also Richardson *et al.*, 1990; Benard, 1991, 1995; Gordon, 1995; Luthar *et al.*, 2000; Henderson and Milstein, 2003).

Thus, we may all be born with a biological or early life experience basis for resilient capacity, 'by which we are able to develop social competence, problem-solving skills, a critical consciousness, autonomy, and a sense of purpose' (Benard, 1995: 1). However, the capacity to be resilient in different negative circumstances, whether or not these are connected to personal or professional factors, can be enhanced or inhibited by the nature of the settings in which we work, the people with whom we work and the strength of our beliefs or aspirations (Benard, 1991; Luthar, 1996; Henderson and Milstein, 2003; Oswald *et al.*, 2003, Day *et al.*, 2006).

Luthar (1996) distinguishes between ego-resiliency and resilience, which also calls attention to the dynamic and multi-dimensional nature of resilient qualities. She argues that the former is a personality characteristic of the individual and does not presuppose exposure to substantial adversity, whereas the latter is a dynamic developmental process and does presuppose exposure to significantly negative conditions (see also Luthar *et al.*, 2000). This distinction implies that resilient qualities can be learned or acquired (Higgins, 1994) and achieved through providing relevant and practical protective factors, such as caring and attentive educational settings, high expectations, positive learning environments, a strong social community, and supportive peer relationships (Glasser, 1965; Rutter *et al.*, 1979; Werner and Smith, 1988; Benard, 1991, 1995; Wang, 1997; Pence, 1998; Johnson *et al.*, 1999; Oswald *et al.*, 2003). In accordance with this distinction, Masten (1994) cautions against the use of 'resiliency' which carries the misleading connotation of a discrete personality trait, recommending that 'resilience' be used 'exclusively when referring to the maintenance of positive adjustment under challenging life conditions' (cited in Luthar *et al.*, 2000: 546).

Thus, there is a considerable body of research in which resilience is acknowledged to be a relative, multidimensional and developmental construct (Rutter, 1990; Howard *et al.*, 1999; Luthar *et al.*, 2000). It is a phenomenon which is influenced by individual circumstance, situation and environment and thus involves far more complex components than specific personal accounts of internal traits or assets alone claim. It is not a static state because 'there is no question that all individuals – resilient or otherwise – show fluctuations over time within particular adjustment domains' (Luthar *et al.*, 2000: 551). This is particularly relevant to understandings of resilience among adults over their work and life span.

Teacher resilience: a relational concept

Historically, advances in understandings about resilience have, as we have noted, been built primarily upon research on children. The empirical work on adults is still in its infancy. Emerging evidence, however, reaffirms that resilience in adults, like that in children, is not associated with personal attributes only (Luthar and Brown, 2007). Rather, it is 'a social construction' (Ungar, 2004: 342) influenced by multidimensional factors that are unique to each context (Ungar, 2004). In his work on cognitive-behaviour approaches to resilience, Neenan (2009) adds that it is not a quality that is reserved for 'an extraordinary few'; it can be learned and achieved by the 'ordinary many' (Neenan, 2009: 7). He advocates the concept of 'routine resilience' to emphasise that resilience comprises cognitive, behavioural and emotional responses to the vicissitudes of daily life. Through an 'active process of self-righting and growth' (Higgins, 1994: 1), it enables individuals to move forward towards their goals and pursue what is perceived to be important to them, 'however slowly or falteringly' (Neenan, 2009: 17). He argues that 'attitude (meaning) is the heart of resilience' (2009: 17).

Drawing upon observations of resilience research in different disciplines, and our own research (Gu and Day, 2007, 2013; Gu and Li, 2013; Gu, in press) we find that teacher resilience has three distinctive characteristics:

1   It is *context specific* in that teachers' resilient qualities are best understood by taking in not only 'the more proximal individual school or classroom context', but also 'the broader professional work context' (Beltman *et al.*, 2011: 190; see also Mansfield *et al.*, 2012). There is abundant evidence in the educational literature which shows that in-school management support for their learning and development, leadership trust and positive feedback from parents and pupils are key positive influences on teachers' motivation and resilience (e.g. Huberman, 1993; Webb *et al.*, 2004; Brunetti, 2006; Leithwood *et al.*, 2006a; Day *et al.*, 2007; Castro *et al.*, 2010; Meister and Ahrens, 2011). Empirical evidence on how successful principals mediate the negative influences of macro-level policy contexts and meso-level external school intake contexts and through this create positive school cultures which nurture teachers' capacity for learning and development is also strong (Leithwood *et*

al., 2006a; Day and Leithwood, 2007; Gu *et al.*, 2008; Robinson *et al.*, 2009; Leithwood *et al.*, 2010; Sammons *et al.*, 2011; Gu and Johansson, in press). For early career teachers in particular, recognition and support of strong school leadership were found in our VITAE research in England (Day *et al.*, 2006, 2007a) to have played a central role in facilitating their professional socialisation into school communities, developing their sense of professional self and sustaining their motivation, commitment and positive trajectories in the school and/or profession (Day and Gu, 2010). The research looked into variations in the work and lives of 300 teachers in different phases of their professional lives in 100 primary and secondary schools over a four-year period. For many new teachers in the VITAE research who were yet to develop their professional identity as a teacher, the way that their schools were often shaped their perceptions of what the reality of teaching was like and also whether their journey into the profession was likely to have 'easy' or 'painful' beginnings.

2   Teacher resilience is also *role specific* in that it is closely associated with the strength and conviction of teachers' vocational commitment; and it is this inner calling to teach and commitment to serve which distinguishes teaching from many other jobs and occupations (Hansen, 1995). In his research on teachers working in inner-city high schools in the United States, Brunetti (2006) defined teacher resilience as 'a quality that enables teachers to maintain their commitment to teaching and teaching practices despite challenging conditions and recurring setbacks' (2006: 813). Moral purposes and ethical values are found to provide important intellectual, emotional and spiritual strengths which enable teachers to be resilient over the course of their careers (Day, 2004; OECD, 2005b; Palmer, 2007; Gu and Day, 2013). Over time, research has also consistently found that teachers' self-efficacy beliefs as to whether they have the capacity to effectively help children learn and achieve are among the most important factors influencing teachers' resilient qualities (Kitching *et al.*, 2009; Morgan *et al.*, 2010; Hong, 2012). In this sense, resilient teachers are not survivors in the profession, because they 'do more than merely get through difficult emotional experiences, hanging on to inner equilibrium by a thread' (Higgins, 1994: 1; see also Gu and Li, 2013). Rather, they display capacity for growth and fulfilment in pursuit of personally and professionally meaningful goals which, as research on teachers and teaching tells us, 'joins self and subject and students in the fabric of life' and connects their 'intellect and emotion and spirit' in their *hearts* (Palmer, 2007: 11).

3   We have learned from teachers themselves that being resilient means *more than 'bouncing back'* quickly and efficiently from difficulties. In addition to the routine pressures and unavoidable uncertainties which feature in many teachers' everyday work and lives (thus the need for 'everyday resilience'), they also face challenges that are specific to their professional life phases. Empirical evidence from Gu and Li's study of 568 primary and secondary school teachers in Beijing, for example, shows that although the scenarios

that challenge them in each phase of their professional and personal lives may be different in nature, the intensity of the physical, emotional and intellectual energy required to manage them may be very similar (Gu and Li, 2103). Given this, it is clear that teachers' ability to be resilient

> is not primarily associated with the capacity to 'bounce back' or recover from highly traumatic experiences and events but, rather, the capacity to maintain equilibrium and a sense of commitment and agency in the everyday worlds in which teachers teach.
>
> (Gu and Day, 2013: 26)

Relational resilience

Teachers' worlds are organised around distinct sets of role relationships: 'teachers with students, teachers with other teachers, teachers with parents and with their school principal' (Bryk and Schneider, 2002: 20). There is strong and consistent evidence from educational research which suggests that the social organisation of the school – when characterised by supportive, trusting and collegial relationships between different stakeholders – fosters teachers' collective capacity, commitment and effectiveness (Bryk and Schneider, 2002; Tschannen-Moran and Barr, 2004; Sammons *et al.*, 2007; Day and Gu, 2010). However, as yet, how such relational resilience influences teachers has not been sufficiently investigated.

Empirical evidence from neuroscience and psychology foregrounds the role of relationships in building and developing resilience in adverse and everyday circumstances. Neuroscientists' discovery of the social brain reveals that 'we are wired to connect' (Goleman, 2006: 4) and provides a biological basis for understanding the importance of good quality relationships in maintaining a sense of positive identity, well-being and effectiveness in our daily work and lives. Goodwin (2005), writing from a psychological perspective, maintains that 'close relationships act as important "social glue", helping people deal with the uncertainties of their changing world' (2005: 615, cited in Edwards, 2007: 8). In positive psychology, particular attention has been given to the importance of relationship-based assets and their contribution to resilience (Masten, 2001; Gorman, 2005; Luthans *et al.*, 2007). Luthar (2006) too argues that '[r]esilience rests, fundamentally, on relationships' (2006: 780).

> Relationships lie at the 'roots' of resilience: when everyday relationships reflect ongoing abuse, rancor, and insecurity, this profoundly threatens resilience as well as the personal attributes that might otherwise have fostered it. Conversely, the presence of support, love, and security fosters resilience in part, by reinforcing people's innate strengths (such as self-efficacy, positive emotions and emotion regulation) with these personal attributes measured biologically and/or behaviourally.
>
> (Luthar and Brown, 2007: 947)

As yet, however, most psychological studies of resilience have been slow to move away from a 'separate self' model of development (Jordan, 2004), which tends to continue to imply that resilience resides largely within the person (Luthar and Brown, 2007). Relationships are seen as an external, 'given' asset, resource or protective factor which has a substantive influence on individuals' personal attributes and through this, the development of their well-being, self-efficacy and resilient qualities (Engh *et al.*, 2006; Luthar, 2006; Taylor, 2007). The emphasis on the benefits of relationships is thus placed upon the individual who is in need of support; and the focus of investigation tends to be narrowed down in a 'one-directional way from the point of the view of the individual looking for support from another individual or group' (Jordan, 1992: 1). The underlying problem of this approach is that it fails to address fully the role of individual agency and capacity in maintaining connection and/or forming reconnection with secure, trusting and enduring attachments to others.

In contrast to the 'traditional' definition of resilience, Jordan (1992, 2004, 2006, 2012) has proposed a model of relational resilience to emphasise that 'resilience should be seen as a relational dynamic' (1992: 1). She argues that 'resilience resides not in the individual but in the capacity for connection' (2012: 73). A toxic cultural system which denies the importance of connection for growth is detrimental in two inter-related ways: on the one hand, it devalues our need for others and impedes our ability to turn to them for support in distress (Jordan, 2010); on the other hand, it challenges 'our capacity to form supportive and resilience building relationships' (Jordan, 2012: 74). Drawing upon recent discoveries in neuroscience studies, Jordan (2012) argues that despite the pressures in dysfunctional cultures which block the natural flow of disconnection-connection, our brains' robust ability to change can enable people to rework back into healthy connections, achieve more secure attachment and through this 'begin to shift underlying patterns of isolation and immobilization' (2012: 74). Therefore, for Jordan, being resilient does not necessarily mean 'bouncing back' to a previously existing state; rather, it entails 'movement through and beyond stress or suffering into a new and more comprehensive personal and relational integration' (Jordan 1992: 1). Mutual empathetic involvement, empowerment and efforts to discover a path back to connection are at the core of this movement; and personal transformation (i.e. positive and creative growth) and social change which promote greater connection and mutually enhanced relationships and growth are the ultimate consequences (Jordan, 2004).

Jordan's relational model of resilience resonates powerfully with the conceptualisation of caring and trusting relationships in the educational literature, especially in relation to the ways in which they influence teachers' sense of commitment, resilience and effectiveness. Noddings (2005) argues that a caring relation is, 'in its most basic form, a connection or encounter between two human beings – a carer and a recipient of care, or cared for' (2005: 15). Solomon and Flores's (2001) work on trust adds to her argument in emphasising that a trusting relationship is 'cultivated', 'a matter of human effort' and thus 'never something "already at hand"': 'it can and often must be conscientiously created, not simply taken for granted' (2001: 87). By extension, once trusting and open professional relationships have been created, nurtured and developed within the school gates and beyond, they may function as *'bonding social capital'* which, as research shows, not only facilitates coordinated actions between individuals, but also allows people to pursue their goals, and serves to bind the organisation together and through this, improve its efficiency (Putnam, 1993; Field, 2008; Hargreaves and Fullan, 2012). For teachers, social relationships and networks in and between workplaces bring intellectual, spiritual and emotional resources which they can use to enhance their collective efficacy and shared beliefs of professional control, influence and responsibility and, ultimately, improve the achievement of their students (Goddard, 2002; Goddard *et al.*, 2004; Mawhinney et al., 2005).

The conceptual strengths of using the relational model of resilience to examine teachers' work and lives are threefold. First and foremost, the model acknowledges the relational nature of teachers' professional worlds and the important role of supportive relationships in sustaining their sense of well-being and commitment in the profession. Second, by placing relationships at the centre of teachers' work and lives, it acknowledges that a collective sense of collegiality, efficacy and effectiveness is an outcome of their joint, collaborative efforts which connect them intellectually, emotionally and spiritually and which, at the same time, enable the seeds of deeper trusting and caring relationships to grow and flourish among them. Last but not least, it reminds us that the role of school leaders in creating favourable organisational structures and conditions which nourish collaborative efforts for learning is of paramount importance for teachers to achieve a sense of fulfilment and success with their students.

Conclusions

We conclude, therefore, that resilience is not a quality that is innate. Rather, it is a construct that is relative, developmental and dynamic, emphasising the positive adaptation and development of individuals in the presence of challenging circumstances (Rutter, 1990; Howard *et al.*, 1999, Luthar *et al.*, 2000). It is both a product of personal and professional dispositions and values and socially constructed. It encompasses a sense of purpose and entails meaningful actions and participation. In addition, it develops along with and manifests itself as a result of a dynamic process within a given context. The social dimension of teacher resilience recognises the interactive impact of personal, professional and situated factors on teachers' work and lives and contextualises teachers' endeavours to sustain their professional commitment.

An individual may demonstrate resilience in a certain context and/or in a certain professional/life phase, but fail to display similar qualities when time or space changes. Personal lives and working contexts may become unstable (e.g. failing health and classroom behaviour problems) in unpredictable ways. However, whether the sudden changes are perceived as adverse conditions by the individual may vary depending on his/her scope of experience at the time of change, perceived competence and confidence in managing the emerging conditions, views on the meaning of engagement, and the availability of appropriate support within the context of change.

For teachers whose everyday professional worlds are inherently characterised by uncertain and unpredictable circumstances and scenarios, to be able to maintain their commitment to teaching and focus upon high quality teaching practices means more than recovering quickly and efficiently from difficulties. In this 'everyday' sense, resilience is not a rare quality that is reserved for the heroic few. Over the last decade, although statistics continue to suggest that teaching is one of the most stressful professions in the twenty-first century (HSE, 2000, 2011; PricewaterhouseCoopers, 2001; Nash, 2005) and that it has experienced relatively higher turnover compared to many other professions (Ingersoll, 2003; Ingersoll and Perda, 2011), there is also consistent evidence which shows that many teachers in the profession have managed to weather the often unpredictable 'storm' of school and classroom life (Patterson and Kelleher, 2005) and sustain their commitment to make a difference to the learning lives of their students over a professional life span (e.g. OECD, 2005b; Day *et al.*, 2007a). In this 'over time' sense, resilience is not a quality that is fixed.

Teachers in different phases of their professional lives are likely to face distinctively different influences, tensions, professional and personal concerns (Day and Gu, 2010). Although the ways in which they build and sustain their vocation, commitment and resilience are complex and continuous, their capacity to do so may also fluctuate depending upon the effects of a combination of workplace-based and personal influences and also their cognitive and emotional capacities to manage these influences. In analysing what kept 73 per cent of the 300 VITAE teachers committed in the profession (Day *et al.*, 2007a), resilience emerged as an intellectually and emotionally important concept which brought us to the heart of the quality retention issue. By linking the concept of resilience with the multi-layered relational contexts of teachers' work and lives, we were able to explore in greater depth how establishing connections with colleagues and students produces collective intellectual and emotional capital for their job fulfilment and commitment; and to identify the critical role of school leaders in creating conditions for the seeds of trust, openness, collegiality and collective responsibility to grow and flourish on their school site. Resilience in this relational sense is the culmination of collective and collaborative endeavours.

In the following chapters, drawing upon a wide range of evidence from the educational literature and beyond, we will examine in detail how a sense of vocation can provide many committed teachers with internal drive, strength and optimism to help every child learn on every school day. We will also explore how individual, relational and organisational factors mediate the impact of the changing social and policy landscapes and influence the ways in which teachers sustain their capacity to make a difference to the success of their pupils. We will suggest, also, that whilst the capacity to be resilient is a necessary condition for sustaining quality in teaching, without moral purpose and the support of colleagues and school leaders it is unlikely to contribute to building and sustaining quality teaching. Finally, by demonstrating the significant associations between teachers' sense of resilience and their effectiveness, as perceived by themselves as well as measured by the progress of their students' academic outcomes, we will endeavour to show why resilience matters to our teachers, schools and above all, pupils, and through this, to contribute to current debates among policy makers, academics and the teaching profession about how high quality teachers may be nurtured and retained and how schools might build and sustain success.

2 Why the best teaching and learning in schools requires everyday resilience

Drawing upon evidence from the research and policy literature, this chapter will show that results-driven policy agendas in many countries have increased the pressures on schools, not only to raise the standards of teaching but to ensure that teaching itself is target driven and compliant to more explicitly instrumentalist agendas. In addition, it will show how the changing socio-cultural conditions in which students live have combined to place increased external accountabilities, work complexity and emotional workload on teachers. In the twenty-first-century world of the teacher notions of the autonomous, 'activist' professional are said to be challenged by neo liberal, 'performativity' agendas (Ball, 2003; Sachs, 2003a). We do not challenge this evidence but examine how it might affect teachers' capacities and capabilities to teach to their best.

'Visible learning'

In his synthesis of over 800 meta-analyses relating to student achievement, John Hattie (2009) found that"

> the act of teaching reaches the epitome of success *after* [our emphasis] the lesson has been structured, after the content has been delivered, and after the classroom has been organised. The art of teaching, and its major successes, relate to 'what happens next' – the manner in which the teacher reacts to how the student interprets, accommodates, rejects, and or reinvents the content and skills, how the student relates and applies the content to other tasks, and how the student reacts in light of success and failure apropos the content and methods that the teacher has taught.
>
> (Hattie, 2009: 2)

One of the major findings in his analysis is that increasing the amount of feedback to the teacher:

> about what students can and cannot do ... is more powerful than feedback to the student ... [but that] ... increasing the amount of feedback in order to have a positive effect on student achievement requires a change in perceptions

of what it means to be a teacher ... and necessitates a different way of interacting and respecting students.

(ibid.: 4)

He goes on to refer to Marzano's (2000) findings that '[e]xceptional performance on the part of teachers not only compensates for average performance at the school level, but even ineffective performance at the school level' (Marzano, 2000: 81).

So we might conclude that ensuring the well-being of teachers is paramount to the intellectual well-being and progress needs of their pupils. A tired, disenchanted or depressed teacher is unlikely to have the intellectual and emotional energy and agility necessary to engage in the complex activities which Hattie finds necessary to the best teaching and learning:

> When these professionals see learning occurring or not occurring, they intervene in calculated and meaningful ways to alter the direction of learning to attain various shared, specific, and challenging goals. In particular, they provide students with multiple opportunities and alternatives for developing learning strategies based on the surface *and* deep levels of learning.
>
> (Hattie, 2009: 22–3)

To achieve this, Hattie continues, teachers need to be passionate, absorbed in the process of teaching and learning. Passion:

> requires more than content knowledge, acts of skilled teaching, or engaged students to make the difference ... It requires a love of the content, an ethical caring stance to wish to imbue others with a liking or even love of the discipline being taught, and a demonstration that the teacher is not only teaching but learning-typically about the students' processes and outcomes of learning.
>
> (Hattie, 2009: 24)

Over a lifetime, most workers, regardless of the particularities of their work context, role or status, will need at one time or another, for shorter or longer periods, as an everyday feature of their work processes, to call upon reserves of physical, psychological or emotional energy if they are to carry out their work to the best of their ability. Schools and classrooms, especially, are demanding of energy of these kinds, partly because not every student chooses to be there and partly because successful teaching and learning requires cognitive, social and emotional investment by both teachers and students. Given the likely associations between resilience and teaching quality (see Chapter 9), it is all the more surprising, therefore, to find that identifying factors which influence and promote the capacity and capability to be resilient in schools has been largely ignored by governments and researchers in the past who have preferred instead to focus upon problems of teacher stress, burnout and retention. So, for example, whilst the final report of the Skills Tests Review Panel to the Secretary of State for Education in June 2012, commissioned by the English government to review the recruitment and selection procedures, identified the need for new written tests in literacy, numeracy and reasoning, it recommended that so-called 'personal qualities such as oral communication, empathy and resilience' should be 'the responsibility of providers of training' (though not, interestingly, of the schools in which they will spend most of their working lives).

Notwithstanding the difficulties of de-contextualised one-off testing, it does seem to be important to investigate exactly why the capacity and capability to be resilient is important to high quality teaching. Which parent, for example, would want their child to be taught by a teacher whose commitment had become eroded over time? Here is what one experienced VITAE teacher, who had lost heart, said:

> I would say it's [commitment] gone down. The desire to contribute isn't there anymore. I used to be a real race horse. I was working every hour I could, but now I don't feel it's worth it anymore … It's getting harder and harder to get up in the mornings. It's more of a duty to come into school. I used to really, really love the job and a lot of that has kind of worn off now and that has been over the last year. It's been getting less fun and I've been less inclined to try new things and push myself that little extra as I used to do as a teacher.

Developing professional capital

Teachers' work in the twenty-first century especially, if it is to be at its best, requires higher levels of intellectual and emotional energy than ever before. It requires investment in what Andy Hargreaves and Michael Fullan have described as '*professional capital*' (Hargreaves and Fullan, 2012). This is an amalgam of 'human, social and decisional' capital (ibid.: 3). Their work draws upon and extends research by Leana (2011) in New York elementary schools. She found, perhaps unsurprisingly, that strong associations between the combination of individual qualifications (human capital) and talent and 'the frequency and focus of conversations and interactions with peers (social capital) that centered on instruction' (cited in Hargreaves and Fullan, 2012: 3), resulted in pupils making higher gains in mathematics achievement (similar findings to those of Bryk and Schneider, 2002, who found that relational trust was a key factor in pupils' achievement in maths and reading in elementary schools in Chicago; and Karen Seashore Louis who identified organisational trust as a key factor in improving and effective high schools in North America). They define the third element of professional capital, decisional capital, as:

> the capital that professionals acquire and accumulate through structured and unstructured experience, practice, and reflection – capital that enables them to make wise judgments in circumstances where there is no fixed rule or piece of incontrovertible evidence to guide them.
>
> (Hargreaves and Fullan, 2012: 93–4)

A range of research supports the notion that investing in 'professional capital' as defined by Hargreaves and Fullan is likely to result in more highly motivated, self-efficacious, committed and capable teachers. In many ways this is self-evident. After all, in those countries and jurisdictions whose students achieve well in international league tables (e.g. South Korea, Alberta, Canada, Shanghai, Singapore and Finland), teachers have high qualifications and status and in-school collaborations are high. However, as Hargreaves and Fullan note, drawing on our own work among others, **teachers' professional capital varies within and across career phases** (ibid.: 77).

As yet, the research and policy communities have largely neglected consideration of variations in the work and lives of the existing majority of teachers and the question of promoting much needed resilience in times of change remains an overlooked and under-researched area. The chapter will discuss those issues in national and international contexts which challenge teachers' capacities to be resilient.

What is work-related stress?

Work-related stress has been defined as 'the process that arises where work demands of various types and the combinations exceed the person's capacity and ability to cope' (Health and Safety Executive, 2009, cited in Griffiths, Knight and Mahudin, 2009: 11–12). Stress is not just about being busy (a key characteristic of teaching is 'busyness'); it is not just about being challenged (to master new situations or learn new skills); it is not just about facing the challenges of unusual, dramatic events or incidents of a short-term nature. Rather, stress is more likely to result from longer term, persisting adversity: for example, continuing disruption of learning and teaching in the classroom, adverse working conditions or relationships with colleagues. It may even be the result of physical illness, relationships or other circumstances outside the school. Whilst individuals will vary in their capacity and capability to manage stress, changes in work-related attitudes and behaviour are likely to have similar features – for example, loss of confidence in one's ability to do the job well (low self-efficacy); fractured relationships with colleagues; poor time management; loss of efficiency; constant feelings of fatigue; loss of previously high levels of motivation and commitment; emotional uncertainty; social withdrawal; and lower quality work.

> In summary, work-related stress is probably best understood as an unpleasant emotional state that results from an unhealthy transaction between the environment and the person that, if persistent, can lead to the development of both psychological and physical illness. Matters tend to be worse when people are put under prolonged pressure, have little control or flexibility over what they do and are not well supported or resourced … Anyone, in any occupation, can suffer from work-related stress, but it has been commonly reported among teachers, nurses, medical practitioners, public administration

and public sector security-based occupations such as police officers, prison officers and UK armed forces personnel.

(Griffiths, Knight and Mahudin, 2009: 12–13)

It is important to acknowledge not only the negative effects which context can have upon employees but also the costs of these to employers themselves. Evidence suggests that employers in general tend to underestimate the extent of psychological ill-health amongst their staff. Psychological ill-health, whether work-related or not, has been estimated to cost UK employers approximately £25 billion per annum. On average this equates to £1,000 per employee. A small organisation with 50 staff (for example, an average-sized primary school) might lose around £50,000 a year. This figure includes sickness absence and replacement costs, but also the reduced productivity of staff who attend work but who are unwell, a phenomenon known as 'presenteeism'. The Sainsbury Centre for Mental Health's report in 2007 also estimated that 'presenteeism' accounted for at least 1.5 times as much lost working time as absenteeism. Although precise figures for the education sector are not available, it is not unreasonable to assume that the extent of 'presenteeism' there may be as considerable as it is for the workforce as a whole: a substantial number of teachers may be attending work whilst not well. Over time this suggests that they are likely to be less able to teach to their best.

Teacher absence and school culture

One consequence of continuing to teach in adverse circumstances is teacher absence and this can have negative effects on both them and their pupils: 'between kindergarten and 12th grade, a typical student is taught by someone other than the regularly assigned teacher for the equivalent of two-thirds of a school year' (Miller, 2008: 1)

Whilst there is much research on teacher attrition and retention, there is less on teacher absence and its effects. Miller (October 2008), in a policy analysis for the Center for American Progress, a non-partisan research and educational institute, reported that:

- Teacher absence is expensive. With 5.3 per cent of teachers absent on a given day, stipends for substitute teachers and associated administrative costs amount to $4 billion annually.
- Teacher absence negatively affects student achievement. Researchers have found that every 10 absences lowers mathematics achievement by the same amount as having a teacher with one year or two years of experience instead of a teacher with three years to five years of experience.
- Teacher absence disproportionately affects low income students. Students in schools serving predominantly low-income families experience teacher absence at higher rates than students in more affluent communities. Part of the achievement gap is thus due to a teacher attendance gap.

(Miller, 2008: 1)

In England, in the academic year 2010/11, 56 per cent of teachers took some sickness leave, as compared with 52 per cent in 2008/09, with an average of 4.6 days per teacher (DfE, 2012). Whilst rates of teacher absence are higher in the developing world (20 per cent) and lower in the UK (3.2 per cent) and Queensland, Australia (3.1 per cent), the overall costs are likely to be significant. These general figures also mask differences between individual schools with different contexts and cultures. Perhaps not surprisingly, Miller's research found that those schools with high levels of trust (as a measure of professional autonomy) between teachers and school leaders have significantly lower rates of teacher absence.

It might also be the case that there are teachers who are not yet absent from school but whose levels of anxiety are high. Stanley (2012), the Chief Executive of the Teacher Support Network in England, has reported that '[b]etween 2010 and 2011, 19,000 users ... recorded 45,633 incidents ... with 4,589 of these specifically related to anxiety. A further ... 2,180 incidents were logged by people losing sleep over their worries'.

Effects of teacher turnover

It may also be the case that teachers will leave one school for another not only for promotion but also because they have experienced relationships (with pupils and/or colleagues) which have challenged their ideals, beliefs or practices. In a study that estimated the effects of teacher turnover on 850,000 students in New York schools over eight years, Ronfeldt *et al.* (2013) found that pupils in schools with a higher teacher turnover rate scored lower in English language and maths tests than others, regardless of the effectiveness of teachers who had left the school, and that, within this, those in schools in socially disadvantaged communities (which were already lower achieving) scored even lower. This research confirms the work of, for example, Bryk and Schneider (2002) and Johnson *et al.* (2005a, 2005b) who found that the quality of relationships, especially trust, was related to rising levels of pupil engagement and achievement. Of particular interest is the finding that:

> turnover has a broader, harmful influence on student achievement since it can reach beyond just those students of teachers who left or of those that replaced them. Any explanation for the effect of turnover must possess these characteristics. One possibility is that turnover negatively affects collegiality or relational trust among faculty [staff]; or perhaps turnover results in loss of institutional knowledge among faculty that is critical for supporting student learning.
>
> (Ronfeldt *et al.*, 2013: 32)

Rather than ask, 'How can we prevent stress and mental/emotional ill-health?' or 'How can we retain teachers?' the more important questions are, we believe: 'How can we foster resilience so that teachers can have the best opportunities always to seek to teach to their best on every school day?' and 'What types of training, support, work environment, culture, leadership and management practices will facilitate its development?'

Everyday resilience

The more traditional, psychologically derived notions that resilience is 'the ability to bounce back in adverse circumstances', as we have shown in Chapter 1, do not lend themselves to the work of teachers. The capacity to be resilient in mind and action is likely to fluctuate according to personal, workplace, policy challenges and pupil behaviour; and the ability of individuals to manage the situations in which such fluctuations occur will vary. Thus, the process of teaching, learning and leading requires those who are engaged in them to exercise their capacity to be resilient on an everyday basis, to have a resolute persistence and commitment and to be supported in these by strong core values. It is this more positive view of teacher resilience associated with teacher quality which should, we believe, inform policies of selection, recruitment and retention. To teach to one's best over time, then, requires **'everyday resilience'**. This is more than the ability to manage the different change scenarios which teachers experience, more than coping or surviving. It is being able to continue to have the capacity and capability to be sufficiently resilient, to have the desire, determination and energy as well as the knowledge and strong moral purpose which enable teachers to teach to their best.

Yet, whilst many teachers enter the profession with a sense of vocation and with a passion to give their best to the learning and growth of their pupils, for some these become diminished with the passage of time, changing external and internal working conditions and contexts, and unanticipated personal events. They may lose their sense of purpose and well-being which are so intimately connected with their positive sense of professional identity and which enable them to draw upon, deploy and manage the inherently dynamic emotionally vulnerable contexts of teaching in which they teach and in which their pupils learn. In a relatively recent survey by the Teacher Support Network (2008) among teachers in schools in England, for example, teachers reported the damaging impact of these symptoms on their work performance. Issues were, in rank order: excessive workload; rapid pace of change; pupil behaviour; unreasonable demands from managers; bullying by colleagues; and problems with pupils' parents (http://teachersupport.info/news/policy-and-public-affairs/better-health-and-wellbeing.php).

Resilience is not an innate quality or disposition: conditions count

The key messages from a recent interdisciplinary series of research seminars in England are that:

- Teaching at its best is emotionally as well as intellectually demanding work and demands everyday resilience.

- Levels of work-related stress, anxiety and depression are higher within education than within many other occupational groups.
- Rather than focusing upon managing stress, a more productive approach would be to focus upon fostering and sustaining resilience.
- Resilience is more than an individual trait. It is a capacity which arises through interactions between people within organisational contexts.
- Teachers' resilience needs to be actively nurtured through initial training and managed through the different phases of their professional lives.
- Because government has a particular responsibility in relation to teaching standards, it needs to ensure that it establishes national policy environments and provides development opportunities which acknowledge the importance of resilience to high quality teaching (http://www.esrc.ac.uk/my-esrc/grants/RES-451-26-0668/outputs/read/d93b9939-79f3-474f-ad74-911e6a16a160).

Resilience is not a quality that is innate. Rather, it is relative, developmental, dynamic and influenced by context. A range of research discussed in Chapter 1 suggests that resilient qualities can be learned or acquired and can be achieved through providing relevant and practical protective factors, such as caring and attentive educational settings in which school leaders promote high expectations, positive learning environments, a strong supportive social community, and supportive peer relationships. Without such organisational support, bringing a passionate, competent and resilient self to teaching effectively every day of every week of every school term and year can be stressful not only to the body but also to the heart and soul; for the processes of teaching and learning are rarely smooth, and the results are not always predictable.

Reporting on a project which combined insights from the natural sciences with a social constructionist perspective, Ecclestone and Lewis (2014, in press) defined resilience as 'one of several, inter-related constructs that comprise "emotional well-being", including optimism, emotional literacy (especially self-awareness, empathy and emotional regulation), altruism, self-esteem and stoicism' (2014: 2). They argue that resilient systems follow four rules. They:

(A) have the capacity to detect changes which may perturb them
(B) link this detection to a response
(C) respond in a way which is appropriate, and which in some way either ameliorates the effects of the change or adapts the resilient system to withstand them and to recover from them
(D) end the response when the need is no longer present, since the response is one which will require resources

(2014: 2)

Whilst these rules describe how resilient individuals behave and so are useful as a means of diagnosis or even analysis, they take no account of how personal, social and policy conditions and contexts may either increase or decrease the capacity and capabilities of individuals and organisations to apply these rules. To put it a different way, attempts to present resilience as 'fixed individual psychological "attributes" or a set of trainable behaviours' (2014: 8) without considering the broader educational and social contexts, present circumstances and social interactions, are misguided.

Emotional regulation and control of self and others which notions of 'emotional intelligence' (Goleman, 1995) espouse over-emphasise the responsibility of the individual without, at the same time, examining the social structures in which the individual works and which are likely to influence that individual's capacity to be resilient (see Chapter 3 for a critique). Thus '[f]rom a critical perspective, resilience interventions need to position the gendered, classed or raced subjects as able to act upon and change the conditions of their lives and not just to adjust their responses to those conditions' (Ecclestone and Lewis, 2014, in press: 10).

It seems to be clear from this evidence that the capacity and capability to be resilient, allied with knowledge of subject and pedagogy and a strong sense of moral purpose within supportive school and classroom environments, is essential to teachers' ability to sustain the intellectual and emotional energy and commitment that the best teaching demands. If this is indeed the case, it follows that efforts to increase the quality of teaching and raise standards of learning and achievement for all pupils must focus on efforts to build, sustain and renew teacher resilience, and that these efforts must take place in initial teacher training, be promoted at policy levels, through training and developing and, most of all, in the teaching and learning cultures of schools themselves.

Five challenges which test resilience

1. Increases in social problems

In research on teachers from the USA, Australia, New Zealand and England (Scott and Dinham, 2002), teachers frequently commented upon the impact on their professional lives of the increase in social problems, summed by a US classroom teacher as 'the type of students we must face (unlike the classrooms of yesteryear)'. An Australian classroom teacher expressed the same concerns and mentioned students' 'lack of real interest and maturation as well as general and severe behaviour problems associated with the above reasons or due to welfare problems'; and a New Zealand specialist teacher produced a similar list of student difficulties, 'poor family backgrounds – lack of experiences, language, attendance at school, physical/emotional abuse, all factors which severely affect children's progress' (Scott and Dinham, 2002: 18).

The views of the teachers to whom Scott and Dinham referred in 2002 could well have been expressed by teachers more than ten years later. Changes in influences upon different generations of pupils as they come to school are an inevitable consequence of changes in the wider society. According to a UNICEF (2007) report, 16.2 per cent of British children lived below the poverty line, 35.8 per cent reported that they were bullied within a two-month period, 35.3 per cent of 15-year-old pupils aspired to low-skilled work and 30.8 per cent of young people reported that they had been drunk two or more times. The UK was in the bottom third of the rankings in a league of 21 economically advanced countries in its treatment of children as assessed by material well-being, health and safety, educational well-being, family and peer relationships, behaviours and risks, and young people's perceptions of their own well-being. The position in education specifically was 17th out of 21. Despite criticisms of the report's narrow focus (Ansell *et al.*, 2007), this is a worrying trend which, nevertheless, will have consequences for teachers.

What keeps teachers going, according to teachers themselves, is essentially their emotional commitment to the pupils they teach. Hastings and Bham's (2003) research on the relationship between student behaviour patterns and teacher burnout found that students influence teachers' sense of emotional exhaustion, leading to feelings of depersonalisation and lack of personal achievement; and:

> additional responsibilities (e.g. time constraints) to be the strongest predictor of emotional exhaustion, *student disrespect* to be the strongest predictor of teacher depersonalisation and *student lack of sociability* to be the strongest predictor of teachers' lack of personal accomplishment.
>
> (cited in Klassen and Anderson, 2009: 755)

If we are to take the negative findings expressed above even half seriously then we must begin to place the need to foster and support resilience in teachers much higher on the school improvement agenda. For many students, the authority of the classroom (and even school) as a legitimate or primary location for learning, is no longer a 'given'. The traditional role of teachers as knowledge experts is being challenged and, with this, their professional identities. For some, such challenges of change are likely to threaten their sense of self-esteem, resilience and emotional stability.

Whilst a positive sense of identity is essential if teachers are to teach to their best, supportive relationships with colleagues are also known to contribute to teachers' sense of self-esteem, commitment and belonging (Day and Gu, 2010). Moreover, as much recent empirical research internationally has revealed, a sense of individual, relational and collective trustworthiness and trust – through, for example, experiencing a high degree of collegiality in decisions about the curriculum, pedagogy and assessment and participating actively in leadership roles – are important contributors to the quality of teaching and student achievement (Bryk and Schneider 2002; Day *et al.*, 2011).

2. Screen cultures

Pupils in classrooms present an increasing number of challenges, not least those associated with emotional uncertainties in family lives and learning uncertainties associated with their increasing participation in 'screen cultures' and social networking sites which are contributing to a 'blurring' of what, where and how they learn. There can be no doubt that in many countries family norms and expectations have changed and that the influence of new technologies upon pupils is increasingly profound. In many countries, also, teachers are not now accorded respect simply because they are teachers; and what may be learned from teachers in classrooms must compete with what may be learned from the internet, social networks and other information and communication devices:

> In less than the span of a single childhood, we have merged with our machines, staring at a screen for eight hours a day, more time than we spend on any other activity, including sleeping. British adolescents spend an average of six hours a day online, and, according to the Royal College of Paediatrics and Clinical Health, 10- and 11-year olds have access to five screens at home.
>
> (Dokoupil, 2012: 2)

In an article drawing upon several pieces of research on the negative effects of digital technologies and originally appearing in *Newsweek*, Dokoupil raises important issues for teachers. He suggests that the physical wiring of the brains of some of their pupils may have already been affected by their interaction with technologies 'in areas charged with attention, control and decision making'. It is claimed that they may be more impulsive than others as a result of their use of technology. They may feel more isolated and struggle in forming a stable sense of self: 'A Carnegie Mellor University study found that web use over a two-year period was linked to blue moods, loneliness and the loss of real-world friends' (Dokoupil, 2012: 3). It has also been suggested that there are associations between the excessive use of the internet and mobile technology and the reported 66 per cent rise in ADHD and OCD disorders among children and young people in the last ten years (Aboujaoude *et al.*, 2006).

Taken together, even with a 'pinch of salt', these findings suggest that teachers in all schools are likely having to manage new sets of challenges in promoting the learning and achievement of at least some of the pupils in their classes – another situation in which they need to call upon 'everyday resilience'.

3. The pressures of policy

> To a great extent, in the UK and in England in particular, the role of the individual school, and indeed the local education authority, has been subordinated to and by ... national policy initiatives ... [but] ... policy-makers do not normally take account of the complexity of policy enactment environments and the need for schools to simultaneously respond to multiple policy (and other) demands and expectations.
>
> (Braun *et al.*, 2010: 547–8)

The research on which these statements are based problematises the well-established but, nevertheless, naive notion in much of the change literature on so-called problems of implementation of external reform initiatives as perceived by policy makers. Rather, it understands that policies are ' "interpreted" and "translated" by diverse policy actors in the school environment' (Braun *et al.*, 2010: 549). The authors continue: 'putting policies into practice is a creative, sophisticated and complex process ...of interpretation' (ibid.: 549). Because changes in external policy have become a dominant feature in the changing landscape of school governance, curriculum and classrooms over the last three decades in English schools, and because teachers themselves are key mediating agents in their enactment, it is perhaps not surprising that for many, being a teacher and achieving success has become more complex, more highly cognitive and emotionally demanding. One consequence of continuing changes in policy, then, has been a greater need for teachers to have the capacity to be resilient. The authors provide an example of a maths teacher in an average-sized comprehensive school:

> *Roger:* [W]e seem to be doing every initiative there is before it eventually becomes government policy. And some of us feel that maybe sometimes we try and do too much and not focus on some things. I know from colleagues in other schools nearby, you know, they haven't got a clue about PLTS [Personal Learning and Thinking Skills] or anything else ... We're still only satisfactory [in Ofsted terms] and thus, you know, we've got to be seen to be doing really well.
>
> (Braun *et al.*, 2010: 552–3)

4. Standards and accountability

Standards of teaching, learning and achievement appear to be judged by policy makers in England and many other countries to be in almost constant crisis. The emphasis upon standardised tests and examinations and the development of new technologies to compare these within and across schools and countries (PISA, TIMMS) are said to have caused more emphasis upon teaching to the test in classrooms. Teachers, particularly those who work in schools which serve socio-economically and emotionally challenging urban and rural contexts, are caught in the middle between efforts to engage students who may be less willing (or able) to be engaged and satisfying the demands of results-driven agendas by which the relative 'success' of schools and, therefore, teachers may be measured and compared.

Writing in the *Journal of the Royal Society of Arts* in the summer of 2012, Sir Michael Wilshaw, Her Majesty's Chief Inspector of Schools in England, wrote of teachers: 'Teaching is a noble profession that has the power to changes lives, particularly for those disadvantaged young people who need it most ... We need to celebrate diversity, ingenuity and imagination in the way we teach' (Wilshaw, 2012: 17). He wrote of two 'incredibly successful' teachers: 'These teachers were resilient people who withstood the slings and arrows ... unflinchingly. They never let failure get the better of them. They learnt from it and came back stronger, tougher and better' (ibid.: 17). In his 'Teacher's Three-Term Report Card' (see Figure 2.1), he identified ten 'skills' and six 'traits'. We re-produce this here because it illustrates well the key strengths which every teacher will need to teach to their best and which every school will need to support in every teacher, regardless of experience.

It is possible to see Wilshaw's skills and traits in research on effective classroom learning and teaching as, in essence, being complemented by the research of John Hattie (2009) to whose work we referred earlier in this chapter. He found that

School Name:

TEACHER'S THREE-TERM REPORT CARD

Marks: E (90=100%); VG (75–89%); G (60–74%); FG (50–59%); F (35–49%); O (under 35%)

	Session 2011–12				Session 2011–12		
SKILLS	**1st Term**	**2nd Term**	**3rd Term**	**SKILLS**	**1st Term**	**2nd Term**	**3rd Term**
Authoritative				Resilient			
Collaborative				Flexible			
Perceptive				Reflective			
Supportive				Empathetic			
Imaginative				Organised			
TRAITS							
AS AN INDIVIDUAL				**AS A MEMBER OF STAFF**			
1. Keeps control of class				1. Shares ideas with colleagues			
2. Plans lessons effectively				2. Prepared to accept criticism			
3. Shows sensitivity to pupils' needs				3. Good at relationship building			

Teacher's name:

Head teacher's signature:

N.B. The head teacher is always willing to interview parents regarding a teacher's conduct.

Figure 2.1 Teacher's Three-Term Report Card (Wilshaw, 2012: 6).

reciprocal teaching, feedback, teaching pupils meta-cognition strategies, problem-solving and self-verbalisation and self-questioning were practices which had the most positive impacts on pupil learning and that 'these top methods rely upon the influence of peers, feedback, transparent learning intentions and success criteria … using various strategies, attending to both surface and deep knowing' (cited in Hargreaves and Fullan 2012: 52). He provided not a report card but six signposts about good teaching:

i)   Teachers are among the most powerful influences upon learning.
ii) Teachers need to be directive, influential, caring, and actively engaged in the passion of teaching and learning.
iii) Teachers need to be aware of what every child is thinking and knowing, to construct meaningful experiences in light of this knowledge.
iv) Teachers need to know *the learning intentions* and success criteria of their lessons, know *how well they are attaining* these criteria for all students, and know *where to go next* in the light of the gap.
v)   Teachers need to move from single ideas to multiple ideas … such that learners are able to construct and reconstruct knowledge and ideas whatever specific measure is being used at one time.
vi) School leaders and teachers need to create [learning] environments where error is welcomed as a learning opportunity and where discarding incorrect knowledge and understanding is welcomed.

(cited in Hargreaves and Fullan, 2012: 52)

It is all very well to set the standards for outstanding teaching, as Wilshaw's Report Card does, and to identify the traits and behaviours of effective teachers, as Hattie's research does. The reality, however, is that the majority of teachers are unlikely to be able to be outstanding always and that, for most teachers, performance will vary according to circumstances in their classrooms, schools and personal lives.

To be resilient, flexible, reflective, empathetic, imaginative and perceptive – five of Sir Michael's ten necessary 'skills' – and to attain each of Hattie's six signposts requires huge amounts of emotional and intellectual energy and a continuing high level of motivation, commitment and resilience in an environment which is both challenging and supportive rather than energy draining and destructive of the professional self.

5. Higher demand cultures

A study in New Zealand sought to compare primary teachers' workload in 2012 with a similar study carried out 20 years earlier by the same author (Bridges, 1992). Given the increase in government-led reforms, including the introduction of national teaching standards and an emphasis on raising pupils' levels of performance through tests and examinations – a pattern which is repeated across the world as evidenced by the development and use of international comparators

(PISA, TIMMS) – the results were not surprising. The working week for teachers was now reported to be 55 hours as against 50 hours previously; ICT use was taking more time than five years previously, as was time spent in meeting special learning needs of pupils; a majority of principals and senior leaders spent more time in administration tasks; and more teachers than in 1992 reported that they faced very heavy or 'overload' workloads. Although these findings are the result of self-report by the 379 self-selected respondents and so should be treated with some caution, what is especially of concern is the authors' report that 'large numbers of primary teachers – more than half overall – do not feel able to keep going in the way that they are at present' (Bridges and Searle, 2011: 423).

Additionally, work relating directly to the needs of the children and the class, a priority for 51.3 per cent of teachers in 1992, was now a priority for 37 per cent, with demands by 'hierarchy', management and others now a priority for 15 per cent as against 1.5 per cent in 1992: 'My workload tends to be prioritised by those in power telling me what they need to see and when, to prove I do the job effectively, not prioritised by the needs that arise day to day in my class' (in Bridges and Searle, 2011: 424).

Increased workload itself does not necessarily lead to job dissatisfaction and low morale, although it clearly tests teachers' capacity to be resilient. For example, Herzberg's (1966) work suggests that job satisfaction can be high from relationships with pupils and the opportunity to 'make a difference' in their learning and achievement, whereas simultaneously job dissatisfaction can also be high because of poor working conditions or external policy environments (see Chapter 4 for a detailed discussion of the effects of these upon teachers' sense of professional identity). A survey commissioned by ETUCE (2011) of 5,400 teachers in 500 schools across Europe found that UK teachers reported the highest levels of burnout, second highest levels of cognitive stress, above average levels of pupil discipline problems and conflicts with parents. Teachers in this survey also reported the second-highest levels of workload and that these impacted negatively on their personal lives outside school.

While international and national surveys have consistently found associations between increased workloads and job dissatisfaction (e.g. Dinham and Scott, 2000, 2002; Rhodes *et al.*, 2004), there is no necessary cause and effect relationship. Indeed, job satisfaction and dissatisfaction have been found to be the result of interaction between three dynamic factors – core commitment to pupils' learning, school leadership and culture, and societal and policy issues.

Nevertheless, it is reasonable to argue that where workloads increase and where demands for improved performance in tests and examinations persist, these are likely to demand a greater capacity for resilience. When these become constant, it is also likely that reservoirs of care and hope may begin to run dry, unless schools themselves ensure otherwise through supportive, collegial cultures in which building and sustaining teachers' capacity to be and continue to be resilient is central to their mission. This will apply especially to those schools which serve pupils from highly disadvantaged communities (see Chapter 6 for a more detailed discussion of this).

So what was already a stressful job has become more stressful. In England, increased autonomy in schools has gone hand in hand with increased accountabilities to government and transparency to parents. The issue here, however, is not whether schools should be less or more accountable, but rather whether such accountability results in higher standards of teaching, learning and achievement. In considering this, it would seem reasonable to seek teachers' own experiences. If we take it that those who work in 'outstanding', successful schools, as judged by Ofsted, are likely to be at least satisfied in their work, can we also assume that those who work in schools which are judged as 'good' are also satisfied? The answer is 'not necessarily', according to Scott and Dinham:

> We recently had our Ofsted inspection and I have 25% of my teaching staff on stress leave as a direct result. The schools' league table for this LEA (Local Educational Authority) was also just published. There are 120 schools in this city in our category and this school was ranked 33rd. I was very pleased but soon after the results were published, parents were lining up outside my door to demand an explanation as to why we had not done better.
> (English school principal, cited in Scott and Dinham, 2002: 23)

Conclusions

This brief consideration of what teachers who work in intensive policy reform contexts are called to do in order, as they see it, to comply with the rules of success which governments set for schools, illustrates well the need for them to be resilient in relation to what is happening outside their classrooms, over which they have little control, as well as inside the everyday complex worlds of teaching and learning inside their classrooms. A closer examination of levels of teacher resilience reveals positive and negative associations with the influences of school culture, in particular 'trust', 'autonomy', 'collegiality' and 'leadership' which affect whether teachers stay or go. For example, where head teachers are successful, it seems that: (i) attendance and behaviour problems of pupils (and teachers) are minimised as the foundation for building, developing and sustaining cultures of learning and achievement (Day *et al.*, 2011b); (ii) system-wide continuing professional development and capacity building through a range of in-school and out-of-school learning opportunities connecting to individual and organisational needs is an enduring priority (Robinson *et al.*, 2009); and (iii) leadership roles are widely distributed hand in hand with the progressive development of trust.

It seems more than likely that those schools which focus upon building individual and organisational resilience through structures and cultures which promote teachers' self-efficacy, academic optimism, collegiality, professional learning and development and pupil care with achievement are likely to be successful. Whilst a direct cause and effect relationship cannot be claimed, nevertheless these schools are more likely to have greater retention and lower turnover rates and more likely to be able to help pupils become more engaged in learning and to achieve more. We end this chapter, therefore, by posing the two questions with which Bridges and Searle (2011) ended their report and which go to the heart of the need for every teacher to have the capacity to be resilient:

- Do we want our children to be taught by educators who are fresh, energetic and focussed on their needs?
- Do we want to keep our good teachers in the work that they say they love, or do we want to watch then burn out and walk away?

(Bridges and Searle, 2011: 431)

3 Well-being, emotions and the importance of care

Much research internationally has found that personal, workplace and socio-cultural scenarios may either support or threaten teachers' sense of positive, stable professional identity and their perceptions of their effectiveness. There is also ample evidence in the literature which points to the role of resilience in enabling individuals to manage adverse scenarios and fluctuations in their work and lives and through this, succeed and thrive over time. However, the contributions to resilience of its constituent parts – well-being, commitment, emotional energy, academic optimism and care – have yet to be fully explored.

Teacher well-being

Well-being has been defined generally as 'a dynamic state, in which the individual is able to develop their potential, work productivity and creatively, build strong and positive relationships with others, and contribute to their community' (Foresight Mental Capital and Wellbeing Project, 2008: 10). As a result of their work with teachers in Belgium, Aelterman and her colleagues provided an occupation specific definition: 'Well-being expresses a positive emotional state, which is the result of harmony between the sum of specific environmental factors on the one hand, and the personal needs and expectations of teachers on the other hand' (Aelterman *et al.*, 2007: 286).

Just as it is impossible to consider teacher resilience without discussing stress, it is also necessary to consider well-being, since a sense of negative or positive well-being clearly plays a role in both. Indeed, it has been claimed that 'paying direct attention to the well-being of populations is the only way in which societies can truly assess whether the lives of their members are going well or badly'; and that 'since our well-being underpins our collective resilience, and thus our ability to effectively respond to rapid societal changes, in the current context this assessment becomes not just desirable, but critical' (NEF, 2007: 9). What follows for the general population, arguably is especially important for teachers. Without a strong sense of their own well-being teachers will find it difficult to promote the well-being of their pupils. Moreover, whilst well-being may or may not be an essential ingredient in the achievement of success, it would be difficult to argue that it does not play a part. A recent cross-national survey by the New Economics

Foundation (NEF, 2009), an independent think tank, identified two measures of well-being – personal and societal:

Personal well-being
- Emotional (positive feelings and absence of negative feelings).
- Satisfying life.
- Vitality.
- Resilience and self-esteem (self-esteem, optimism and resilience).
- Positive functioning (autonomy, competence, engagement, meaning and purpose).

Social well-being
- Supportive relationships.
- Trust and belonging.

Yet it identified, as countries move through periods of increasing economic, social and environmental uncertainty:

> [a] myopic obsession with growing the economy ... [which] ... has meant that we have tended to ignore the negative impacts on our well-being such as longer working hours and rising levels of indebtedness. It has created an economic system which has systematically squeezed out opportunities for individuals, families and communities to make choices and pursue activities which play a role in promoting positive well-being and flourishing.
>
> (NEF, 2009: 2)

The NEF (2009) found that the United Kingdom ranked 15th of 22 nations in terms of well-being at work and 13th of 22 nations when personal and social well-being scores were combined (2009: 3, 43), and that, within the UK, young people reported very low levels of trust and belonging compared to older people. Thus:

> [t]he science of 'subjective well-being' suggests that as well as experiencing good feelings, people need: a sense of individual vitality; to undertake activities which are meaningful, engaging, and which make them feel competent and autonomous; and a stock of inner resources to help them cope when things go wrong and be resilient to changes beyond their immediate control. It is also crucial that people feel a sense of relatedness to other people, so that in addition to the personal, internally focussed elements, people's social experiences – the degree to which they have supportive relationships and a sense of connection with others – form a vital aspect of well-being.
>
> (NEF, 2009: 9)

A review by Gray *et al.* (2011) of 300-plus international studies found six key school factors which contributed to young people's well-being: i) relationships with teachers; ii) relationships with peers; iii) satisfaction with school; iv) membership of the learning community; v) handling pressure of schoolwork; and vi) thinking 'small' (cited in Gray, 2012: 30). Most, if not all, of these key factors will be influenced by teachers and, in some cases, particular teachers in successful schools:

> the factors which contribute to making a school academically effective are not the same ones which make it a more 'supportive' institution ... somehow we have managed to develop a very lopsided view of schooling. Test and exam results matter – not much else does.
>
> (Gray, 2012: 30)

In a mixed methods study of secondary school students in German secondary schools, Glaser-Zikuda and Fuss (2008) found strong linear effects between six teacher competencies (clarity of instruction, motivational competence, diagnosing task understanding and performance, diagnosing social relations between students, individual progress and achievement, and care) and students' well-being. The higher the students rated all these teacher competencies, the higher was their perceived well-being. The study gives us two messages: first, that to be a good teacher requires the possession of a number of competencies; second that the exercise of these competencies assists in creating a positive sense of well-being and a lessening sense of anxiety about learning among pupils. What it did not investigate are the influences on pupils of teachers who do not have these competencies or who have them but are unable to apply them consistently. In other words, what would be the effect on pupils' sense of well-being if teachers had a low sense of commitment to them or whose reservoir of emotional resilience had been drained? Indeed, in their research and development work on teacher resilience, Henderson and Milstein (2003) stress that it is unrealistic to expect pupils to be resilient if their teachers, who constitute a primary source of their role models, do not demonstrate resilient qualities.

Research into successful primary and secondary schools (e.g. Day *et al.*, 2000: Moos *et al.*, 2012; Leithwood and Seashore Louis, 2012) has also demonstrated that they do indeed achieve success through attention to both academic and 'well-being' needs of their pupils; and that whilst there may not be a direct cause and effect relationship between academic progress and achievement and well-being, there are certainly associations. Head teachers and teachers in these successful schools, as part of their core purposes, believe that 'we develop as human beings in and through our relations with others' (Fielding, 2000: 51):

> Basically there are two kinds of relations through which we develop our humanity. They are functional or task-centred relations and personal or person-centred relations ... both are necessary and interdependent, but one is more important than the other ... the functional ways in which we work

together in schools to achieve personal, communal and educational ends should be transformed by the moral and interpersonal character and quality of what we are trying to do.

(Fielding, 2000: 51–2)

It is the interdependence of the functional with the personal that is so important to good and effective teaching, which can be simultaneously exhilarating and exhausting for teachers. This juxtaposing of the measures of well-being with the increasing complexities of society and work is important in the context of teacher resilience because it points to the different sets of tensions which teachers must manage which may have detrimental effects on their physical and emotional well-being.

Emotional energy

Emotions ... are central to the function of the brain and to the life of the mind.

(Davidson and Begley, 2012: ix)

Good, effective teaching demands the engagement of the head (the intellect), the hand (the pedagogical skills) and the heart (values, beliefs, emotions). Together, these make up what we call, 'the person in the professional'. Teaching is emotionally demanding work because it involves working with the challenges of pupils – who have different motivations, aptitudes and personal histories of learning, who have not necessarily chosen to learn and who do not always place a high value on the subject or teacher. Thus teachers, if they are to continue to be willing and able to teach to their best, need to sustain strong 'emotional energy' (Furu, 2007). Paradoxically, despite a recognition of the importance to teachers of so-called emotional and social intelligence (Goleman, 2006; Salovey and Mayer, 1989), emotional understanding (Denzin, 1984) and emotional literacy (Harris, 2005), policies for promoting teacher quality, development and renewal rarely address the emotional dimensions of their work.

Long ago, Hargreaves and Fullan (1999), among others, identified the importance of acknowledging the significance of the emotional dimension of teachers' work:

Teaching is an emotional practice. It arouses and colours feelings in teachers and students. Teaching not only involves instructing students, but also caring for them, forming bonds and relationships with them ... It is a job where teachers repeatedly put themselves on the line ... [It] is easy to lose sight of teaching's emotional dimension, of the enthusiasm, passion, care, wisdom, inspiration and dedication that make many teachers great.

(Hargreaves and Fullan, 1999: 21)

There are a growing number of empirical studies which focus upon understanding the part played by teachers' emotions in their work (Day, 2004; Hargreaves,

2000; van Veen and Sleegers, 2006; Schutz and Zembylas, 2009; Day and Lee, 2011). There is no doubt, also, that teachers' sense of emotional well-being can influence the energy they bring to their teaching, their motivation, self-efficacy, commitment and care and that this is likely to impact positively or negatively on the motivations and behaviours of their pupils in the classroom. For example, teachers' and pupils' emotions interact and exist in an uncertain dynamic reciprocal relationship. Neither one dominates the other in general, but at particular times, in particular circumstances, one may dominate the other. Below are four possible scenarios which we might consider:

Scenario 1
(Teachers' positive emotions – high self-efficacy, job satisfaction, professional identity, well-being, high emotional energy)

Teacher positive emotions → positive influence → high student engagement in learning

Scenario 2
(Teachers' negative emotions – low self-efficacy, job satisfaction, well-being, emotional energy, uncertain professional development)

Teacher negative emotions → negative influence → low student engagement in learning

Scenario 3
(Teachers' mixed emotions – uncertain sense of self-efficacy, job satisfaction, well-being and professional identity, unstable levels of emotional energy)

Teacher mixed emotions → positive/negative influences → mixed student engagement in learning

Scenario 4
(Students' mixed/negative emotions – disenchantment with learning, school, teacher)

Student mixed emotions → positive/negative influences on teacher and peers → challenge to teacher's emotional energy levels if sustained

Teachers (and their pupils) experience an array of sometimes contrasting emotions in the classroom. In a review of empirical research, Sutton (2000) found that love (as a social relationship) and care, surprise and joy, anger, sadness and fear, excitement and pleasure in pupils' progress and achievements are among the most commonly cited emotions. Thus it is not surprising that, because of the emotional investments which many teachers make in their work, they can experience instabilities or vulnerabilities when control of long-held principles and practices is challenged by policy changes or new expectations for working practices and assessment, when their moral integrity is questioned, or when trust and respect from parents, the public and their students is eroded. Indeed, it has been claimed that vulnerability is a structural condition of teaching (Kelchtermans, 2010). Instabilities create stresses in the emotional fabric of identity, whether the result of personal, socio-cultural/policy or workplace, or a combination of these.

It has been observed that the cognitive and rational competences continue to be privileged (Sharp, 2001). Arlie Hochschild (1983), in a much quoted study, observed the consequences of the suppression of authentic emotional engagement at work upon those employed to help others. Hochschild coined the term 'emotional labour' to describe work which demands that the workers present themselves as 'liking' all their clients, regardless of how the clients themselves respond. She found that the constant presentation of an inauthentic or false emotional self resulted in dysfunctional relationships outside the job itself.

Of course, the work of teaching is not the same as the work of airline stewards or bill collectors, two of the groups studied by Hochschild. However, there are some parallels; and it is easy to see why, as Flintham put it when looking at the work of school leaders, when the 'reservoirs run dry' and emotional energy dips, so too will the levels of authentic engagement by the teacher with the pupils and the engagement by pupils with their learning (see Chapter 7 for a detailed discussion of leadership resilience). Emotions are not only mediated by self-awareness and understanding, but also by working contexts.

Teachers, therefore, need to be resilient, to understand and manage their emotions, and to be supported in doing so during these periods in order that these may be managed in ways that build and sustain resilience. They need to have the capacity and capability to manage emotions (their own and others) as part of a necessary repertoire of inter and intra personal qualities and skills, since they play a key role in pupils' motivation (to learn) and the establishment of trusting relationships (with their teachers). Various authors have explored and explained the nature of emotions (e.g. Damasio, 2004), emotional understanding (Denzin, 1984), emotional literacy (Harris, 2005) and emotional and social intelligence (Salovey and Mayer, 1989; Goleman, 2006). Goleman's notion of 'emotional intelligence', in particular, has become widely popular. Yet it is not without its critics.

Emotional intelligence: a critique

Goleman's (1995) popular, psychologically based notion of 'emotional intelligence' comprises five key elements: knowing one's emotions; managing emotions; motivating oneself; recognising emotions in others; and managing relationships. It is clear that as with his colleague, Davidson, there is a strong emphasis placed upon individual (psychological) capacities and capabilities of emotional self-regulation and the emotional regulation of others. Goleman's work, as McLaughlin points out (2008: 362), 'is based on the idea that individuals ... are largely responsible for the management of their own emotions ... rather than being interdependent'. He argues that 'those who are at the mercy of impulse – who lack control – suffer a moral deficiency: the ability to control impulse is the base of will and character' (Goleman, 1995: xii, cited in McLaughlin, 2008: 355). Emotional intelligence now features regularly in the policy and training literature as being a necessary quality for all school leaders. However, Craig (2007, reported in McLaughlin, 2008: 359–60) has critiqued Goleman's work on the grounds that:

i) He has distorted the original concept of emotional ability, developed by Mayer *et al.* (2004), as a combination of intelligence and emotional skills. He has, 'taken the concept of emotional ability and added to it certain positive personality characteristics, such as warmth, empathy and zeal, which are not substantiated in the original work' (McLaughlin, 2008: 360);

ii) Gardner (1999) has questioned the notion of EI as being a separate form of intelligence, claiming that, 'emotions are part and parcel of cognition ... if one calls some intelligences emotional, one suggests that other intelligences are not – and that implication flies in the face of experience and empirical data' (Gardner, 1999: 71–72);

iii) The labelling of people as 'emotionally intelligent' can create an emotional elite, particularly since, 'there may be an overlap between EI personality and socio-economic status' (McLaughlin, 2008: 360);

iv) The reliability of emotional intelligence tests has been questioned (Sternberg, 2000); and

v) Emotions are seen, in Goleman's work, 'as something much more to be feared, controlled and regulated than celebrated'.

(Craig, 2007: 10)

To this critique, we would add that in terms of the wide range of resilience-related research found in this book and elsewhere, teachers' capacities to be resilient will be influenced by the environments in which they work and the people with whom they work, whether their workplaces are sites in which they are able to flourish or sites which drain them of their emotional energy.

Emotions and health

One of the strongest and most consistent findings in behavioural medicine now is the relationship between positive emotions and health ... there is compelling evidence that the state of your mind affects the state of your body and, more specifically, that emotions influence physiology and therefore health.

(Davidson, 2012: 117, 132)

One strong source of confirmatory empirical evidence for relationships between positive emotions and health is the work of Steptoe *et al.* (2005) reported in *Positive Affect and Health Related Neuroendrone, Cardiovascular and Inflammatory Processes*. They collected and analysed self-report and medical data from 116 male and 100 female civil servants at different points over a three-year period, measuring levels of cortisol, a hormone which helps the body deal with stress, and plasma fibrinogen, a molecule which is 'implicated in inflammation and coronary disease' (2005: 120). They found that the participants who reported themselves to be the least happy 'had cortisol levels that were, on average, 48% higher than those who rated themselves as the most happy ... [and that] ... the least happy participants also had a hugely elevated plasma fibrinogen response to two stress-inducing tasks' (2005: 12). Other medical scientists have also found associations between levels of happiness and the development of the common cold (Cohen *et al.*, 2003). They found that those participants with the highest levels of self-reported positive emotions (happy, cheerful, calm, at ease, lively and energetic) as against those with negative emotions (sad, depressed, nervous, hostile), and who had the largest number of positive social interactions, 'were nearly three times less likely to develop a cold' (2003: 121).

Although it is important to remember that 'associations' do not imply 'cause and effect', these and other studies signal emerging objective biological evidence which seems to complement many claims by educational researchers on the importance of relationships between teachers' motivation, sense of self-efficacy and job fulfilment – in other words, associations between their emotional health and their ability to be energetic, committed and resilient in their work in classrooms.

The emotional life of the brain

In *The Emotional Life of Your Brain* (2012), Davidson and Begley examined why people respond differently to life events by applying techniques of neuroimaging and other methodologies. Their findings are in welcome contrast to those who have claimed that cognition, reason and logic, and emotion 'run on separate, mutually independent brain circuitry' (2012: 24). They suggest that differences in response relate to the individual's 'emotional style', a 'constellation of reactions and coping mechanisms that differ in kind, intensity and duration' (2012: 24); and that it is possible for individuals to learn to change the habitual patterns of their responses. If such findings are trustworthy, then they have clear implications for those who are concerned with building teachers' capacities and capabilities to be resilient.

Davidson is a neuroscientist and director of the University of Wisconsin's Center for Investigating Healthy Minds and has identified *'emotional style'* as 'a consistent way of responding to the experiences of our lives' (Davidson 2012: xi). Unlike many psychologically derived classification schemes, emotional style, he claims, 'is governed by specific, identifiable brain circuits and can be measured using objective laboratory methods' (2012: xi). We are particularly interested in this work because the six dimensions of emotional style which arise from Davidson's research in affective neuroscience relate closely to educational research on teachers' work, lives and effectiveness. The dimensions of emotional style which he identified are:

- Resilience: how slowly or quickly you recover from adversity
- Outlook: how long you are able to sustain positive emotion

- Social intuition: how adept you are at picking up social signals from the people around you
- Self-awareness: how well you perceive bodily feelings that reflect emotions
- Sensitivity to context: how good you are at regulating your emotional responses to take into account the context you find yourself in
- Attention: how sharp and clear your focus is

(2012: xii)

Davidson claims that these dimensions are not always immediately apparent at an individual's conscious level. Whilst he elaborates on each of these six, drawing upon an impressive range of empirical research which reveals physical connections between the mind and the body, we focus here on what he found about resilience.

Referring to 'resilience' he notes that 'with few exceptions, we do not pay attention to how quickly we recover from a stressful event' (2012: xiii). This 'fits' both with our own finding that teachers need 'everyday resilience' and extends it by the observation that 'we experience its consequences'. For example, teachers with a low capacity for resilience may be slow to recover from a negative experience during a lesson or disagreements or disputes with colleagues, and this may adversely affect their teaching for the rest of the day or longer: whereas teachers with a high capacity for resilience are likely to recover more quickly. Davidson's claims that people respond differently to experience resonates with our own observations that generalised formulae for either identifying resilience in aspiring teachers or providing generic training, development and support opportunities are unlikely to result in success. Instead, it is far more likely that self-knowledge by teachers and knowledge of individual teachers by school leaders is a necessary part of building and sustaining individual and organisational capacities for resilience (see Chapter 6 for a more detailed discussion of workplace influences). It is also the case that the relative influence of the six dimensions of emotional style can change and that this will be influenced by personal, workplace or policy changes:

> Emotional style is the result of brain circuitry that is laid down in our early years by the genes we inherit from our parents and from the experiences we have. But that circuitry is not forever fixed. Although emotional style is ordinarily quite stable over time, it can be altered by serendipitous experiences as well as by conscious, intentional effort at any point in life, through the intentional cultivation of specific mental qualities or habits.

(2012: 10)

The resilience recovery continuum: fast or slow?

Davidson builds on his observation that resilience may fluctuate according to circumstance by suggesting that, even within differences in individuals' resilience histories, there is a 'recovery' continuum, from 'Slow to Recover', which can prevent individuals from moving on following a setback, to 'Fast to Recover' in which individuals are able to recover quickly and put the negative experience behind them. It is not necessarily the case, though, that being fast to recover is always positive, for, as Davidson points out, '[i]n order to have a healthy emotional life, you need to be able to feel and respond to your own emotions, which is difficult to do if you move on too quickly' (Davidson, 2012: 242). Moreover, teachers need to be able to respond empathetically to those pupils or colleagues who are slower to recover from setbacks and so are less able to function well for longer periods, if they are not to be perceived as uncaring.

Davidson found, also, that '[r]esilience in the little things is ... a good indicator of resilience on bigger ones' (2012: 47). In schools we may see everyday resilience (in the little things) and being fast to recover as indicators of and contributors to emotional health and a sense of well-being (not complacency), both of which are fundamental to teachers' motivation and capacity to teach at their best.

Contexts that challenge well-being

> [T]eaching is fundamentally characterised and constituted by vulnerability. Vulnerability in that sense is not so much to be understood as an emotional state or experience (although the experience of being vulnerable definitely triggers intense emotions), but as a structural characteristic of the profession.
>
> (Kelchtermans, 2009: 265)

Geert Kelchterman's small-scale qualitative and conceptual research over a number of years provides further compelling evidence of the consequences on teacher professionalism and teachers' emotions of 'regulation, quality controls, policy demands' and what others have called the increasingly performativity, results-driven agendas of governments worldwide (see Chapter 2). Whilst risk and vulnerability are part of the everyday worlds of teachers, as policy-led demands increase and conditions of working change (as, for example, expressed through increasing transparency of teaching and learning processes, performance management and close monitoring and measuring of pupils' progress and achievement), so the sense of vulnerability to external and well as classroom pressures may increase. Such vulnerability may threaten teachers' sense of job satisfaction, fulfilment and well-being, affect their motivation and even cause them to question their competence to 'make a difference' in the learning lives and achievements of their pupils. Longer-term effects may be seen in what Huberman (1989) identified among secondary mid-career teachers in Switzerland as a 'lowering of energy and interest' (1993: 38) and disenchantment in the final phase of their teaching: 'A reason why teachers are vulnerable to burnout is that they regularly engage in dealing with highly complex and emotional structures that expose them to emotionally draining and discouraging experiences' (Pyhältö *et al.*, 2011: 1102).

In a study designed to explore what challenged Finnish secondary school teachers' sense of occupational well-being and what caused burnout, Pyhältö *et al.* (2011) examined the teacher-working environment 'fit' on the basis that a good fit was likely to contribute towards job satisfaction whilst a poor fit was likely to increase the risk of burnout (see also Cable and Edwards, 2004). Whilst it is unlikely that there will be a single cause for teacher burnout, it is, nevertheless, important to take the notion of 'teacher-working environment fit' seriously, since it is likely to relate both to teacher retention or turnover and especially to levels of teacher motivation and commitment. Moreover, where the 'fit' between teacher and environment is poor, this may be associated with conflicts in values between the teacher and colleagues, teacher and principal, or teacher and pupils. The authors analysed interviews with 68 teachers of primary- and secondary-aged pupils in nine case study schools across Finland. Not surprisingly, they found that the levels of reported 'exhaustion, cynicism, inadequacy and alienation' varied. However, the authors did find that 'more than half of the teachers' descriptions (61%) were related to becoming more cynical and feelings of being alienated from their work' (Pyhältö *et al.*, 2011: 1104) and that there were four environments which were associated with these:

1   Teacher-pupil interaction.
2   Interaction within the professional community.
3   Teacher-parent interaction.
4   School system, including school reforms and administration (leadership).

These authors, although working in an entirely different psychological research tradition, found that 'burnout', like 'hopefulness' (Bullough and Hall-Kenyon, 2011b), is not only an individual trait or characteristic, but is also a 'social, collective and relational ... phenomenon' (Pyhältö *et al.*, 2011: 1108) and that whilst 'burnout' is a condition which develops over time,

> it is important to note that teachers' perceived lack of emotional energy, feelings of insufficient competence or distant and acerbic attitude towards the students, parents or colleagues are constructed horizontally in schools' everyday practices. Burdening episodes are often embedded in school practices in such a way that members of the school community may not even be aware of them.
>
> (Pyhältö *et al.*, 2011: 1108)

The same applies to the erosion of commitment, hope and resilience. Factors that contribute positively or negatively to these are likely to be cumulative and context-specific. Thus, when we consider how the capacity and capabilities to be resilient may be built and sustained, teachers themselves and school leaders need to have a continuing focus upon self-reflection, and interpersonal relationships which include attention to teachers' emotional as well as intellectual and practical well-being. Although it is a truism, processes or organisational improvement are unlikely to be successful without equal attention being given to the professional care of all staff as individuals – not only in terms of the physical environment for teaching and learning but also the human environment in which emotional energy is nurtured and sustained, 'hopefulness' flourishes and commitment grows.

Eraut *et al.* (2004, 2007), in researching workplace learning, provide a model which, when read in the context of the need for resilience, indicates the fine balance of interaction between the challenges for the individual of maintaining confidence in themselves and commitment to their work, and the way in which the work is structured, expectations of performance, relationships and levels of support and feedback (see Figure 3.1).

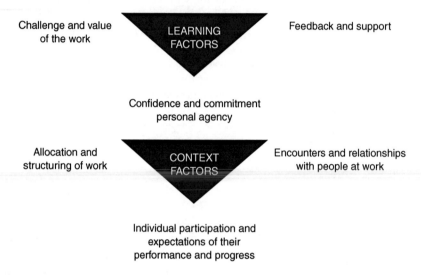

Figure 3.1 Factors affecting learning at work: the Two Triangle Model.

As with other researchers, the authors conclude that a sense of professional autonomy and control is a key contributor to high self-efficacy and job satisfaction – and in the context of this book – a contributor also, to teachers' capacity to be resilient.

Writing about the 'Job-Demand-Control-Support' model (Karasek, 1979; Karasek and Theorell, 1990), from which Eraut takes his inspiration, Caspersen (2013: 30) notes that 'when jobs are highly demanding and provide high levels of control, there is great potential for learning ... but, when demands are high and control is low, stress and poor health result'. However, he points to later research in the Netherlands (Taris *et al.*, 2003) which suggests that there is an important difference between demands by others and control. Job demands by others may have a negative effect on learning, whereas the reverse is the case with job control. We know, also, from the work of Eraut *et al.* (2004, 2007) and others that the social contexts of teaching may have positive or negative influences and that, within these, individual resilience histories are likely to play their part. Figure 3.2 is a tentative model which we have constructed in order to understand the relationships between demands, control, autonomy, self-efficacy, job fulfilment, social contexts and resilience.

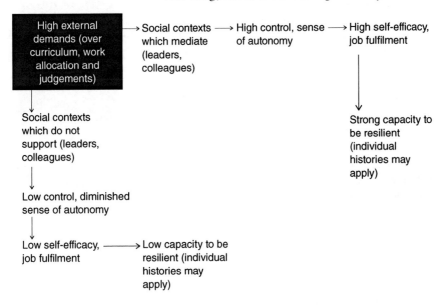

Figure 3.2 How external job demands, and social mediation interact to build or reduce self-efficacy, job fulfilment and the capacity to be resilient.

Academic optimism: more than a positive personal trait

> Teacher sense of academic optimism is individual teachers' beliefs that they can teach effectively, their students can learn and parents will support them so the teacher can press hard for learning...
>
> (Beard *et al.*, 2010: 1136)

As a result of carrying out a number of studies in the USA, based upon Bandura's (1994) self-efficacy theories and Seligman's (1998) notion of 'learned optimism', and building on their earlier research, these authors found not only that collective academic optimism, which is a 'latent' property of successful school cultures, includes student achievement but that it is also a factor at the level of individual teachers. The authors conceive academic optimism as the product of interactions between a focus on learning (academic emphasis), collective efficacy, and trust in parents and pupils. Trust qualities are indicated by benevolence, reliability, competence, honesty and openness (Hoy and Tschannen-Moran, 1999), and these are able to be nurtured within school cultures and structures, which are enabling:

> [E]nabling bureaucracies in schools manifest(ed) themselves through shared authority within established roles, two way communication, seeing problems as opportunities, respecting differences, engendering trust, learning from mistakes and welcoming the unexpected ... trust in the principal, absence of

role conflict, truth telling, teacher sense of power, authentic interpersonal relationships among teachers, and open communication between teacher and principal.

(Hoy and Sweetland, 2001; in Beard *et al.*, 2010: 1138)

So there seems to be a clear association between teachers' capacity for developing and sustaining academic optimism (academic emphasis, self-efficacy and trust) and the way their leaders promote this through their influence upon school structures and cultures. In relation to teachers' contributions to student learning, this work may be said to be complemented by Bryk and Schneider (2002) who identified four social conditions present in improving elementary schools in Chicago:

1 teachers who have a 'can do' attitude;
2 relationships with parents;
3 collaborative work practices; and
4 high expectations.

Whilst many teachers may enter the profession with a strong sense of academic optimism, this may be reinforced or eroded over time by positive or negative workplace influences. Academic optimism, therefore, is more than a personal disposition to 'expect to have positive outcomes, even when things are hard' (Carver and Scheier, 2002: 233).

Hope, resilience and the capacity to teach well

Bullough and Hall-Keynon (2011b) suggest that, at least in the USA as in many other countries, governments place an over-reliance on pupil test scores on standardised tests and examinations as the most accurate means of assessing schools' relative performance; and that this has led to: i) an increased perception by teachers that they will be punished if their pupils underperform when compared to other schools in their own and other systems internationally; and ii) an increased implicit threat in government school improvement initiatives of more punishment if teachers do not work more efficiently in order to ensure that pupil test scores rise. Such increases in the functionalist purposes of teachers' work are not confined to the USA and these have, it may be argued, been inadvertently spread by the development of systems for international comparisons of pupils' progress and attainment.

Below we provide examples of what some researchers have found about the effects of results-driven cultures upon how (some) teachers view their work within externally dominated policy contexts:

- '*Defensive*' teaching (Bracey, 2009) where frequency of external monitoring is high, risk taking is low, conservatism high. Extreme examples of this would be a continuing emphasis upon 'teaching to the test' and the use of a limited range of teaching approaches rather than, for example, independent learning or problem-solving activities.

- *'Threat rigidity'* (Olsen and Sexton, 2009) where school management structures stress conformity within highly centralised control mechanisms and where innovative thinking is not promoted.
- *'Data saturated'* classrooms and schools, where the emphasis is upon the generation of detailed information about pupil progress and achievement to enable target setting and high levels of close, almost atomistic monitoring, often against assessment templates. No criticism of data collection, analysis and use in itself is implied here, unless such data is tied only to a functionalist, efficiency and linear view of learning where pupils and teachers drown in data to the exclusion of broader educational purposes and processes.

Bullough and Hall-Kenyon (2011a) explore the effects of what they see as malevolent contexts on teacher motivation and well-being, and their sense of 'hopefulness' (2011a: 128). They draw upon the work of Lazarus (1991) to distinguish between optimism and hope:

> The difference between hope and optimism is logically substantial ... In hope, the belief that circumstances could get better goes hand-in-hand with anxiety about the potential for a negative outcome ... In optimism as it is usually defined, however, there is little or no room for doubt. One is confident that everything will work out well.
>
> (Lazarus, 1991: 672)

They designed and implemented a survey of pre-service and in-service elementary school teachers with a range of teaching experience. The survey itself was based upon a 'Hope Scale' which, 'combines self-reports of agency'; 'a sense of successful determination in making goals in the past, present and future'; and pathways, 'a sense of being able to generate successful plans to meet goals' (Snyder *et al.*, 1991: 570). Our belief is that these terms have a likely association with teachers' capacity for and ability to build and develop resilient qualities. Whilst the findings from their work were more 'suggestive' than 'definitive' (Bullough and Hall-Kenyon, 2011b: 137), the authors concluded that teachers may remain hopeful even when they are not satisfied with their working conditions but that, over time such hope – which the authors associate with their sense of vocation – may become eroded. Alongside this, their optimism, commitment and resilience may decline (Schaufeli and Buunk, 2003):

> Constant striving for control over events without the resources to achieve it can take a toll on the individual who faces an objective limit to what can be attained regardless of how hard she works. If optimism is to survive as a social virtue, then the world must have a causal texture that allows this stance to produce valued rewards. If not, people will channel their efforts into unattainable goals and become exhausted, ill, and demoralised.

> Or people may re-channel their inherent optimism into attainable but undesirable goals.
>
> (Peterson, 2006: 127)

They conclude that:

> [m]aintaining and deepening teachers' investment in and commitment to teaching are crucially important to improved practice and, therefore, of central importance to any successful effort at school improvement ... policies which strengthen teachers' hopefulness are likely good for children.
>
> (Bullough and Hall-Kenyon, 2011b: 137)

If schools want not only to find but also to keep teachers who are knowledgeable, enthusiastic, optimistic, committed and persistent in their belief that they can make a difference in the learning lives of the pupils they teach, then nurturing high self-efficacy and emotional competencies through activities which build the capacities for resilience and the capabilities to manage in everyday as well as exceptional adverse circumstances is essential – not least because, as Tait (2010: 71) suggests, '[r]esilient attitudes and responses to teaching challenges could conceivably be valuable predictors of success in and commitment to a teaching career'.

Reservoirs of care: resilient teachers, resilient pupils

It is a truism to state that the best teaching reflects the combined application of the head (knowledge, intellect), the hand (classroom competences, teaching and learning strategies) and the heart (professional and personal commitment based upon a set of moral and ethical principles). Thus, reason and emotion, the cognitive and affective, are interdependent, indistinguishable in the 'flow' of high quality teaching and learning (Csikszenthmihalyi, 1996). One element that is key to all good teaching and learning is the quality of the relationship between teacher and pupil. A key contributory factor in establishing, growing and maintaining this relationship is a belief by the pupil that the teacher 'cares', not only about the subject that is being taught but also about the pupils. Teaching, as Hargreaves observed long ago, involves, 'human nurturance, connectedness, warmth and love' (Hargreaves, 1994: 175).

We conclude this chapter, therefore, by highlighting the need for teachers to have what we term *reservoirs of care* in order for them to begin to meet these challenges, for we know that this is an essential quality recognised in the best teachers by their pupils:

> [T]he most frequently encountered non-family, positive role models in the lives of resilient children were favourite teachers who took an interest in them, were not academic instructors but were also confidants and positive models for personal identification ... Thus achievement in school is made

more likely when: teachers teach for mastery; curricula are relevant to students' present and future needs; authentic assessment practices are used; democratic classrooms are created where students contribute to the rule-making and governance; rational, humane and consistent behaviour management techniques are adopted; teachers are warm, approachable, fair and supportive and a range of ways of being successful are made available to students.

(Howard *et al.*, 1999: 313–18)

We use this quotation as a means of making explicit the potential influence of teachers in building their students' capacities to be resilient, but also because it signals, at least implicitly, the combinations of qualities, knowledge and skills or competences which teachers need and must apply in order to promote their emotional well-being. They are the detailed demonstration of what, in general terms, are so often known as 'care and support'.

The teaching profession is ... not merely a technical or cognitive practice but also fundamentally social, i.e. relational and emotional, intimately intertwined.

(Aspfors and Bondas, 2013: 243)

In their mixed methods study of Finnish primary-school early career teachers, Aspfors and Bondas identified three characteristics of relationships and the positive and negative ways in which these were experienced by the teachers:

- *Caring about* emphasises the importance of being cared for and acknowledged as a new teacher by others.
- *Reciprocity* focuses on the reciprocal actions between persons involved in the school community (openness, dialogue, exchange, receptivity, attentive listening).
- *Caring for* is the new teacher's own caring for those surrounding them, especially their pupils. It is relational and task-oriented.

(based on Aspfors and Bondas, 2013)

We reproduce below the table which they constructed (Table 3.1) because it reveals the conditions which exist within schools for building upon these three essential relational characteristics of teaching in ways which are likely to promote commitment (and thus, retention) and ways which are likely to lead to job dissatisfaction, diminished commitment or exit.

Whilst this Finnish research focuses upon newly qualified primary school teachers, it may, we believe, be equally applied to those with more experience, since 'caring about', 'reciprocity' and 'caring for' are all key parts of teachers' professional identities and all may be said to contribute to teachers' resilience.

Table 3.1 Categories of characteristic relationships and tensions of paradoxes experienced by NQTs

Relationship	Tensions of paradoxes

Caring about	*Nurturance*
	    Vital and nurturing leadership
	    Collegial reception and support
	    Positive recognition
	Exclusion
	    Lack of recognition and trust
	    Harassment and the need of putting your foot down
	    Demanding contacts and legal proceedings

Reciprocity	*Expansive*
	    Reciprocal collaboration
	    Open and positive atmosphere
	Restrictive
	    Sporadic contact and resistance
	    Different perspectives and one-way communication

Caring for	*Joy*
	    Close and fruitful relationships with pupils
	    Inspiring and rewarding learning and development
	    Full of confidence and respect
	Exhaustion
	    Demanding classroom management and upbringing
	    Challenging pupil behaviour
	    Difficulties meeting individual needs

(Aspfors and Bondas, 2013: 246)

Conclusions

Care in the classroom can only be successful if it is embedded in knowledge of the person for whom one is caring and, within this, an ambition for that person to learn and achieve well. It requires trust and trustworthiness to be nurtured and sustained:

> When we confirm someone, we identify a better self and encourage its development. To do this we must know the other reasonably well. Otherwise we cannot see what the other is really striving for, what ideal he or she may long to make real. Formulas and slogans have no place in confirmation. We do not post a single ideal for everyone and then announce, 'high expectations for all'. Rather, we recognise something admirable, or at least acceptable, struggling to emerge in each person we encounter.
>
> (Noddings, 1998: 192, in Smith, 2004)

When we examine individual and collective acts of care, it is clear that these require considerable resilience. It seems then, that good teaching requires more than the possession of technical competences. Indeed, we have never met a good, effective teacher who does not demonstrate care in his or her teaching. In this sense, good teaching can never be 'emotional labour', where individuals present one set of public feelings (e.g. of friendliness, intimacy) whilst suppressing others in order to carry out their work (Hochschild, 1983). Rather, it is emotional work which requires a genuine desire and 'capacity for connectedness' (Palmer, 1998: 13) on the part of the teacher. If the 'emotional well-being of young people is deeply bound upon the processes of inclusion, teaching and learning, and community building in schools and classrooms ... [and] ... is inseparable from the quality of the relationships between teachers and pupils and pupils and pupils' (McLaughlin, 2008: 365), then it is not only incumbent upon teachers themselves to be resilient but also on school leaders to ensure the necessary enabling conditions for teachers' own capacity and capability to be resilient to grow.

The opportunities to care are much richer for primary school teachers with a whole class responsibility than for secondary school teachers with many classes to teach. Nevertheless, the energy required to enact in teaching the integration of an ethic of individual as well as collective care whilst managing pressures of performativity is considerable – another potential drain on emotional reservoirs and a reason why a focus upon building and sustaining teachers' capacity to be resilient is central to the work of school leaders. Yet, as with hope and commitment, so the capacity to care may be eroded over time, either by the constant challenges posed by pupils who are hesitant to learn, by colleagues who are unsympathetic to the level of personal investment in pupils, or by the teacher's own reservoir of care running dry as a result of too much investment in the values and practices which the best teaching means to them, with too little return on their investment (NEF, 2009: 9).

Part II

Building resilience in teachers

Contexts count

4 Identities and commitment in the workplace

The role of the vocational self

Over time, teachers are likely to face many challenges in building and sustaining their identities as effective and committed professionals, classroom practitioners and members of their school communities. The first part of this chapter will, therefore, examine associations between teachers' sense of identity in the different settings in which they work and the positive and negative influences in these which may challenge their capacities to be resilient over a career span. The second part will focus upon the inner landscape of the teaching self and identify the contributions of educational values and moral purposes to the capacity to be resilient. Within this, and drawing upon considerable empirical data internationally, we will discuss how a strong calling to teach may add to teachers' capacities to sustain their motivation, commitment and effectiveness in a variety of school and personally and professionally challenging contexts. We will show that teachers' intrinsic motivation and emotional commitment to provide the best service for their students is associated with their sense of identity; and that it is teachers' inner vocational drive which helps them to find strength and power to be and to remain intellectually and professionally committed and resilient.

Identity and resilience

Professional identity should not be confused with role. Identity is the way we make sense of ourselves to ourselves and the image of ourselves that we present to others. It is culturally embedded. There is an unavoidable inter-relationship, also, not only between professional, role and organisational identities but also between the professional and *personal selves* because '[d]eveloping a professional identity involves finding a balance between the personal and professional side of becoming a teacher' (Pillen *et al.*, 2012: 8).

In much educational literature it is recognised that the broader cultural, policy and social structures in which teachers live and work, the emotional contexts, as well as the personal and professional elements of teachers' lives, experiences, beliefs and practices are integral to one another; and that there are often tensions between these which impact to a greater or lesser extent upon teachers' sense of agency (the ability and resolve to pursue one's goals). These in turn affect teachers' sense of professional, role and organisational identities. Previous research has either suggested that identities are stable (Nias, 1989), affected by work contexts (Beijaard, 1995) or fragmented (MacLure, 1993). The research reported in this chapter found that identities are neither intrinsically stable nor intrinsically fragmented, but that they can be more, or less, stable depending both upon the capacities of teachers to manage a number of influences within a number of scenarios and the nature of the support provided in the workplace.

> Building an identity consists of negotiating the meanings of our experience of membership in social communities. The concept of identity serves as a pivot between the social and the individual, so that each can be talked about in terms of the other. It avoids a simplistic individual–social dichotomy without doing away with the distinction. The resulting perspective is neither individualistic nor abstractly institutional or societal. It does justice to the lived experience of identity while recognising its social character – it is the social, the cultural, the historical with a human face.
>
> (Wenger, 1998: 145)

If we accept Wenger's notion of identity as a 'pivot between the social and the individual' in investigating the component parts which influence and are influenced by resilience, then identity needs to considered in terms of the extent to which teachers are able to exercise agency both internally (in terms of their sense of vocation) and within the social structures of the workplace.

Teachers spend much of their time in the complex learning environments of classrooms, leading and managing others' learning. However, their participation in classrooms is different from their participation in staffroom life, in the enactment of externally initiated polices, and different again from their participation in social settings outside school. They thus may be said to have 'multi- belongings':

> As such a nexus, identity is not a unity but neither is it simply fragmented … Considering a person as having multiple identities would miss all the subtle ways in which our various forms of participation, no matter how distinct, can interact, influence each other and require co-ordination.
>
> (Wenger, 1998: 159)

We may consider these multi-belongings in terms of three distinct but overlapping identities – the professional, the role and the organisational. Here we draw upon the work of Stets and Burke (2000) and Burke and Stets (2009), who have argued that differences between identity theory and social identity theory are 'more in emphasis than in kind' (Stets and Burke 2000: 224) and that they overlap in three areas: social identity, role identity and person identity: 'People possess multiple identities because they occupy multiple roles, are members of multiple groups, and claim multiple characteristics, yet the meanings of these are shared by members of society' (Burke and Stets, 2009: 6).

The identification of these is a further development of our previous empirical research in which we found that the relative stability or instability of their sense of identity was influenced by changes in the policy/socio-cultural, professional/ personal and situational (workplace) scenarios which teachers experienced. Where one of these dominated, more energy was required to manage this and so teachers would be likely to have less energy to manage all three. Where two dominated, the efforts to manage all three well were greater. In other words, their capacity to manage the anticipated and unanticipated challenges in each of these scenarios (at different times and in different circumstances) required different degrees of resilience (Day *et al.*, 2007a; Day and Kington, 2008). Further consideration of our data led us to the conclusion that the personal, policy/socio-cultural and situational are not only the settings in which teachers work but also constitute their key identities.

By *professional identity* we mean how teachers regard themselves in relation to the community of teachers to which they belong. We include in this teachers' *personal identity.* Although this is, of course, so much broader and more complex in itself, we believe that it is also a part of the professional identity of every teacher. Later in this chapter, we will discuss, in relation to this, the key parts played by teachers' moral purposes and vocational selves in sustaining commitment to the profession of teaching and to their capacities for resilience. By *role identity,* we mean how teachers see themselves in the particular role they play as classroom teacher, subject leader, head of department, faculty or as a member of the senior leadership team. By *organisational identity,* we mean how teachers see themselves as members of their school or department. There are connections here with teachers' sense of pride and loyalty, motivation to work for the greater good of the school. There may also be connections with teacher retention.

Managing competing discourses in shaping and enacting professional identities

Professional, role and organisational identities are in part expressed through the way teachers are able (with and without the support of others) to mediate and manage what Judyth Sachs calls 'two competing discourses':

> The management discourse gives rise to an entrepreneurial identity in which the market and issues of accountability, economy and effectiveness shape how teachers individually and collectively construct their professional identities. Democratic discourses, which are in distinct contrast to the managerialist ones give rise to an activist professional identity in which collaborative cultures are an integral part of teachers' work practices. These democratic discourses provide the conditions for the development of communities of practice.
>
> (Sachs, 2001: 159)

Although this is a helpful means of understanding the broader context of teachers' work, the ways in which such discourses are mediated and managed through professional, role and organisational identities are more complicated than Sachs suggests. Teachers' work and lives will be influenced by their personal and social histories and belief systems as well as their current workplace experiences of shifts in personal settings, externally initiated policy and social conditions.

MacLure concluded from her research that, at times of intense demands for change, these represent 'sites of struggle' and that 'each teacher also partially constructed that context according to his or her biographical project, that is, the network of personal concerns, values and aspirations against which events are judged and decisions made' (MacLure, 1993: 314). If this is so, the demarcation between 'managerialist' and 'democratic' becomes less clear cut. Some teachers, for example, may place themselves in close agreement with managerialist agendas, others less so; some may be in close agreement with democratic discourses and yet others less so, since these may threaten their existing, less democratic identities.

One example of the diverse and complex nature of teachers' views about their sense of professional, role and organisational identities may be found in the results of two large-scale surveys of teachers in England administered in 2003 and 2006. These revealed that teachers' views were multi-layered, consisting of:

> an inner core of strong, shared beliefs and commitments; an intermediate set of coherent but contested components of professionalism; and an outer layer of disparate elements which are generally highly disputed and which remain unintegrated into broader ways of thinking.
>
> (Swann *et al.*, 2010: 549)

The surveys found that at the intermediate level, for example, 'teaching as collaboration with others' (2010: 567) attracted only 'modest levels of agreement' (2010: 567); that there was 'a wide divergence of opinion among teachers' (2010: 568) concerning the importance of autonomy; and that between 2003 and 2006 there had been 'a significant weakening of support' (2010: 568) for this.

Our own empirical work adds to this and develops that of Sachs and others by suggesting that work contexts are also important in the shaping and re-shaping of professional, role and organisational identities. We see this clearly in the experiences of beginning teachers (Flores, 2004; Flores and Day, 2006) but also more experienced teachers, which we will discuss in Chapter 5. For example, it is clear that in each of their six professional life phases (see Chapter 5 for a summary of these) there are teachers whose commitment is rising or stable and those whose commitment is declining. These commitment trajectories are also associated with the positive and negative scenarios which they experience and their capacity and capability to mediate and manage these. Thus, professional, role and organisational identities (how teachers see themselves and how they would like others to see them) may, also, be stable and unstable, and positive or negative. In the same way that associations between 'well-being', 'emotional style' and resilience are important, so also are associations between identity, commitment and resilience.

Identity, commitment and resilience: issues of stability and change

Commitment theory (Becker, 1960; Kanter, 1972) conceptualises how individuals make choices and these are based on 'how individuals "orient" themselves to the costs and rewards involved in participating in the culture, to the emotional attachment to others within the culture, and to the "moral compellingness" of the norms and beliefs of the system' (Kanter, 1972: 68, cited in Torres, 2012: 120). So, looking at identity and commitment through the lens of socio-cultural theory (Eisenhart, 2001), we can immediately see that there is a likely connection, for example, between the relative stability of a positive sense of identity and the relative stability of a positive commitment. Thus, where the relative stability of the scenarios in which teachers play out their identities is challenged, it is likely, also, that levels of commitment will be affected. The same would be true in reverse. That is, where levels of commitment are challenged, for example by work overload, poor conditions for teaching and learning or external policies which challenge existing values and practices which are viewed as efficacious and successful, then it is likely that teachers' professional identities will be negatively affected:

> Commitment is not something that teachers have when they enter and lose when they leave. Rather, commitment is constantly developing and evolving throughout a teacher's career. Commitments change as teachers experience different factors and circumstances in their various contexts. Retention involves individuals' conceptions of what it means to be a teacher along with how they interpret what happens in their personal lives and in the school cultures in which they work.
>
> (Torres, 2012: 120)

The clear implication is, then, that there are associations of influence between teachers' professional, role and organisational identities and commitment and resilience. As Brunetti's (2006) study on the resilience of teachers in one inner-city high school in the USA shows, managing and sustaining each of these and the associations between them must be understood in the context of leadership and collegial support. Commitment and devotion to students and pursuit of personal and professional fulfilment were found by Brunetti to be two primary reasons for teachers' decision to remain in the classroom and also at a school where challenges, difficulties and feelings of frustration were often experienced on a daily basis. A strong belief in social justice and a desire to do their part for the society drove their commitment and were clear characteristics of their professional identities. However, it was the support from school leadership and colleagues that had enabled them to sustain hope and resolve in the face of difficult circumstances and continue to fulfil their professional responsibilities as they saw them.

As we have seen earlier in this chapter, previous research by the authors and colleagues (Day *et al.*, 2007a; Day and Kington, 2008; Day, 2011) identified different scenarios with which teachers are likely to engage in each phase of their working lives. Importantly, building upon a hypothesis of relationships between variations in teachers' work and lives, their identities and their commitment and effectiveness (Figure 4.1), it found empirical associations between teachers' positive and negative sense of professional identity, the ways in which these impact upon their sense of efficacy, agency, well-being and job satisfaction, and their perceptions of effects on pupils.

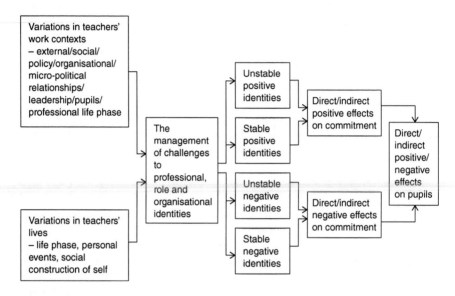

Figure 4.1 Relationships between identity, commitment and effectiveness.

It has been claimed in previous small-scale, short-term, snapshot studies of teachers, usually experiencing extremely challenging circumstances (e.g. Troman and Woods, 2001; Stronach *et al.*, 2002), that they lead lives of stability and instability at the same time. However, our previous research, which analysed teachers' responses to different scenarios over a three-year period (Day *et al.*, 2007a), suggested a more nuanced picture. Whilst there were undoubtedly tensions caused by the relative dominance of one or more key influences or challenges to existing identities in three scenarios, many teachers were able to manage these and thus maintain stability within what from the outside seemed to be, and were, vulnerable, unstable environments. It seems, therefore, that existing professional identities are more or less vulnerable at different times and in different ways according to teachers' capacity to manage the interaction of a number of policy, workplace and personal challenges.

Teachers' professional, role and organisational identities themselves may be seen, then, as being subject to influence by existing socio-cultural policy, workplace and personal influences and changes within and between these (Day *et al.*, 2007):

1 Socio-cultural/policy influences/changes. These reflect cultural, social and policy expectations of teachers and teaching, and the educational ideals, ethical and moral purposes of the teacher. These are subject to the influence of changing policy and social trends as to what constitutes a good teacher, classroom practitioner etc., and may contain a number of competing and conflicting elements such as local or national policy, continuing professional learning and development, workload, roles and responsibilities etc.

2 Workplace or socially located influences/changes. These are located in the micro-politics and social relationships of specific school, department or classroom contexts and are affected by local conditions, i.e. pupil behaviour, the quality of leadership, support and feedback in teachers' immediate work context.

3 Personal influences/changes. These are located in life outside school and are associated with personal histories, present lives, family, social relationships and personal sense of efficacy and vulnerability.

Whilst such influences and/or changes may create instabilities in teachers' identities, these are not always necessarily negative. They can, for example, stimulate a re-evaluation of current thinking and practices that may no longer be the most effective in changing work situations. For example, a beginning teacher or a teacher who moves schools or takes a new role will inevitably experience a period of instability, as will a teacher who has to learn new knowledge about teaching or adopt new teaching, monitoring and/or assessment strategies. Indeed, as we have seen, Kelchtermans (2009) argues that vulnerability is a structural condition of teaching. However, the longer a sense of negative instability persists as a result of the dominance of one or more clusters of influence, the more unlikely it is that the teacher will be able to manage the others.

Professional, role and organisational identities held by teachers will, then, be the consequence of how they manage these changes within and across particular classroom, school and policy environments and life and career phases. Teachers may at any time and over time experience tensions as a result of the challenges to existing identities (values, practices, sense of professionalism) which change may represent. The strength of teachers' job fulfilment, well-being, self-efficacy and vulnerability, commitment, and their capacity to be resilient will be affected but not necessarily determined by these changes. Each of these will be mediated by teachers' cultural traditions, sense of vocation/moral purpose/values and agency and the interaction between these and their working environments. According to Burke and Stets (2009), 'humans maintain a steady and stable environment in the face of disturbances, and they do so by changing their actions (output) to make their perceptions (input) match a reference standard' and this has implications for stress and self-esteem. Managing such temporary (or persisting) challenges of change, whether negative or positive, to professional, role or organisational identities will require additional time and emotional energy from teachers. However, the extent to which they are able to draw upon these in order to sustain or renew their positive sense of identity is likely to be influenced by the nature of the support in the workplace.

There are implications from these findings for policy makers and school leaders. Teachers need to be committed and resilient in order to sustain their sense of effectiveness in what are emotionally as well as intellectually demanding and often changing work contexts. These are associated with their sense of positive or negative professional, role and organisational identities. When challenges of change are unacknowledged or poorly managed, either nationally by policy makers, within the school by school leaders, or by teachers themselves, instabilities in existing positive identities are likely to increase. Alongside these, challenges to continuing professional, role and organisational effectiveness are likely to grow. It is important, then, for policy makers and school leaders, if they really want the enactment of system-wide school and curriculum change and improvement agendas to succeed, to factor into their planning their potential positive and negative destabilising effects upon teachers' identities. The kind of environments in which individuals in schools are more likely to flourish are not those which Bullough and Hall-Kenyon (2011b) among many others, identify as threatening, fearful or alienating, but ones in which trust, engagement, optimism and hope grow – what have been described as 'professional learning communities' (see Chapter 6 for a discussion of this).

The call to teach

> It is obvious that no one becomes a teacher because of salary, respect, or prestige. Nor do they enter the profession to help students pass standardized tests or to teach them to fill in the blanks. No, people come into teaching for good and noble reasons, reasons that are hard to remember in the present context. Most of us probably had teachers who opened our eyes, our hearts, and our minds, and we know the enormous difference that teachers, when given the chance, can make in the lives of their students. Clearly, matters beyond the technocratic goals of schools today bring people to teaching, and keep them there.
>
> (Nieto, 2010: ix)

What is clear from this and a range of research over time (Bernstein, 1996; Wenger, 1998; Castells, 1997; Hall, 1996; Melucci, 1996; MacLure, 1993; Hargreaves, 2000; Beijaard *et al.*, 2004) is that a stable, positive sense of professional, role and organisational identities, which we have discussed in the first part of this chapter, is likely to be based upon clear sets of educational values, beliefs and practices which place care and achievement of pupils at the centre, and that this is a key factor in teachers' capacities to be resilient.

There is overwhelming evidence in the literature on teachers' work and lives which shows how commitment to children's learning and achievement functions as a strong internal drive which enables many teachers to remain meaningfully engaged in the profession over time. For them, those snapshot memories of children's success, whether big or small, give them immense 'pleasure' and 'joy' and provide them with sustained emotional strength to teach to their best. Also, for them teaching is more than just a job. It is a 'lifestyle'. Hansen (1995) argues that in contrast to a profession which has an emphasis on public recognition and larger rewards, the language of vocation 'takes us "inward" into the core of the [teaching] practice itself', that is 'what many teachers do, and why they do it' (1995: 8). The following thoughts about teaching from a teacher in Nieto's research probably provide the best testimony to Hansen's observation:

> Maintaining my enjoyment and passion for teaching for over 20 years can be attributed to several reasons, two of which include the love and respect I have for my students and my personal need to remain intellectually alive. However, the principal reason why I continue to enter the classroom with energy and a sense of hope lies in how I view what I do. Teaching is not just my profession; it is my calling; it is my mission.
>
> (Nieto, 2003: 128)

In the VITAE study in England the large majority of the 300 teachers in different phases of their professional lives (Day *et al.*, 2006, 2007a) reported an initial strong calling to teach and continued enjoyment of working with children and watching them grow. Their intrinsic motivation and emotional commitment to provide the best service for their students were associated with an ethic of care for the well-being of their pupils. This was at the heart of what they did and how they lived their lives in the profession.

However, to continue to exercise care over a professional life span demands considerable intellectual and emotional commitment. Palmer (1998) proposed three important interwoven paths in the inner landscape of the teaching self: intellectual, emotional and spiritual. He explained that the teacher's inner quest to help pupils learn, their feelings and emotions which promote or hinder the relationships between them and their pupils and their hearts' longing to be connected with the work of teaching, form the essence of their inner terrain. In developing his view, we argue that a key notion that connects the three paths of teachers' inner worlds is that of 'vocation' or 'calling'. The testimonies of the four teachers in Hansen's classic study (1995) are illustrations of many of the meanings 'characteristically associated with helping others learn and improve themselves intellectually and morally' (1995: 15). Such enthusiasm and love for the children had not only drawn many VITAE teachers into teaching, but also provided them with the inner strength to continue to teach to their best in the face of the challenges created by work-life tensions. Teachers' inner vocational drive, as Hansen (1995) observes, fuels teachers' personal resources with 'determination, courage, and flexibility, qualities that are in turn buoyed by the disposition to regard teaching as something ... to which one has something significant to offer' (Hansen, 1995: 12). More importantly, because it is associated with a strong sense of professional goals and purposes and 'an inner incentive which prevents

[the] person from treating his work as a routine job with limited objectives' (Emmet, 1958: 254–5), it helps turn 'the focus of perception in such a way that the challenges and the complexities in teaching become *sources of interest* in the work, rather than barriers or frustrating obstacles to be overcome' (Hansen, 1995: 144).

In their work on the resilience of more than 500 teachers in primary and secondary schools in Beijing, Gu and Li (2013) found that what was also embodied in teachers' vocational commitment was a strong desire for continuing professional learning and development. For example, when reflecting on her 23 years in teaching, a mid-career teacher in their research felt that the most rewarding periods of her career were those years when she was deeply involved in training, research and development, endeavouring to make a difference to the pupils' learning. Those were very difficult years because she had to juggle constantly between work and family commitments. Yet where possible, all her evenings and weekends were spent on research into teaching and learning: 'But it was worth it, especially when you look back at it now, because I helped the children learn and I also helped myself mature more quickly as a professional.'

Indeed, because of these very acts of learning for her and the others in that research, teaching became, not a string of repetitive chores and duties that they had to deal with, but rather 'an open-ended series of new opportunities and possibilities' (Hansen, 1995: 144) in which they saw their confidence growing, their capacity to spark their students' interest in learning improving and, subsequently, their sense of moral, personal and intellectual fulfilment deepening.

Conclusions: self-efficacy, emotions and resilience

There has been relatively little research which has focused upon relationships between self-efficacy, the emotional aspects of teaching and teacher identities (see Day and Lee, 2011; Isenberger and Zembylas, 2006; Noddings, 2005, 2010; O'Connor, 2008; Schutz and Zembylas, 2009; Sutton and Wheatley, 2003). We have shown in Chapter 3 that emotions play a key mediating role in the capacities and capabilities of teachers to be resilient; and that they are the necessary link between the social structures in which teachers work and the ways they act; the ways they construct and, at times re-construct their identities:

> [E]motion is a necessary link between social structures and social actors. The connection is never mechanical because emotions are normally not compelling but inclining. But without the emotions category, accounts of situated actions would be fragmentary and incomplete. Emotion is provoked by circumstance and is experienced as transformation of dispositions to act. It is through the subject's active exchange with others that emotional experience is both stimulated in the actor and orienting of their conduct. Emotion is directly implicated in the actor's transformation of their circumstances, as well as the circumstances' transformation of the actor's disposition to act.
>
> (Barbalet, 2002: 4)

As we have seen in Chapter 3, there are close connections between a positive sense of identity, a strong sense of moral purpose, emotional maturity and well-being. The academic progress and achievement of pupils is more likely to be supported by teachers who have a sense of professional well-being, are committed and able to teach to their best; and possess the emotional energy, optimism and hope which enable them to manage a range of internally and externally generated challenges for continuing improvement: in other words to be resilient. The close connection between cognition and emotion which runs through each chapter in this book represents a view that the two should not and cannot be treated as separate components when examining teachers' and pupils' lives. The health of both play an important role in how teachers see themselves and how they form, develop and sustain (or do not sustain) their sense of professional, role and organisational identity:

> Discussions of emotionality in teachers' work form a counter-discourse to the technical rationalist emphasis on teacher standards. Whilst standards seek to define and prescribe the professional role that teachers play, teachers' identities are complex and socially situated within lived experiences.
>
> (O'Connor, 2008: 125–6)

The capacity to be resilient, whether in everyday classroom life or in more extreme and unusually testing circumstances, also suggests the possession of high self-efficacy beliefs and a sense of optimism. This kind of teacher is a person who, as Davidson (2012), in writing about his second dimension of emotional style, 'outlook', puts it, maintains 'a high level of energy and engagement even in the most trying circumstances ... pleasure from a life that, objectively, could easily be a source of unhappiness or anxiety ... Outlook reflects how long and how well you can sustain positive emotions' (2012: 48–9).

However, in research in the Netherlands which drew upon data from the Netherlands Working Conditions Survey of 2010, Roosmarijn *et al.* (2014, in press) found that the proportion of respondents from the educational sector agreeing with the statement, 'I can meet the psychological demands of my work', was significantly lower than the average for all sectors; and the proportion of those who perceived emotional workload, time pressure and frequent unnecessary administrative tasks as negative factors was the highest of all sectors. Moreover, significantly more respondents from the education sector than all other sectors also stated that measures to reduce stress and emotional work were insufficient.

In the USA, Melanie Tait (2008) focused on the relationship between resilience and what she calls two human strengths – personal efficacy and emotional competence. She points to the literature on risk and resilience in which researchers agree that 'risk factors contribute to psychological distress while protective factors moderate the effects of adversity' (Tait, 2008: 59). Like Benard (2004), Hong (2010), and Tschannen-Moran and Hoy (2001), she suggests that teachers with high self-efficacy are likely to have more capacity for resilience than those with low self-efficacy: 'Efficacy beliefs influence teachers' levels of effort, goal setting, persistence, resilience, willingness to try new ideas and strategies, enthusiasm, organisational, planning, fairness and commitment to teaching' (Tait, 2008: 59).

Support from within the school (mentoring, guidance, feedback and encouragement from a collegial community, whether in the department, faculty or school) is likely to strengthen a sense of self-efficacy, belonging and loyalty to the school and the profession itself as part of the growth of teachers' stable, positive professional, role and organisational identities.

Such teachers are likely to have a strong sense of self and in their identity as professionals who are recognised as having 'the capacity to judge, to act and to take responsibility' (Kelchtermans, 2009: 266) for decisions about the academic progress and well-being of the pupils in their classrooms which may be threatened.

> Perceived self-efficacy is concerned with people's beliefs in their capabilities to exercise control over their own functioning and over events that affect their lives. Beliefs in personal efficacy affect life choices, level of motivation, quality of functioning, resilience to adversity and vulnerability to stress and depression. People's beliefs in their efficacy are developed by four main sources of influence. They include mastery experiences, seeing people similar to oneself manage task demands successfully, social persuasion that one has the capabilities to succeed in given actualities ... Ordinary realities are strewn with impediments, adversities, setbacks, frustrations and inequities. People must, therefore, have a robust sense of efficacy to sustain the perseverant effort needed to succeed. Succeeding periods of life present new types of competency demands requiring further development of personal efficacy for successful functioning. The nature and scope of perceived self-efficacy undergo changes throughout the course of the lifespan.
>
> (Bandura, 1994: 71)

This long extract from Bandura's seminal work is important because it highlights the relationship between individual's sense of self, their belief that they can affect pupils' learning lives, regardless of particular circumstances, and the influence of work contexts and life changes upon their capacity to be resilient. It links, also, to work which associates individual and collective academic optimism and hope with the capacity to teach well.

This chapter has explored the nature of teachers' professional, role and organisational identities, and in particular the part played in teachers' capacity for resilience by their vocational selves; how these are important as a means of furthering understandings of the job of teaching and what it means to be a teacher striving to be effective in changing policy, workplace and personal contexts. Teachers' self-efficacy, their emotional commitments to their students, colleagues and schools may be influenced by the extent to which they are able to manage and, where appropriate, adapt existing identities in testing times. What we have tried to establish are the ways in which teachers' inner worlds of professional identity and vocation influence their capacity to learn and to teach to their best over the course of their careers. To teach at one's best over time is not easy. As Nieto (2003) observes:

> Even under the best of circumstances, teaching is a demanding job, and most teachers do not work under the best of circumstances. The enthusiasm and idealism that bring them to teaching dissipate quickly for many. This is not a new problem.
>
> (Nieto 2003: 3)

What has become clear to us in exploring associations between teacher identities and teacher resilience is the integral role of teachers' vocational self in enabling them to continue to be committed to making a difference to the lives of their pupils at a time when the contexts of teaching are populated with centrally monitored and controlled performativity agendas and initiatives. The concept of vocation offers a lens which takes us closer to the inner landscape and professional identities of many teachers who have managed to maintain their 'courage to teach' (Palmer, 2007). It also enables us to understand what many teachers do and why they do it in their classrooms and schools. What we have observed from the accounts of these teachers is that their drive and strong sense of agency enable them to be activist professionals (Sachs, 2003a, 2003b), rather than victims of their social and educational contexts; and that their 'missionary zeal' (Nias, 1999: 225) enables them to find emotional strength and power to learn, to teach, and through this, to fulfil their integrity and commitment to make a difference over time.

5 Teacher development, retention and renewal

> It is imperative that schools find effective ways to retain teachers, but it is neither possible nor necessarily desirable to retain all teachers ... While the term retention has positive connotations, suggesting that retention is inherently 'good', it is worth noticing that school administrators and policymakers are interested in the retention of quality teachers.
>
> (Scheopner, 2010: 262)

Attracting, developing and renewing effective teachers are issues of global concern (OECD, 2005b). We define 'effective teachers' as those who have the necessary knowledge and competencies to engage pupils, cause them to learn and achieve to the limits of their potential and beyond and invoke in them a love of learning. Yet to fulfil this definition of effectiveness, teachers themselves need to be highly motivated, for:

> what leads an individual to start a type of behaviour, to direct it towards specific objectives and to support it both intensely and persistently is explained by needs, values and motives which have to be satisfied.
>
> (Müller *et al.*, 2009: 577)

Thus, understanding how effective teachers may develop and be renewed is a critical factor in successful organisational development. We saw in the previous chapter that schools need to pay attention to personal, workplace and socio-cultural and policy factors which may influence teachers' sense of professional identity. These factors may also influence their intrinsic and extrinsic motivation. *Intrinsic* motivation has been defined as:

> doing something because it is inherently interesting or enjoyable ... an inherent tendency to seek out novelty and challenges, to extend and exercise one's capacities, to explore and to learn.
>
> (Ryan and Deci, 2000a: 55, 2000b: 70, cited in Müller *et al.*, 2009: 578)

In contrast, *extrinsic* motivation regulates behaviour 'in order to attain a separable outcome' (Ryan and Deci, 2000b: 71, cited in Müller *et al.*, 2009: 578).

Whilst these interact at different times and in different ways, it is the former – *intrinsic* motivation – which is said to characterise teachers who have a strong sense of vocation or 'calling'. It is these teachers, as we have shown in Chapter 4, who are likely to be resilient in ways which others may not. However, even their resilience, born out of and strengthened by their high levels of commitment, is unlikely to be inexhaustible. It will be enhanced or diminished by the quality of their working environment, the relative autonomy with which they are trusted to organise and conduct their work in classrooms, the support they receive from school leaders and colleagues, the culture of the department and school, and the success which their pupils achieve.

A recent review of the psychological literature on teachers' professional identity found that it was composed of six elements: values, commitment, self-efficacy, emotions, knowledge and beliefs, and micro-politics (Hong, 2010: 1531); that, whilst erosion in each of these was a factor, *emotional burnout* was the key cause of drop out; and that conditions of work in individual schools actively influenced the decision to stay or to leave:

> Unfulfilled commitment, lack of efficacy, unsupportive administrators, and beliefs emphasising teachers' heavy responsibilities were contributing factors for emotional burnout.
>
> (Hong, 2010: 1539)

In a later qualitative study of seven teachers who stayed and seven who left teaching during their first five years, using the same psychological lenses, Hong (2012) found that whilst both groups experienced similar challenges (classroom management and effective delivery of lessons), 'leavers showed weaker self-efficacy beliefs than stayers, who tended to get more support and help from school administrators' (2012: 417). Hong concluded that,'[t]he stayers and leavers showed different resilient attitudes and responses to challenging situations'. It is worth referring to this conclusion in detail, since it provides insights into the ways in which teachers' psychological constructs (values, beliefs, self-efficacy, commitment, emotions) influence and are influenced by their working environments, and the extent to which different teachers are able to manage (or not manage) such dynamic interactions:

> When leavers faced the challenges of managing the classroom and handling students' misbehaviours, they often experienced diminished self-efficacy beliefs, attributed the difficulty to their own personality or characteristics and experienced emotional burnout. However, under the same challenging situation, stayers could still maintain strong self-efficacy beliefs with the help and support of administrators. Additionally, they strategically set emotional lines or boundaries between themselves and students, so that

they would not take negative events personally or get burned out. Regarding content-specific beliefs, leavers held the belief that they were heavily responsible for students' learning, not realising students' own role and effort in the learning process.

(Hong, 2012: 431)

Table 5.1 opposite identifies three key motivators which attract teachers to the profession initially – job characteristics, working conditions and professional image – and shows how these may become degraded over time, causing them to leave. The final column on the right shows how five 'key determinants' can 'leverage' the motivation of teachers over the course of their careers: task system; leadership system; reward system; social system; and professional development system.

Professional life phases: characteristics and trajectories

Teachers are likely to experience different challenges in different professional life phases and the ways in which they – and their leaders – are able to manage these are likely to affect their job satisfaction and fulfilment. We know from a range of research, for example, that teachers' may lose heart over time as a result of: i) tensions in relations with pupils and parents; ii) excessive externally imposed initiatives and reforms; iii) increases in bureaucracy; and iv) negative images of teaching in the media (Smithers and Robinson, 2003).

Strong identification with the teaching fades over time. It seems that the initial enthusiasm for teaching cannot, unfortunately, be maintained over the years. More experienced teachers' regret, on a systematic basis, that the professional image of teaching has deteriorated over the course of their career.

(Müller *et al.*, 2009: 591)

Teachers' commitment and resilience are mediated by their capacities and capabilities to advance their pupils' learning successfully and the kinds and quality of the support they receive in managing different professional, role and organisational identities in the different and sometimes competing 'scenarios' in which they live and work and by their needs and concerns, as we have seen in Chapter 4. It follows that school leaders: i) need to be aware of these 'scenarios' and 'phases' if they are to plan for CPD (continuing professional development) which is relevant and effective; that ii) CPD will need to represent a range of both formal and informal learning and development opportunities; and iii) that CPD interventions must 'target' both instrumental needs and those designed to support teachers' commitment and resilience. The VITAE research (Day *et al.*, 2007a) found that teachers' work and lives spanned six professional life phases and that each had its own challenges to their commitment and resilience.

Table 5.1 Transversal issues to attract, develop and retain teachers' commitment and motivation

Transversal issues	Motivations for entering teaching	Motivations for leaving teaching	Motivational inducement systems involved
Job characteristics	Little job routine Working in a social network providing various human contacts (students, colleagues, parents) An evolving and demanding job Transmission of knowledge to young people	Increasing work load (e.g. increasing diversity of tasks, more administrative work) Increasing number of meetings Dissatisfaction with content and the way that institutional reforms have been implemented Too much effort going into disciplining rather than into teaching students Student behaviour	Task system (e.g. job definition, job description) Leadership system (e.g. change implementation) Professional development system (e.g. enhancement of teacher's competencies) Task system (e.g. evolution of teacher's responsibilities and professional activities) Social system (e.g. perception of teacher's role in society)
Working conditions	Autonomy in pedagogical choices and activities Autonomy in performing teaching activities	Lack of autonomy and flexibility Lack of hierarchical support Lack of flexibility	Task system (e.g. structures and processes to carry out professional activities) Professional development system (e.g. opportunities to acquire skills and knowledge) Leadership system (e.g. guidance and support to carry out professional activities) Social system (e.g. teamwork and feedback procedures) Reward system (e.g. pay and working conditions)
Professional image	Identification with teaching profession	Degradation of teaching profession's image	Task system (e.g. vision creation and mission development) Social system (e.g. shared vision and set of norms)

(Müller *et al.*, 2009: 592)

1. Professional life phase 0–3 years – commitment: support and challenge

Sub-groups:

a   Developing sense of efficacy; or
b   Reduced sense of efficacy.

The outstanding characteristic of the large majority of teachers (85 per cent) was their high level of commitment to teaching. Two sub-groups were observed within this professional life phase: one with a developing sense of efficacy and the other with a reducing sense of efficacy.

Teachers who had an 'easy beginning' benefited from a combination of influences that were more positive than those for teachers who experienced 'painful beginnings'. Teachers in both groups reported the negative impact of poor pupil behaviour on their work.

For new teachers who were struggling to survive the challenges of a new professional life in the reality of the classroom, the impact of combined support from the school/departmental leadership and colleagues was highly significant in helping to build their confidence and self-efficacy and deciding the direction of their next professional life path.

CPD activities in relation to classroom knowledge were most frequently reported as having a positive impact on their morale and as being significant to the stabilisation of their teaching practice. These activities included school/department-based training and INSET days, external (NQT) conferences, and visiting and working with teachers in other schools.

The key influences on these teachers' potential professional life trajectories were found to be the level of support, recognition of their work and the school culture.

2. Professional life phase 4–7 years – identity and efficacy in the classroom

Sub-groups:

a   Sustaining a strong sense of identity, self-efficacy and effectiveness;
b   Coping/managing identity, efficacy and effectiveness; or
c   Vulnerable and declining: identity, efficacy and effectiveness at risk.

An important feature of teachers in this phase in the VITAE research was that promotion and additional responsibilities had already begun to play a significant role in teachers' perceived identities, motivation and sense of effectiveness. Most teachers (78 per cent) in this phase had additional responsibilities and particularly stressed the importance of promotion to their growing professional identity. This suggests that for many teachers this professional life phase is not a stabilisation period. Rather, it is a period in which teachers, whilst consolidating their professional identities in their classrooms, also have challenges beyond these.

An important difference between sub-groups a) and b) was that the latter group had a stronger concern over their ability to manage their heavy workloads. Teachers in sub-group c) felt that their identity, efficacy and effectiveness were at risk because of workload and difficult life events.

Support from the school/departmental leadership, colleagues and pupils continued to be of importance to teachers in this phase who demonstrated a primary concern about their confidence and feelings of being effective. In contrast with professional life phase 0–3, there were more frequent references made to heavy workload, which was seen as reducing their teaching effectiveness. The need for classroom knowledge and knowledge of external policies was markedly less, role effectiveness similar, and CPD which focused upon professional and personal development needs had become more important.

3. Professional life phase 8–15 years – managing changes in role and identity: tensions and transitions

Sub-groups:

a   Sustained engagement; or
b   Detachment/loss of motivation.

This professional life phase, described by some as being populated by 'the most overlooked group in the entire teaching profession' (Hargreaves and Fullan, 2012: 72), marks a key watershed in teachers' professional development. Although they are likely to more established, confident and competent, these teachers are beginning to face additional tensions in managing change in both their professional and personal lives. The majority of teachers in VITAE, for example, were struggling with work-life tensions. Most of these teachers in this phase had additional (79 per cent) out-of-classroom and out-of-school responsibilities and had to place more focus upon their management roles. Heavy workloads also worked against the continuing improvement of their classroom teaching.

Sub-group a) contained teachers who were sustaining their engagement and whose expected trajectories were career advancement with increased self-efficacy and commitment (human capital investment). The combined support from leadership, staff collegiality (high social capital), rapport with the pupils and engagement in CPD were contributing factors in this sub-group's positive sense of effectiveness.

Around half of the teachers in sub group b) reported a lack of support from leadership (50 per cent) and colleagues (60 per cent) – low social capital. Adverse personal events and tensions between work and life were also important issues. Other key characteristics of this sub-group included: giving up management roles because of adverse personal events (e.g. ill health, increased family commitments); decreased motivation and commitment leading to early retirement (e.g. one late entrant and one 'career-break' teacher); and, disillusionment/low self-efficacy/ decreased motivation and commitment.

4. Professional life phase 16–23 years – work-life tensions: challenges to motivation and commitment

In common with the previous two professional life phases (4–7 and 8–15), excessive paperwork and heavy workload were seen by these teachers as key hindrances to their effectiveness. In contrast with teachers from the earlier professional life phases, events in personal lives, coupled with additional duties, had a stronger impact on the work of this phase, and as a consequence, a larger proportion of teachers were struggling with a negative work-life balance. Teachers in this phase were categorised into three sub-groups on the basis of their management of the challenges of work, life and home events:

Sub-group a):   Teachers who had seen their motivation and commitment increase as a result of their further career advancement and good pupil results/relationships and who were most likely to see their motivation and commitment continue to grow (primary = 63 per cent; secondary = 32 per cent);

Sub-group b):   Teachers who maintained their motivation, commitment and sense of effectiveness as a consequence of their agency and determination to improve time management and who were most likely to cope with work-life tensions in their next professional life phase (primary = 30 per cent; secondary = 37 per cent);

Sub-group c):   Teachers whose workload, management of competing tensions and career stagnation had led to decreased motivation, commitment and perceived effectiveness and whose career trajectories were expected to be coupled with declining motivation and commitment (primary = 4 per cent; secondary = 27 per cent).

In addition to work-life tensions, the combined negative effects of pupil behaviour, personal events, policy, leadership and CPD had strongly contributed to sub-group c) teachers' decreased motivation and career stagnation, particularly those in secondary schools.

5. Professional life phase 24–30 years – challenges to sustaining motivation

Teachers in this phase were facing more intensive challenges to sustaining their motivation in the profession. Eighty-eight per cent had additional leadership responsibilities. Deteriorating pupil behaviour, the impact of personal life events, resentment at 'being forced to jump through hoops by a constant stream of new initiatives', taking stock of their careers (and lives) and length of service in the school were key influences on the effectiveness of teachers in this phase. However, not all teachers were disenchanted. On the basis of their levels of motivation, two sub-groups were identified:

Sub-group a): Teachers who had sustained a strong sense of motivation and commitment (primary = 59 per cent; secondary = 45 per cent) and who were most likely to continue to enjoy an increase in their self-efficacy, motivation and commitment;

Sub-group b): Teachers holding on but losing motivation which was most likely to lead to a sense of detachment and early retirement (primary = 41 per cent; secondary = 55 per cent).

Role effectiveness activities continued to be important. Classroom knowledge updates were important to teachers in this phase; and more general professional/personal development needs were of great importance.

6. Professional life phase 31+ – sustaining/declining motivation, ability to cope with change, looking to retire

Pupils' progress and positive teacher-pupil relationships were the main source of job satisfaction for these teachers. Teachers in this phase were categorised into two sub-groups.

Sub-group a): Teachers whose motivation and commitment remained high despite or because of changing personal, professional and organisation contexts and whose expected trajectories were strong agency, efficacy and achievement (primary = 64 per cent; secondary = 64 per cent);

Sub-group b): Teachers whose motivation was declining or had declined and whose expected trajectories were increased fatigue, disillusionment and exit (primary = 37 per cent; secondary = 37 per cent).

Not only were supportive school cultures of crucial importance to teachers' sense of effectiveness across all six professional life phases but, for teachers in this professional life phase, in-school support (high social capital investment) played a major part in teachers' *continued engagement* in the profession.

The VITAE study found that, statistically, it was more likely that pupils of teachers in the later phases of their careers (24+ years experience) achieved at or below expectations than those of pupils in the early and middle phases, thus challenging the notion that expertise necessarily increases with experience. The VITAE study also found an association between experience and commitment trajectories such that those teachers in the later phases were more likely to be less committed than those in the early and middle phases. Based on this and other research internationally (e.g. Nieto, 2003; Borman and Dowling, 2008; Weiss, 1999), it is clear that self-efficacy, motivation, commitment, job fulfilment, morale and the quality of the support in workplace environments are key factors associated with teacher development, quality retention and renewal across all career phases. Scheopner's (2010) review confirms the findings of VITAE (Day *et al.*, 2007a) that retention strategies should focus on 'building and sustaining teacher quality and effectiveness over the whole of their careers' (2010: 254) since it is, above all, retaining teachers' commitment that is most likely to lead to the retention of quality teaching.

In the next part of this chapter, we draw upon a range of selected research drawn from different countries in which the demands for higher standards and more accountability are continuing to increase. We use these as a means of illustrating the complexity of teachers' work and the challenges which they face now and which are likely to continue to increase in every phase of their working lives. The texts provide examples of the tensions between the emotional and rational environments which teachers need to manage and the interactions between schools, personal and policy contexts which have positive and negative influences upon their capacity to be and remain resilient:

Uncertain futures: the first five years

> Given the current climate of high levels of teacher attrition, it is critically important that we understand what keeps early career-teachers in the profession.
> (Peters and Pearce, 2012: 249)

No matter what mode of pre-service preparation that they have experienced, when faced with the on-going, everyday myriad of challenges to intellect, expertise and emotional stability which responsibilities for pupils' care, learning and achievement pose, it is not surprising that many early career teachers feel overwhelmed. In Australia, for example, a relatively recent survey reported that 45.6 per cent could not envisage themselves being a teacher in ten years' time (Australian Education Union, 2006, cited in Peters and Pearce, 2012). It is important, therefore, to examine the key positive influences which are likely to ensure that, in Huberman's (1993) terms, new teachers have 'easy' rather than 'painful' beginnings.

In the USA, Ingersoll (2003a) reported that 30 to 50 per cent of new teachers leave the field within their first five years; and the Alliance for Excellent Education (2004) found that 14 per cent leave at the end of their first year, 33 per cent within three years and 50 per cent within five years. Similar rates of attrition have been noted in Australia (Ministerial Council on Education, Employment, Training and Youth Affairs, 2003), Canada (McIntyre, 2003), England (DfES, 2005) and China (Changying, 2007). Although many studies have been carried out to find the reasons for such high attrition, most have focused upon the negative effects of pupil characteristics and work conditions: for example, inadequate support, frustration with the politics and micro politics, workload, pupil behaviour, excessive bureaucracy. There have been fewer studies on how teachers view of themselves as professionals, and their sense of identity, might influence their decisions. Taken together, though, the research suggests that it is a combination of causes, rather than the impact of one single event, which leads to what might be called an erosion of a teacher's sense of professional self or identity:

> a teacher's decision to discontinue teaching is generally not such an immediate choice resulting from a single event. Rather, such a career decision tends to be closely associated with the teacher's own sense of self and identity as a teacher, which have been constructed, challenged, and modified throughout pre-service teacher education and in-service teaching experience.
>
> (Hong, 2010: 1531)

This view of a *process of identity erosion* leading to a decision to leave teaching altogether, or to remain in teaching but to provide less energy or commitment of the heart, to modify or reconfigure one's sense of identity as a protective strategy, seems to be consistent with research which identifies teachers' sense of professional identity or sense of professional self as being a key factor in teachers' motivation, commitment and effectiveness (Day, Elliott and Kington, 2005; Day, Kington, Stobart and Sammons, 2006; Lasky, 2003, 2005; Van den Berg, 2002; Watson, 2006; Beijaard *et al.*, 2004; Johnson, 2003; Bullough *et al.*, 1991; Kelchtermans, 1993).

Many other studies report how the initial optimism and hope with which many teachers enter the profession – one of the few in which new teachers carry as much responsibility in the classroom as their more experienced colleagues – may turn to pessimism as the everyday realities of teaching in the classroom alongside target setting and results-driven cultures begin to deplete reserves of emotional and physical energy levels. Witness, for example, the negative experience of one new teacher in the USA:

> New teachers (in the school) get the difficult kids that no-one wants to teach. They get the split classes, they get the portables ... when you look at the business community, you'd never think of starting someone new off with that many strikes against them. And they wonder why people quit after five years. It's because you're treated, I don't want to say badly, but you're not supported in a lot of different things.
>
> (Tait, 2008: 68)

Less visible in research on teacher resilience, retention, quality and commitment are the stories of those teachers in their early years who begin to lose heart as the combination of high motivation to teach and the effects of fulfilling this begin to conflict with their personal lives. Here is one such story from England:

> I love teaching but I think I am having an identity crisis. It all began when I received a text from an old friend inviting me to a catch up.
>
> 'Fantastic!' I thought, but wait, it was on a Sunday night. Given that I now live a three hour train ride away from my old friends, I decided to

decline on the basis that I needed to be back in London preparing for school the next day.

This makes me sad. Looking back over the past year and a half, I have realised that I can probably count the amount of times I have been out with my old friends on one hand.

Apparently I am not alone. I know NQTs (Newly Qualified Teachers) who have given up sports clubs, social events, friends' birthdays and more, because their lives have just been completely and utterly consumed by the career we have chosen to embark upon.

Thinking back over what my life has consisted of over the past year, term time seems to be this massive black hole, void of social interactions outside of the school sphere. My friends and family must think I'm on another planet, as I enthusiastically try to postpone social events until half-term or Easter.

After five days on manic loop, Saturday and Sunday are spent recovering from the emotional, mental and physical strain of the week while simultaneously attempting to be a little more prepared for the next. Before I know it, Monday has returned to haunt me and it starts all over again.

When I chose teaching as a profession it was because I did not want to spend the majority of my time doing something I did not care about. Teaching is something I enjoy and am passionate about but, if I have no time to do anything else at all with my life, am I anything but a 'teacher'?

I can feel my identity slipping from my grip; what if the only version of me left is the one who stands at the front of the classroom every day? I want to be a teacher but I also want to be other things – a girlfriend, sister, friend, daughter.

I am scared that I am slowly morphing into just 'teacher' and all these other parts of me are fading away or hibernating in term times, ready to pop out over half term or holidays with the hope that loved ones will still be exactly where I left them and not put out by the weeks of neglect and lack of calls.

I love being a teacher and I cannot think of any other job that would give me the same degree of satisfaction and challenge. But I have to say, the way I am feeling this week, roll on half term.

(*Secondary Education*, 15 February, 2013)

We wonder what will happen to this teacher over the longer term. Will she learn to manage the personal and professional domains of her life differently, so that she is able to gain fulfilment from both? Will she begin to put less emotional, mental and physical energy into her work, avoiding a possible spiral to excessive stress and anxiety but perhaps no longer teaching to her best? Will her capacity for resilience remain as it is now, or will it decline and, with it, her commitment?

There is much writing about the 'struggles' which many new teachers experience as they move from being student teachers to teachers-in-practice (e.g. Huberman, 1993; Flores, 2004; Kelchtermans and Ballet, 2002) but rather less empirical research on how they manage the different tensions which they experience as they adjust to contributing full-time to school and classrooms, not only through what they know about subject, pedagogy and learner, but through who they are as educationalists and colleagues (their educational beliefs, their social skills, their motivations and work ethics). Fuller and Brown's (1975) seminal research on the initial phase of teaching found that it was likely to consist of four stages: i) *pre-service concerns* where new teachers identity more with themselves as students rather than teachers; ii) *survival concerns* where new teachers are concerned with how to manage the classroom and whether pupils like them (caring versus tough behaviour); iii) *teaching concerns* where new teachers recognise that being a teacher means more than preparing lessons and teaching them in isolation from others; and iv) *student concerns* where new teachers try to engage in more differentiated, personalised teaching and learning.

Pillen *et al.* (2012: 10) found 13 dilemmas experienced by beginning teachers. Not all new teachers experienced all of these dilemmas, but most (60 per cent) reported that they had experienced tensions between:

- wanting to take care of students versus being expected to be tough
- wanting to invest in a private life versus feeling pressured to spend time and energy on work
- experiencing conflicting orientations in terms of learning to teach.

In order to manage these and other tensions successfully, rather than just 'cope' with them, beginning teachers need to develop very early on – and preferably with the explicit support of their school – the capacities and capabilities for everyday resilience.

The impact of working conditions on 'teachers of promise'

The next source of evidence is a study of primary and secondary school teachers in New Zealand during their first nine years of teaching. Its authors (Lovett and Cameron, 2014, in press) built on the results of Susan Moore-Johnson and her colleagues' research with teachers in their first two years in the USA (Johnson, 2004; Johnson *et al.*, 2012). This found, perhaps unsurprisingly, that a key factor in enjoyment and retention was support from experienced colleagues.

> The subordination of teachers to ... externally mandated priorities for professional learning could seem overwhelming, yet in the midst of these regulations, the individual and collective agency of teachers should not be underestimated.
>
> (Ambler, 2012: 181)

The purpose of this more extended research in New Zealand was to find what built teachers' sense of engagement and pedagogical well-being and what worked against it. The authors found that teachers, like those in the VITAE study in England (Day *et al.*, 2007a), experienced varying levels of support from principals and colleagues and that these and their workplace conditions were 'fundamental to the way teachers feel about their work, to their ability to promote student learning and to their desire to take on leadership responsibilities' (Lovett and Cameron, 2014). Below we provide one negative and one positive illustration from this research of the ways in which teachers' work, lives and resilience can be affected by school conditions:

> I am absolutely loving working in this school. I feel supported just the right amount, and left alone just the right amount too, to get on and do a good job. There is a good work/life balance encouraged and modelled at the school; teachers are respected and treated as professionals.
>
> (Lovett and Cameron, 2014: in press)

> There is a 'culture of fear' in my school, where some teachers feel afraid to make even the smallest mistake, for fear of losing their jobs and perhaps even having their careers tarnished ... several teachers have been disciplined unnecessarily and in a way which has not maintained their ... dignity, nor even allowed them to easily move on to another job.
>
> (Lovett and Cameron, 2014: in press)

Examining the boundary between the inner and outer lives of early-mid career teachers

The third study examined challenges to the personae or identities of teachers in early-mid career phases in Northern Ireland. The lens through which they were examined was self-study. Its author acknowledged, as we do here, that crucial to teaching to one's best is 'sustaining professional commitment, nurturing a passion for teaching and children, generating hardiness and renewing a sense of moral purpose' (Leitch, 2010: 329) and that there is an unavoidable inter-relationship between professional and personal, cognitive and emotional identities (Day *et al.*, 2007b: 105). Using mask-making as a research medium, teachers were invited to 'tell their stories' (2007: 335) through the making of and reflection upon the mask. This research is both unusual and important, for it reaches into the inner selves of teachers which are rarely revealed using more conventional means of inquiry. So, for example, a beginning teacher in her early years revealed that:

> I pretend outwardly in my professional role that I have no tensions at all, while inwardly all those tensions ... are ripping the fabric of my life ... I'm a chameleon, changing all the time.
>
> (quoted in Leitch, 2010: 336)

Another teacher in the second professional life phase found herself 'at odds with the approach of the school to the children' (2010: 340):

The kids need more than that, you know, they ... need to be understood and educated rather than contained and trained. If I can teach effectively then I want to develop a close and genuine relationship with my pupils. If this is deemed so wrong then I am at a loss as to how to teach!

(quoted in Leitch, 2010: 341)

A third, in the middle 'watershed' years of his teaching and head of a science department, created a mask which represented a life in which he managed the private agony of a personal accident, and the impact of working in a challenging school context, 'no-one, outside my departmental colleagues, appeared interested in my recovery once back at school':

The outer mask appears as a bleary-eyed face. It has a visible crack running diagonally across it. Others see these tired eyes resulting from my family life. It never occurs to them that these are also a result of adapting to perpetual changes in the school and the reforms to the curriculum being introduced. For me, this (crack) is the consequence of my accountability as head of department, demands for exam performativity and the fault-lines created by recent restructuring by senior management – changes which were more punishing than anyone was aware of.

(quoted in Leitch, 2010: 344–5)

In another small-scale, qualitative study of resilience and loss in work identities, the authors (Kirk and Wall, 2010) suggest that the 'profound structural changes in education' (2010: 629) which have been described earlier in this book (see Chapter 2) have caused teachers in mid-career to rethink once stable identities, and re-orientate themselves around 'the new needs and demands of an increasingly bureaucratised and commodified education sector' (2010: 629). Their research drew upon accounts of recently retired teachers. They reported that, despite living through challenges which had been demoralising, uncomfortable and difficult, they had demonstrated 'considerable resilience in maintaining their personal identities as teachers' (2010: 633) as a result of their depth of feeling of care, vocation and child-centredness (2010: 633). They had thus, despite a sense of loss, maintained their core identities as professionals.

Veteran teachers: adaptation, regeneration and hardiness

In the fourth study which we report, Cohen (2009) provides detailed portraits of the work and lives of two veteran teachers in an American high school. Both had taught for over 25 years and both were regarded as highly successful. Cohen found that their commitment was as strong as ever, both through their continuing love of the subjects they taught and of their pupils. She identified three themes of endurance:

1   Putting the self first

> Some considerable degree of self-involvement – of narcissism – is vital to teachers' long term survival, particularly in difficult schools where psychic rewards are experienced less frequently.
>
> (2009: 481)

2   Useful amnesia

> One key to my longevity is to always assume the best about every kid. They may very quickly provide me wrong, but at least I start out assuming the best ... Whatever happened yesterday, it's gone. You *have* to assume the best.
>
> (2009: 481)

3   Love of subject

> More than altruism, more than patience, more than love of kids, a 'passion for subject' may be the most critical trait in retaining a particular type of devoted, veteran urban teacher.
>
> (2009: 483)

Whilst these teachers are not presented as typical of veteran teachers and whilst the school in which they worked was situated in an urban community, the advice given by this researcher that, 'if urban schools are to retain more great teachers longer term, they need to find ways to *generate* hardiness' in their staff would equally ring true for all schools. Cohen's use of Maddi's (2002, 2006) work on hardiness is located in positive psychology, and is defined as 'a dispositional factor in persevering and enhancing the performance and health despite stressful conditions' (Maddi, 2002: 76).

Contrary to this study, the VITAE study in England found that not every teacher had been able to generate and sustain 'hardiness' (Day *et al.*, 2007b) and that teachers in what we termed 'later' professional life phases (judged to be 24+) were more likely to lose their sense of commitment. Moreover, the students of those teachers were more likely to progress and achieve at or below expectations than those of teachers in early and middle professional life phases. Within this general pattern, however, the study did find that there were teachers in the later professional life phases who were able to sustain their sense of commitment; and that this was associated with their continuing positive classroom relationships, sense of vocation, enabling school leadership and the collegiality of colleagues.

Individuals, such as those successful veteran teachers in Cohen's (2009) study and an earlier classic study by Nieto (2003), conform to Maddi's (2006) findings that 'hardy' people are those who tend to be most committed, have a strong sense of control over their working environment and feel comfortable with challenge. Yet there are other veteran teachers who have experienced less success and whose narratives reveal somewhat different stories. Some may have only 'survived'.

Staying and impact power: teachers in urban schools

In 'Reflection on their first five years of teaching: understanding staying and impact power', Tricarico, Jacobs and Yendol-Hoppey (2012) examined the preparation and induction experiences of urban elementary school teachers engaged in 'The Transition to Teaching' five-year programme in one school district in Florida. The research took place in a national context where the rate at which teachers were leaving the profession within their first five years in urban schools was running at 50 per cent in urban schools – roughly twice the rate of those in other schools (see also Chapter 7 for a more detailed discussion of the particular challenges faced by those who work in urban schools in challenging socio-economic contexts). The researchers were interested in both teacher success and survival:

> Survival and success are two different things. Survival means that you are pleasing the system and abiding by the many expectations that are important to the administration and bureaucracy of the system. Succeeding is the important part, but it is very different. Succeeding is about the kids' learning.
> (Yendol-Hoppey *et al.*, 2009: 11.
> Cited in Tricarico, Jacobs and Yendol-Hoppey, 2012: 7)

The authors found that survival skills were necessary to build *staying power* and that success skills contributed to *impact power*. They made and tested through their research four assertions. The first three focused upon individual teacher dispositions, not dissimilar to those identified by Wilshaw (see Chapter 3). The fourth examined the social contexts of teaching:

i)   Teachers with 'staying power' and 'impact power' in high poverty schools enter with and maintain an unrelenting persistence, a strong work ethic, and a sense of calling to work with children in high need contexts;

ii) Teachers with 'staying power' and 'impact power' in high poverty schools do not wait for resources to be offered but assertively seek out the specific resources they believe they need to strengthen their teaching practices and provide them necessary support;

iii) Teachers with 'staying power' and 'impact power' attribute their success to strong professional knowledge specifically targeted at differentiation of instruction for diverse students and family communication;

iv) Teachers with 'staying power' and 'impact power' seek teacher leadership opportunities to enhance schools but often face barriers to their success.
(Tricarico, Jacobs and Yendol-Hoppey, 2012: 13–29)

The first three of these assertions identify the power of teachers' passion for teaching in schools in challenging urban communities and their strong work ethic and unwavering commitment. The authors found that it was the combination and interaction of these which created 'staying' and 'impact' power. However, the fourth assertion identified, according to the authors, 'three serious barriers which would cause them to, "imagine and generate" a new type of "staying" and "impact" power during the next stage of their careers' (2012: 9).

- Reduction of bureaucracy
- Make everyone (principals, coaches, teachers, families, district administrators, community, and children) do their jobs
- Create a culture where change and improvement are rewarded

(2012: 29)

A quote from one of the teachers illustrates this well:

> For example, the culture of the school, from the students to the adults, needs to become more cohesive. We're very small, so you'd think it would be simple to have everyone on the same page. Even if we're not reading from the same line, just have us on the page, common goal. Sometimes the goals and visions get shaded. Unfortunately, people kind of go in their own direction. I want to work on motivation, team-building, cohesiveness. You have to have teacher buy-in, staff buy-in for things to happen, and lately [it] just hasn't been the case. That's one thing I would like to change. In time, the kids see that and then everybody kind of jumps on board.
> (Ruth, in Tricarico, Jacobs and Yendol-Hoppey, 2012: 28–29)

It is a rare teacher who can sustain staying and impact power through relying entirely upon their own resources, whatever the strength of their 'calling', however dedicated they may be. They need, as we indicate elsewhere in this book, high quality leadership and working conditions which support and reward in order to sustain initial enthusiasm, expand their knowledge and expertise and continue to care.

> Along the years we acquire a temporal perspective. We have experienced evolution and change ourselves. I know individuals in other schools who did not change, but rather have prolonged a particular point in time indefinitely. Our adaptation to changes in the environment enables our survival.
> (Eilam, 2009: 500)

Others, supported by the environment, may have continued to flourish:

> 'We have created a narrative of faith and trust among ourselves; we ask, suggest, criticise, and accept each other's ideas and comments, veterans and teachers alike'.
> (Eilam, 2009: 505).

Teachers who work in schools serving high need communities

Our final example focuses on the special circumstances of teachers who work in urban schools which serve socio-economically disadvantaged communities and how they might be helped to build their capacity to be resilient, 'to adjust to situations that require adaptation and to view the situations as opportunities to continue learning, even under the most adverse of conditions' (Huisman *et al.*, 2010: 484–5). Teachers in these schools often face excessive demands to improve the performance of pupils who, relative to other more advantaged pupils, are already well below national requirements for achievement in literacy and numeracy:

> Whilst all novice teachers experience a degree of stress in their jobs, those teaching in urban schools often cite stress resulting from the chasm they experience between what they perceived their work to be ... and the reality of their classrooms.
>
> (Huisman *et al.*, 2010: 484)

Pupils in these schools often need intensive and sustained individual attention as they struggle to manage emotionally and economically unstable home and community environments with the demands at school; and it is, perhaps, not surprising that many schools serving disadvantaged communities have a higher teacher turnover, especially among teachers in their early years who simply cannot cope with the intensity and complexity of the learning expectations and demands, blaming poor pupil behaviour, lack of in-school support and parental disinterest (Bullough, 2005).

The authors draw upon '*positioning theory*' (Harré and van Langenhove, 1999), in which '[t]he person first takes ownership in solving the situation, then continues to look for and solve situations as the success feeds the desire to make a difference' (1999: 486). They distinguish between resilient and non-resilient teachers:

> Although resilient teachers may disengage at times, their sense of failure is temporary and they always re-engage with the situation in order to try something else. Resilient teachers expand the values that are part of their background to include the values of the culture where they are teaching ... They change their expectations of the children, not to lower them, but to meet them in a different way. Non-resilient teachers may position themselves as the victim and blame their failure to succeed on the circumstances of the situation. Eventually, these teachers disengage and their sense of failure becomes permanent; they do not seek opportunities to re-engage.
>
> (Huisman *et al.*, 2010: 486)

Although this was a relatively small-scale qualitative study, based upon interviews with only 12 (female) teachers in their first or second year of teaching in 12 urban elementary schools in the USA, the themes which were perceived to contribute to teacher resilience resonate with those identified in other studies of urban school teachers (Brunetti, 2006; Castro *et al.*, 2010). Whilst these may be regarded as desirable for beginning teachers in a range of schools, it is likely that for those in school in urban settings, they are essential:

1   *Significant adult relationships:* urban teachers rely, perhaps more heavily than others, on colleagues, especially senior colleagues, who listen to them, provide appropriate emotional and practical support, mentor and coach, fostering hope rather than despair.

2   *Mentoring others:* sharing their on-going experiences with colleagues engaged in similar work.

3   *Problem-solving:* analysing the reasons, for example, why pupils' behaviour is poor or expectations low, as a means of generating innovative solutions.

4   *Hope:* examining what they have learned in the first year as a means of planning for improvements for the next. A teacher in the study spoke of the role of her mentor in this:

> I think [she] has given me hope because she told me that 90 per cent is you. It's not the kids, it's you. I didn't want to hear that, but I realised it was true. Because you know I was dealing with the situation ... I was responding to the situation, but not taking control and preventing problems. I was passive to it. Now, I'm trying to see problems before they happen. Trying to be good with my curriculum. Trying to be more engaging ... trying to just ... just ... to teach. I want to be the best!
>
> (quoted in Huisman *et al.*, 2010: 491)

5   *High expectations:* placing a priority on students' learning, maintaining a belief-in-practice that they can and will achieve success, rather than allowing negative external conditions or present attitudes of pupils to cause expectations to fall.

6   *Socio-cultural awareness:* embracing biases and prejudices about educating in disadvantaged urban schools within and outside the immediate community, and choosing to be there in the moral certainty that all children, and especially those in these communities, should have the opportunity to be taught by good, committed teachers.

7   *Professional development:* actively seeking informal and formal opportunities to learn – a commitment to lifelong learning not only from the individual but also the school.

Conclusions

These snapshots of the inner beliefs, emotions and feelings of teachers in different phases of their careers and lives, working in different school environments and in different countries, provide powerful images both of the strength of their commitment to their work and the costs of this commitment. They also illustrate that resilience is more than the immediate ability to bounce back in response to acute challenges. It is the ability to sustain quality and renew commitment over time. Taken together, these research reports also provide powerful illustrations of the social and psychological dimensions of teacher resilience: 'Just as individuals create the enclaves ... in which they relate, so too these environments may come to exercise a formative impact upon individuals and social identities' (Dixon, 2001: 601).

Klassen and Anderson (2009) explored changes in the level of job satisfaction and the sources of job dissatisfaction among 210 secondary school teachers in eight schools in England in 2007, using a survey conducted in 1962 as a 'point of comparison' (Klassen and Anderson, 2009: 749). They did so because, like others (e.g. Rhodes *et al.*, 2004; Jesus and Lens, 2005), they believe that they influence teacher motivation and commitment and, importantly in the context of our focus, teacher resilience: 'it is likely that changes in the sources of dissatisfaction gradually erode how satisfied teachers feel about their work' (Klassen and Anderson, 2009: 753). They found that what teachers in 2007 reported differed, and differed in perceived importance, in three main respects from those in 1962:

1   job satisfaction was lower
2   the sources of job dissatisfaction were different
3   the views of male and female teachers were more unified.

Responses in 2007 were focused much more upon time constraints and pupils' behaviour and attitudes as primary sources of dissatisfaction. The authors found, as with our own work on variations in the work and lives of teachers (Day *et al.*, 2007b), that the sources of teachers' job satisfaction are embedded in a series of interdependent, interactive and reciprocal relations (with self, pupils, school and policy) and are more complicated than Herzberg's (1966) or Nias' (1981) models suggest. Rather, they found that the quality of the work culture was a major influence, especially the development and leadership by principals in teacher learning communities (Talbert and McLaughlin, 2006). As we have seen in the previous chapter, in the USA, for example, Brunetti (2006) found that the most important motivational force for staying in teaching among teachers with more than 12 years' experience was the support they received from school leadership; whilst Fullan (1999) has noted that teachers tend to attribute their resilience to multiple support systems within and without collegial school environments.

The best schools are the finders and keepers (Moore-Johnson and The Project on the Next Generation of Teachers, 2004) of committed teachers for the profession. Raising teachers' expectations of themselves and providing targeted support for their learning and development needs are keys to increasing their sense of well-being, morale, motivation, commitment and retention, and through these, achieving better learning outcomes for pupils. In the next chapter we will explore how workplace factors promote (or hinder) teachers' sense of resilience in more detail.

6 Workplace factors which promote resilience

So far in this book we have established that teachers who develop systems of self-management (which is founded upon a high degree of self-awareness, which itself is an on-going, renewing evidence-based, reflective process) are likely to be academically optimistic, with a sense of positive self-efficacy and well-being, professional identity, commitment, emotional energy and moral purpose. They are also likely to have a strong sense of agency and job satisfaction or, better yet, job fulfilment. We have shown, also, that because teaching and teaching effectively is necessarily intense, complex and exhausting (as well as invigorating) work, everyday resilience which goes beyond 'coping' and 'survival' is necessary. So resilience as it has been defined traditionally – the ability to bounce back in adverse or extreme circumstances – is insufficient to understand how and why many teachers are able to flourish and teach to their best.

In this chapter we will turn to a close examination of workplace factors and explore the ways in which school conditions, cultures and interactions influence resilience in teachers. We have found in our work with teachers that the longevity of their commitment and resilience cannot be understood in isolation from the support available in their workplace environments which helps them learn well and teach to their best. We have seen teachers who start out with a strong desire to serve but, sadly, as time goes by, become disappointed and less committed in their schools – 'do their job, nothing more, nothing less ... [and] ... the sacred fire that once lit their work becomes a smoulder' (Hamon and Rotman, 1984, cited in Huberman, 1993). We endorse Kennedy's observation that:

> educational researchers and policy makers may be overestimating the role of personal qualities in their quest to understand teaching quality. In their effort to understand classroom-to-classroom differences in student learning, they may focus too much on the characteristics of teachers themselves, overlooking situational factors that may have a strong bearing on the quality of the teaching practices we see.
>
> (Kennedy, 2010: 591)

We have extended the factors which influence teachers' willingness and capacities to sustain commitment to include influences of professional life changes (see

Chapter 4). We have shown how teacher vocation, moral purpose, well-being, self-efficacy, commitment, emotional energy and sense of professional identity are closely related to job fulfilment and are predictors of teachers' retention as well as having an important influence on pupils' engagement with learning and achievement. As teachers feel more confident, efficacious and stable in their classroom identities and practices, they then enter a phase where they confidently begin to take on additional responsibilities and experiment with new things at work. These responsibilities are often accompanied with greater expectations of themselves as well as their schools and, as they grow older, greater family commitments and work-life tensions. Thus, the scenarios that challenge teachers in each phase of their professional and personal lives may be different in nature (see also evidence from Mansfield *et al.*'s 2012 study). However, the intensity of the physical, emotional and intellectual energy required to manage them can be very similar.

Teaching is essentially a social endeavour that is influenced by pupils, colleagues and professional networks within and beyond the school gates. Findings from recent research in psychology, neurology and education collectively point to the importance of good quality relationships and social capital in maintaining a sense of positive identity, well-being and effectiveness in teachers' work and lives. So, quality teach*ing* as against quality teach*ers* will be influenced, as Kennedy reminds us, not only by the 'enduring personal qualities that they bring with them'; it will also be 'a function of schedules, materials, students, institutional incursions into the classroom, and the persistent clutter of reforms that teachers must accommodate' (2010: 597). Thus, in this chapter we will focus on the influence of workplace colleagues and school leaders on teachers' capacities to be resilient. We will demonstrate through illustrations drawn from practice how the presence, quality and range of learning and development opportunities in professional learning communities may help nurture teachers' individual and collective motivation; and we will hypothesise a relationship between self-efficacy and academic optimism, well-being, job fulfilment, a sense of identity, belonging and commitment, which enable them to build, sustain and renew their capacity to be resilient.

Early years' teacher attrition and even later decline of commitment can be considered as the result of personal choice in the light of unexpected negative experience (the 'reality shock' which many writers, e.g. Flores and Day, 2006, have observed over the years) or a deliberate, premeditated decision (where the teacher never intended to commit to a career in teaching). More often than not, however, there will be multiple causes, for example, lack of leadership or colleague support, such that a new teacher may feel under-valued, isolated, lonely or alienated from colleagues and membership of the wider profession (Schlichte *et al.*, 2005), persistent behavioural issues with students, salary and conditions of service or status (Smith and Ingersoll, 2004; Borman and Dowling, 2008; Guarino *et al.*, 2006). Supportive colleagues, leaders and school cultures and structures which provide appropriate induction support can, of course, nurture confidence and a sense of belonging which will have the effect of minimising possibilities of emotional exhaustion and build capacities and capabilities for resilience (Johnson *et al.*, 2010). Problems of status may be associated with the process of seeing themselves as 'teacher' as against 'student' or 'student teacher'. Studies in Finland (Grubb, 2007), USA (Johnson, 2004; Markow and Martin, 2005), UK (Smithers and Robinson, 2003), Taiwan (Wang, 2004), China (Wriqi, 2008) and Australia (Johnson *et al.*, 2010) all identify workplace conditions as having a key influence. It is important, then, to examine the workplace factors which cause teachers to stay rather than move on or leave the profession entirely.

Workplace and self-efficacy

The influence of school cultures upon the well-being, learning and achievement felt by pupils and teachers is, by all accounts, immense and, for teachers, particularly associated with their sense of self-efficacy:

> Just as individual teacher efficacy may partially explain the effect of teachers on student achievement, from an organisational perspective, collective teacher efficacy may help to explain the differential effect that schools have on student achievement. Collective teacher efficacy, therefore, has the potential to contribute to our understanding of how schools differ in the attainment of their most important objectives – the education of students.
>
> (Goddard *et al.*, 2004: 483)

A range of research internationally supports the view that a strong sense of efficacy contributes to teachers' abilities to plan for and conduct their work well, to be flexible in their classroom teaching, to form strong interpersonal relationships and to be satisfied with their work (Klassen *et al.*, 2010; Caprara *et al.* 2006). However, a large-scale Norwegian study of primary and middle-school teachers found that their sense of efficacy and technical mastery do not in themselves necessarily lead to a sense of job satisfaction: 'We found that being able does not guarantee satisfaction, if (despite the good practice) one fails to experience the positive effect of feeling self-efficient' (Moe *et al.*, 2010: 1151). The social environment is important, then, and resilience can be fostered or diminished through the environment (for example, leadership interventions in establishing and nurturing structures and cultures). Recent European research on the impact of psychosocial hazards on teachers at their workplace (ETUCE, 2011) found that 'a higher job satisfaction is presumed to decrease the chances of stress' (ETUCE, 2011: 19) among teachers. Moreover, and perhaps not surprisingly, the same research found that the factors that had the strongest impact upon job satisfaction were 'trust and fairness' in the workplace, followed by 'sense of community', 'meaning of work', resources and 'workprivacy conflict' (i.e. the compatibilities or incompatibilities of working and private lives).

In a recent review of 33 studies internationally published within the last 20 years, Scheopner (2010) identified the important influence of the workplace environment on teachers' self-efficacy.

> Simple solutions will not suffice. Self-efficacy is vitally important; teachers must experience a sense of effectiveness. Teachers need to feel supported, in compensation that acknowledges the work that they do, from colleagues and principals who encourage and assist them, and in realistic expectations of what they can accomplish ... Teachers value supportive relationships with their colleagues, but structures are needed to encourage teachers to work together, take advantage of one another's feedback, expertise and knowledge.
> (Scheopner, 2010: 274–5)

Arguably, there is a close association between levels of resilience and stress and attrition; and these are also likely to be related to conditions in the workplace. In a 25-country review of teacher retention, the OECD (2005b) found that poor working conditions (workload; pupil behaviour; resources; parental support) were often the reasons teachers gave for leaving the profession (2005b: 199). Rates of supply and attrition vary internationally and across particular geographies and subject areas. For example, in many 'industrialised' nations, attrition is greater in socio-economically challenging rural and urban areas, whereas lack of supply, poor working conditions and health issues (e.g. HIV/AIDs) are key factors in developing countries (Rinke, 2008: 3). Even so, those schools which are successful have a higher rate of retention in all areas, regardless of geography and socio-economic circumstance.

We know also from a range of research that there are variations in the work, lives and effectiveness of teachers (Day *et al.*, 2007b) and that peers, head teachers, personal events and changing policy and social conditions are key positive and negative factors in their willingness and abilities to sustain their commitment. Susan Moore-Johnson and her colleagues (2004) identified the school culture as playing an important role in decisions by new teachers to stay or leave teaching and that collegiality and emotional support from colleagues are factors in their retention (Moore-Johnson *et al.*, 2004; Hobson and Ashby, 2010). In school cultures which are less collegial, new teachers are likely to feel isolated, become disillusioned about their place in the school and begin to question their own abilities to be effective in the classroom (Flores and Day, 2006). However, it is the school leader who is likely to exercise, indirectly or directly, most influence.

Research has also shown is that it is a sustained sense of commitment that has kept many teachers enthusiastic and professionally fulfilled over the course of their professional lives. Teachers' job fulfilment is a satisfying state of mind which they attribute to the reward they derive from the ways in which their professional capacities have enabled them to bring about their pupils' engagement, learning and sense of successful achievement (Gu and Li, 2013). Pupils' appreciation of their effort connects their hearts and minds with the very people whom they care about and care for. In this sense, whether or not teachers are drawn into teaching because of their love of the subject or children is perhaps relatively less important. Once they have entered teaching, what becomes more important is whether they are able to sustain such love, and/or whether their schools are able to provide the kinds of support which enable them to enjoy both their passion for their subject and the pleasure of seeing their pupils learn and achieve over time.

What we have seen in the literature and heard from many enthusiastic, hopeful and committed teachers with whom we have worked is the importance of continuing informal and formal opportunities for their professional learning and growth – so that they *can* continue to develop their capacity to teach, expand their horizons as professionals within and outside their classrooms, and through these, enjoy a strong sense of professional fulfilment. Narrative accounts of such teachers have led us to believe that they are resilient but that resilience is about much more than survival. Resilient teachers are not only those who survive. Rather, they are activist professionals who strive to make a difference in intellectual, cultural and social environments which provide them with the opportunities and support which cause them to feel that their potential for further improvement is regularly challenged by themselves and others and that their contributions to individuals' learning and achievement and to the collective learning and achievement enterprise of the school are recognised and valued. Below we provide an overview of how the influences discussed in this chapter and throughout the book combine to contribute to teachers' capacities to be resilient (Figure 6.1):

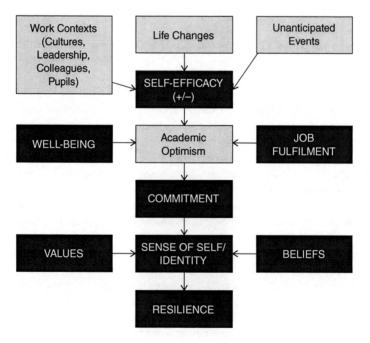

Figure 6.1 Influences on teachers' capacity for resilience.

The head teacher's influence

> [S]chools where the principal was able to inspire a common sense of purpose among teachers and where student disorder was kept to a minimum were schools in which teachers felt a greater sense of efficacy. In addition, principals who used their leadership to provide resources for teachers and to buffer them from disruptive factors but allowed teachers flexibility over classroom affairs created a context that allowed strong self-efficacy beliefs to develop.
>
> (Tschannen-Moran and Hoy, 2007: 947)

This finding about influences on the self-efficacy of novice and experienced teachers complements earlier claims that organisational efficacy (the collective sense of self-efficacy in a department and/or school) is a distinguishing feature in assessing the effect of schools on pupil achievement. In a survey in the USA which investigated why 40 to 50 per cent of all beginning teachers leave teaching with five years, Ingersoll and Smith (2003) found that 39 per cent of these left for a better job or another career and 29 per cent left because they were dissatisfied with teaching itself – problems of pupil behaviour, little support from school leadership, poor pupil motivation and lack of a sense of participation in school and classroom decision making. Ingersoll and Smith's (2003) findings that the quality of school leadership and management 'play a significant role in the genesis of school staffing problems but can also play a significant role in their solution' (2003: 5) are important and confirm those, also, of Australian researchers (Scott *et al.*, 2001).

Question: What do we know about the link between effective teaching and good principals?

> Linda Darling-Hammond: If you ask teachers, 'What kept you in a school that you're in?' or 'What caused you to leave?' … leadership and support is one of the most critical elements because everything the teacher does is framed by the way the leadership operates. It is possible to be an effective teacher in a poorly led school but it's not easy. That takes a toll. And it is possible to become an even more effective and successful teacher in a well-led school.
>
> (The Wallace Foundation, January 2013: 18)

A range of research reveals that the influence of the school head on student progress and achievement is second only to that of the classroom teacher (Leithwood *et al.*, 2006b) and that successful, effective heads/principals place a high priority on establishing the optimal conditions for teaching and learning (Robinson *et al.*, 2009). Tschannen-Moran's (2004) study of trust in elementary schools in the USA also identifies the pivotal contribution made by school principals to teachers' self-efficacy – a key factor in teachers' capacity to be resilient.

Thus, school cultures, and especially school leaders, play a vital positive or negative role in creating the conditions which actively promote teachers' commitment and resilience. They do so through a persistent emphasis on the creation and support of learning and development opportunities which take into consideration individually and organisationally identified needs and priorities.

Investing in the person

We saw in Chapters 3 and 4 that teachers' sense of psychological/emotional health (wellbeing) and identity play important roles in their capacity for resilience. Thus, the principal's investment in the teacher-as-person as well as the teacher-as-professional is important. The VITAE research into variations in the lives, work and effectiveness of teachers in England (Day *et al.*, 2007b) found an abundance of evidence from teachers of all ages and experience of the contribution made by school leaders to their continuing commitment to the school.

Peters and Pearce (2012) investigated the conditions which promote primary and secondary school teacher resilience and retention in the first two years of teaching. Through interviews with school leaders and teachers in 59 schools in two states of Australia, they found that 'a strong emerging theme is how relationships with principals influence teachers' feelings of personal and professional well-being, with both negative and positive effects reported' (Peters and Pearce, 2012: 249). In their paper they present the stories of two teachers. The first, Jasmine, had been successful in her first year but suffered from two severely adverse personal life events in her second year which placed enormous demands on her time outside school and threatened her capacities to be resilient. Her principal, aware of this, played a pivotal role in her support:

> Everybody's family goes through things – things happen that you can't plan for and they're very family oriented in this school and it's made a lot easier for me knowing that they're going to support me … It's also the principal himself, taking a one-on-one approach and having conversations with me about it.
>
> (cited in Peters and Pearce, 2012: 253)

The importance of the contributions of colleagues and leaders to teachers' on-going sense of emotional well-being and commitment has been widely documented (Wood, 2005; McCormack and Thomas, 2003; Gu and Day, 2007). However, they may also have negative effects:

> When new teachers perceive they are not well supported in their management efforts by colleagues, including the School Executive, they rapidly become disillusioned about the efficacy of the school's infrastructure, and their own capacities as effective leaders.
>
> (Manuel, 2003: 147, cited in Peters and Pearce, 2012: 254)

The second story provided by Peters and Pearce (2012) is of Audrey, at her first school, who had been 'left alone to struggle with situations … [the worst class groups] ... for which she felt she had not been well prepared' (2012: 255); and at her second school, 'felt completely alienated and isolated': 'I was just being told "this isn't good enough" and "that's not good enough"' (2012: 255).

Peters and Pearce (2012), among others (e.g. Blackmore, 1996; Gu and Day, 2007; Wood, 2005; Crawford, 2009) point to prevailing pressures of 'performativity', market-driven policies and increased workload pressures which may cause school leaders to become pre-occupied with measurable performance at the expense of attention to teachers' emotional well-being. This was clearly the case with Aubrey. However, a range of research on successful school leaders – and indeed, the 2012 Ontario Leadership Framework (Leithwood, 2012) – shows that they, like Jasmine's principal, recognise the importance of attending to the needs of the person within the professional. Peters and Pearce provide a useful 'aide memoire' for leaders. Whilst they use this for career resilience of early career teachers, we believe that it can be applied to those in all phases of their careers:

- take a personal interest in [early career] ... teachers' welfare and development;
- actively participate in their employment and ongoing induction;
- model and foster relationships that are 'trusting, generous, helpful and cooperative' (Barth, 2009: 9);
- lead the development of school cultures that are supportive of the learning and well-being of staff and collaborative processes;
- take a 'humanistic' approach to mentoring which acknowledges the importance of building self-esteem while also developing professional knowledge and skills.

(Peters and Pearce, 2012: 260)

In our own research on successful school leadership (Day *et al.*, 2011), we observed that a sense of individual and collective resilience was a key characteristic. Not only did individual teachers express a strong sense of academic optimism, hope, agency, collegiality and positive identity but, in quantitative terms, more stayed than left the schools, there were fewer absences, pupil attendance and behaviour were non-problematic (though in some schools they had been in the past) and test and examination scores were on an upward trajectory – regardless of school location. Importantly, teachers did not feel isolated and there was a strong sense of collective efficacy, defined by Bandura (1997) as:

a group's shared belief in its conjoint capabilities to organise and execute the course of action required to produce given levels of attainments ... similar to self-efficacy, collective efficacy beliefs affect group performance in diverse fields of functioning such as business, sports, politics, and education.

(Bandura, 1997: 477)

Performance is, of course, a source of job satisfaction, dissatisfaction and fulfilment and may be associated with well-being, as we have shown in Chapter 3.

What is important to note is that efficacy is context specific (Goddard *et al.*, 2004) and that this is likely to be affected, positively and negatively, by colleagues, pupils, leadership and the culture of the school. In research on novice and experienced teachers in the USA:

> Stronger self-efficacy beliefs have been found among teachers who perceived a positive school atmosphere ... and a strong press for academic achievement among the staff in their schools ... Moreover, sense of community in school was the single greatest predictor of teachers' level of efficacy.
>
> (Tschannen-Moran and Hoy, 2007: 946)

Investing in learning

A key influencing condition is the provision of opportunities for professional learning and development which, in successful schools, go far beyond the traditional (and narrow) view of professional learning and development promoted, primarily, through attendance at formal 'in-service' courses and conferences. In the USA, for example, Wood (2005) found that principals played five roles in the induction of early career teachers: '(a) culture builder; (b) instructional leader; (c) coordinator/facilitator of mentors; (d) novice teacher recruiter; (e) novice teacher advocate/retainer' (2005: 39). National policies in some countries (e.g. UK) also ensure a maximum 80 per cent teaching load for new teachers and formal mentoring schemes, though it should be noted that variability in quality within this has been reported (Jones, 2002; Bubb and Earley, 2006).

Much emphasis in school leadership research is placed upon the virtues of 'instructional leadership' (e.g. Heck and Hallinger, 2005, 2009; King and Newman, 2001; Robinson *et al.*, 2009) in which successful principals have been identified as having a key focus upon improving classroom teaching and learning. This has been supported by the findings of an international 'best evidence synthesis' of empirical studies (Robinson *et al.*, 2009). Here, the effect sizes of five key dimensions of effective leadership were calculated, with by far the largest being participating in and promoting continuing professional learning and development (Figure 6.2).

Inclusive learning

The recognition that successful schools are led by many, rather than a few, is exemplified in the almost evangelical rush towards distributed leadership. Unfortunately, writings on distributed leadership seem often to focus upon the forms and levels of distribution without also a consideration of the social and emotional infrastructures needed for this to be successful. It takes time to build trust. Our own large-scale empirical research on the impact of school leaders on pupil outcomes found a relationship between levels of trust and trustworthiness and the extent to which leadership was distributed (Day *et al.*, 2011).

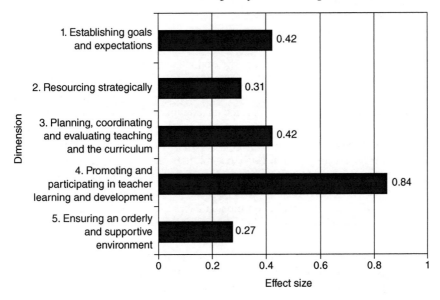

Figure 6.2 The difference leadership can make (Robinson *et al.*, 2009: 39).

Metaphors of professional learning and development

Roosmarijn and her colleagues (2014, in press), use four 'resiliency-related' theories from outside the educational sector in exploring teacher and school resilience:

1 *Resilience engineering:* 'variability in performance is normal and ... the challenge is to cope with this variability in a flexible, robust and mindful way'.
2 *Organisational mindfulness:* 'mindful engagement is built around the principles of anticipation and the principles of containment'.
3 *Human resource management:* 'If we want to enhance resilience, we ... need transformational leaders and employees that want to align their personal goals with the organisational goals'.
4 *Resilience as a social system;* 'If we want to enhance resilience, we can either focus on diminishing risk factors (employee internal and external stressors) ... or enhance resources like supportive networks, problem solving ability, appraisal and harmony (protective factors)'.

They suggest that, taken together, these theories point to the need to use multi-level approaches in building resilience capacities and that these approaches – anticipating, monitoring, responding and learning – are needed for individuals, teams and schools to develop resilience.

In the context of our consideration of capacity building for resilience and its constituent components of self-efficacy, optimism, emotional energy, trust and motivation, it is worth briefly examining four metaphors of continuing professional learning and development identified by Judyth Sachs (Sachs, 2011). The first two are oriented towards 'training', the third and fourth towards teacher learning:

1   *CPD as retooling.* This is seen as the dominant training model, based upon a 'practical' competency view of teaching in which ideas, knowledge and techniques learned can be immediately applied to the classroom. It represents 'a skill-based, technocratic view of teaching' (Kennedy, 2005: 237) and 'is likely to promote a limited conception of teaching and being a teacher' (Day, 1999: 139).
2   *CPD as remodelling.* This is seen by Sachs as being 'more concerned with modifying existing practices to ensure that teachers are compliant with government change agendas ... [it] ... reinforces the idea of the teacher as the uncritical consumer of knowledge and operating at the level of improving specific skills as these relate to immediate classroom practice' (2011: 5).
3   *CPD as revitalising.* Here the focus is upon teacher renewal, providing opportunities for teachers to reflect upon why they came into teaching in the first place, examining beliefs and practices, perhaps through professional development networks, or participation in practice-based enquiries.
4   *CPD as re-imagining.* This represents what Sachs calls 'a transformative view of teacher professionalism' (2011: 7) which acknowledges the complexities of being a teacher. It seeks to develop in teachers their own 'critical and transformative capacities' (2011: 7). Here, teachers may participate in collaborative activities in collegial environments which 'support open minded inquiry, reflection ... they support teachers in validating their knowledge and building on it' (2011: 8).

We reproduce Sachs' CPD Grid opposite (Table 6.1). As we reflect upon this, and upon the kinds of learning opportunities available to teachers, we do not consider it contentious to suppose (as Sachs found in her research reported above) that in many countries, in many schools – especially in reform-intensive times – it is the tooling and remodelling orientations which dominate. Yet our own research has found that in effective and improving schools (which have higher teacher retention rates and in which teachers seem to be more optimistic, self-efficacious and collegial), there is a balance across the four kinds identified. Key to success in each of these is an acknowledgement that learning and development is a reciprocal process in which both individual and organisational needs are negotiated and for which both the individual and the organisation share responsibility.

> Identifying teachers' agendas is crucial to learning and change; ... teacher learning needs to be inquiry oriented, personal and sustained, individual and collaborative, on and off site; ... CPD means a range of learning opportunities appropriate to needs and purposes; ... these need to be supported by school cultures of inquiry and be evidence based, where evidence is collected and interrogated which acknowledge the complex worlds of teaching and learning, teachers and learners.
>
> (Day and Sachs, 2004a: 26)

Table 6.1 CPD Grid

	Retooling	Remodelling	Revitalising	Reimagining
Driver/trigger	Accountability and control by government	Compliance with government change agenda	Professional renewal	Professional reinvention
Purpose	Upgrading of skills	Modify existing practices	Rethink and renew practices	Transformative practices
Conception of CPD	Transmission	Transmission	Transitional	Transformative
Responsibility	System	School/district	Individual teacher	Teachers
Focus	Professional development	Professional development	Professional learning	Professional learning
Learning processes	Passive recipient of knowledge	Uncritical consumer	Collaboration	Mutual engagement and knowledge creation
Approaches	One-off seminars, outside expert	Programmes devised by an external expert over an extended time	Collaborative learning circles, networks, action research	Practitioner enquiry or action research, enquiry as stance
View of teaching	Teacher as technician	Teacher as craft worker	Teacher as reflective learner	Autonomous professional
Professional outcomes	Improved teaching skills	Updated discipline knowledge or pedagogical skills	New approaches to pedagogy and learning	Production of new knowledge
Type of professionalism	Controlled	Compliant	Collaborative	Activist

(Sachs 2011: 162)

Capacity building for resilience

> Efforts at school reform require more than a focus on students – it requires that school employees work together in new and different ways that promote and reinforce inclusiveness, collaboration, innovation, and support for one another.
>
> (Bowen *et al.*, 2007: 206)

Bowen and his colleagues developed and tested an instrument for assessing schools as learning organisations. They found that two components of this – 'actions' and 'sentiments' – could be regarded as 'leverage points in supporting the ability of schools to work more effectively as "output driven organisations"' (Bowen *et al.*, 2007: 206). We reproduce them in Table 6.2 as a means for reflection.

School leaders are particularly influential in building, sustaining and renewing individual and collective resilience, for it is their responsibility to create supportive studies for individuals' learning through influencing the intellectual, ethical, social, political and emotional environments in which learning takes place. However, as we will show in the next chapter, school leaders themselves need not only to build the capacity for resilience in others, they also need to be able to call upon their own capacity to be resilient if they are to lead successfully.

What, then, does research tell us about the ways in which resilience may be built and supported in individual teachers through organisational cultures, structures and actions? What individual concerns need to be taken into account? Just as the best teaching 'personalises' students' learning agendas, so the best professional development activities will personalise the resilience needs of teachers. Most, though not all, of these are likely to focus upon and be shaped by the contexts in which they work and the pupils whom they teach. Their level of commitment, sense of identity, self-efficacy, sense of optimism and hope and job fulfilment at any given time will have accrued from a range of personal experiences and practice-based knowledge. These constitute what have been called 'funds of knowledge' (Gonzalez *et al.*, 2005). It follows that a key purpose of in-school professional learning directed to building, sustaining and renewing their resilience should focus upon assisting teachers to revisit their purposes, 'unpack' and

Table 6.2 Actions and sentiments for assessing schools as learning organisations

Action	Sentiment
Team orientation	Common purpose
Innovation	Respect
Involvement	Cohesion
Information sharing	Trust
Tolerance for error	Mutual support
Results orientation	Optimism

interrogate their values, intentions and practices, in order to assess current challenges and the levels of emotional energy they are able to give to their work, together with their sense of well-being and effectiveness.

> Capacity is a power – a 'habit of mind' focused on engaging in and sustaining the learning of people at all levels in the educational system for a collective purpose of enhancing student learning in its broadest sense. It's a quality that allows people individually and collectively, routinely to learn from the world around them and to apply this learning to new situations so that they can continue on a path towards their goals in an ever-changing context.
>
> (Stoll, 2009: 125)

Whilst we would support fully this statement, we would wish to make explicit the need, as part of capacity building, to engage the hearts as well as the minds of people at all levels in the system in order that their emotional energies, their capacities to be resilient, would be built, sustained and renewed; for without a strong sense of motivation, self-efficacy, commitment, key components in resilience, it is unlikely the 'habit of mind' will be sufficient to enhance student learning: 'Learning what is necessary to live cannot be untangled from living in a manner that allows you to learn: learning and living are inextricably connected' (Andrews, 2006, in Collinson, 2008: 443).

Moreover, capacity itself is built through processes which enable and ensure that teachers' knowledge, expertise, commitment, well-being and job fulfilment grow and are renewed (Darling-Hammond, 2005). In other words, capacity-building strategies themselves will only be successful if they enhance social cohesion, trust and shared responsibilities, and, alongside these, a commitment to continuing professional learning and development.

Mitchell and Sackney (2000) identified three 'spheres' of capacity: personal, interpersonal and organisational, arguing that school leaders must build all of these synchronistically. For example, organisational structures need to be built which will enhance conditions for teaching and learning in the classroom whilst at the same time openness and trust will need to be nurtured among staff, students and parents. It is important to note, also, that personal, interpersonal and organisational capacities for resilience are neither innate nor static. They will fluctuate according to the benign or alienating professional norms and social ties (Bryk *et al.*, 2010; Hargreaves, 2011). Moreover, whilst capacity for resilience may be said to be an inner quality of competent teachers and effective leaders, it is not inexhaustible. Understanding the conditions and actions necessary to build and sustain teachers' (and leaders') capacities to be resilient and the component parts of resilience itself is, therefore, important for all those who are concerned with the quality of teaching, learning and achievement.

In recent years, Bruce Johnson and his colleagues in South and Western Australia have conducted extensive research into early career teacher resilience, claiming, then correctly, that 'what is lacking in the literature currently is an in-depth understanding of the interplay of personal and contextual factors around early career teachers' experiences' (Johnson and Down, 2012: 2). Our own work (Gu and Day, 2007, 2013) supports their critique of what they call 'mainstream conceptions' of resilience research as being: i) reductionist approaches which seek to 'reduce complex human interactions to discrete independent and dependent variables that focus on isolated aspects of life' (Johnson and Down, 2012: 4) which ignore broader social, political and economic contexts in which teachers work; ii) hyper-individualism approaches which 'individualise analyses of risk and successful adaptation' (2012: 5) on the assumption that all individuals, regardless of circumstance, should be able to be resilient through their own efforts; and iii) normativity approaches which ignore the implicit (often middle-class) beliefs, interests and assumptions about what is, for example, 'good' or 'bad' for early career teachers – as Johnson and Downs say, 'what puts them at risk personally and professionally' (2012: 7). Drawing on the work of Wright Mills (1959), they suggest that:

> [t]he life of an individual cannot be adequately understood without references to the institutions within which his biography is enacted ... To understand the biography of an individual, we must understand the significance and meaning of the roles he has played and does play; to understand these roles we must understand the institutions of which they are a part.
>
> (Wright Mills, 1959: 178–9)

Their work identified five conditions or influences on early career teachers – relationships, school culture, teacher identity, teachers' work and policies and practices. However, importantly, their work shows that the positive or negative experiences of teaching (Huberman (1993): 'easy' or 'painful' beginnings) which early career teachers experience is likely to be the results of a complex interplay between these, rather than any single condition. From this, Johnson and his colleagues developed a 'Framework of Conditions Supporting Early Career Teacher Resilience' (Johnson *et al.*, 2012); and we re-produce this in Fig. 6.3.

Conclusions

Clearly, capacity building is about more than creating a vision, setting directions, distributing leadership, restructuring the working day or upgrading facilities and resources available for classrooms. Whilst these are important contributors, shaping of learning cultures, building individual relational and organisational trust and building capacity, through opportunities for growth and renewal are fundamental to teachers' capacities and capabilities for resilience. School principals:

POLICIES & PRACTICES

Policies and practices refer to the officially mandated statements, guidelines, values and prescriptions that both enable and constrain ECT wellbeing. ECT resilience and wellbeing are enhanced when policies and practices show a strong commitment to social justice, teacher agency and voice, community engagement, and respect for local knowledge and practice.

To enhance ECT resilience, it is important to:

Provide relevant, rigorous and responsive pre-service preparation for the profession
- Foster stakeholders' collective ownership of preparation, induction and ongoing learning
- Provide diverse, rigorous and carefully planned pre-service professional experiences
- Ensure coherence between on-campus courses and the dynamic demands of the profession

Create innovative partnerships and initiatives that assist smooth transitions to the workforce
- Support professional development suitable to the school context
- Acknowledge the value of previous professional experiences and expertise
- Provide additional professional and financial resources for complex school settings

Implement transparent, fair and responsive employment processes
- Notify school appointments in a timely manner
- Provide opportunities for continuity of employment
- Ensure equitable access to support, resources and learning opportunities
- Provide professional development that equips school leaders to support ECTs

TEACHERS' WORK

Teachers' work refers to the complex array of practices, knowledge, relationships and ethical considerations that comprise the role of the teacher. ECT resilience is promoted when the focus is on understanding the complex, intense and unpredictable nature of teachers' work rather than on individual deficits and blame.

To enhance ECT resilience, it is important to:

Acknowledge the complex, intense and unpredictable nature of teachers' work
- Attend to the physical, intellectual, relational and emotional dimensions of teachers' work
- Acknowledge that teachers' work is demanding and tiring

Develop teachers' curriculum and pedagogical knowledge and strategies
- Provide opportunities for collaborative planning, teaching, assessment and reporting
- Allocate space and structures for teachers' critical and reflective work
- Focus on student diversity, passions and interests
- Promote innovative and engaging curriculum practices

Provide support to create engaging learning environments
- Take collective ownership of students' wellbeing and behaviour
- Develop beliefs and practices that engage students and encourage constructive behaviours
- Create collaborative and democratic learning environments
- Make authentic connections between students' learning and their life-worlds

Ensure access to appropriate ongoing support, resources and learning opportunities
- Provide equitable and timely access to needs-based professional learning
- Support the development of pedagogical beliefs, values and practices
- Provide adequate release time from face-to-face teaching

SCHOOL CULTURE

School culture refers to the values, beliefs, norms, assumptions, behaviours and relationships that characterise the daily rituals of school life. ECT resilience flourishes in schools that promote collaborative relationships, professional learning communities, educative forms of leadership and democratic decision-making.

To enhance ECT resilience, it is important to:

Promote a sense of belonging and social connectedness
- Practise affirmation
- Recognise and value diverse perspectives, practices and backgrounds
- Foster trust and goodwill
- Minimise isolation
- Take collective responsibility for teacher wellbeing and safety

Develop educative, democratic and empowering processes
- Promote distributive leadership
- Work through problems respectfully
- Include all school personnel regardless of employment status
- Establish a commitment to social justice

Provide formal and informal transition/induction processes
- Appoint mentors/coaches/buddies
- Provide ongoing induction
- Apply equitable processes regardless of length and nature of appointment
- Promote understanding and appreciation of the different roles in the school

Develop a professional learning community
- Promote opportunities for risk taking and innovation
- Provide environments and resources that optimise teaching and learning
- Provide opportunities for collaborative learning
- Take collective responsibility for student behaviour, learning and wellbeing

RELATIONSHIPS

Relationships refers to the social and professional networks, human connections and belongingness experienced by ECTs. Schools that value relationships focus on the complex emotional needs of ECTs and encourage social exchanges that foster respect, trust, care and integrity. ECT resilience benefits significantly when these values are evident in policies and practice.

To enhance ECT resilience, it is important to:

Promote a sense of belonging, acceptance and wellbeing
- Foster relationships based on mutual trust, respect, care and integrity
- Help manage personal and professional challenges and conflicts
- Encourage involvement in professional and community networks
- Value support from family, friends and peers

Place student–teacher relationships at the heart of the teaching–learning process
- Develop positive and democratic relationships with students
- Involve parents/caregivers in their children's learning
- Enjoy interacting with students and celebrate their successes
- Develop learning communities where everyone encourages each other's learning
- Celebrate student innovation and success in and beyond the classroom

Foster professional growth
- Value the personal strengths and resources of teachers
- Give specific, constructive and timely feedback
- Give explicit affirmation and acknowledgement
- Support communication with parents/caregivers/community

Promote collective ownership and responsibility for professional relationships
- Cultivate a generosity of spirit
- Share responsibility for maintaining positive relationships
- Create time and spaces for dialogue and collaboration

TEACHER IDENTITY

Teacher identity refers to the development of one's awareness and understanding of self as a teacher. Teacher resilience is enhanced when ECTs engage in processes of self-reflection and self-understanding that sustain their personal and professional identity, while at the same time developing a robust teacher identity.

To enhance ECT resilience, it is important to:

Understand the interplay between personal and professional identities
- Recognise that personal and professional identities are interconnected
- Recognise that teachers' identities are produced in particular social and cultural contexts
- Understand the evolving nature of personal–professional identities
- Recognise that emotions are an integral part of identity development

Engage in self-reflection
- Accommodate new and different ways of thinking
- Challenge and develop beliefs, assumptions, values and practices
- Negotiate the contradictions and tensions of teaching
- Employ proactive coping strategies

Foster a sense of agency, efficacy and self-worth
- Commit to the ethical and moral purposes of teaching
- Develop a high level of social and emotional responsiveness
- Maintain hope and optimism
- Promote work-life balance and wellbeing
- Seek help and support

Johnson, Down, Le Cornu, Peters, Sullivan, Pearce, Hunter – (2012)

Figure 6.3 A framework of conditions supporting early career teacher resilience.

determine to a certain degree which information is emphasised or even allowed into the organisation, which knowledge is discussable or undiscussable, how knowledge is disseminated, whether members participate in sense-making and decision making, whether leadership is shared, and how the development and well-being of members is nurtured.

(Collinson and Cook, 2007: 139)

So, for example, in revitalising and re-energising staff, leaders will need to 'establish both respect and personal regard when they acknowledge the vulnerabilities of others, actively listen to their concerns, and eschew arbitratory actions' (Bryk and Schneider, 2002: 137). Teachers respect principals, also, when they model their personal values in what they say and what they do. 'How' leaders foster over time personal and interpersonal relationships in building capacity is as important as what they do to achieve this. As Bryk and Schneider note, 'the history of power relations between a principal and her or his faculty can strongly influence a staff's willingness to undertake some new reform' (Bryk and Schneider, 2002: 5).

Their work, like that of other researchers (Day *et al.*, 2007b; Gu and Day, 2007, 2013; Gu and Li, 2013), is a reminder of the key role in nurturing and shaping teachers' resilience of school leaders in promoting supportive school cultures and providing strong and consistent support for all teachers' emotional and practical selves, but especially those in their early years whose professional sense of self and whose capacities to be resilient may not yet be fully formed. It is also a reminder, perhaps by default, that much of the existing research focuses upon 'teachers' and 'schools', rather than 'good or outstanding' teachers and schools in which nurturing, building and sustaining teachers' sense of positive identity and capacities and capabilities to be resilient within challenging, but supportive cultures of and conditions for teaching and learning might be expected to be the norm. The next chapter, therefore, focuses upon the relationship between resilient leaders and resilient schools.

Part III

Why teacher resilience matters

7   Resilient leaders, resilient schools

Much of the research and writing about teachers' work and lives focuses on the role played by school leaders in, for example (as we have shown in Chapter 6), creating and developing working conditions, cultures and structures in schools and classrooms through which teachers' capacities for resilience may be built. However, little has been written about the need for leaders themselves to be resilient. This chapter will draw upon a range of national and international empirical research into successful leadership in which we have been involved, which provides insights into the positive and negative influences upon leaders' own self-efficacy, sense of commitment, well-being and capacities for resilience. We will suggest that resilience is an essential quality and a necessary capacity for leaders to lead to their best. This is so in part because of the innate complexities of leading and managing in schools; in part because of the influence that heads must exercise with a range of stakeholder groups and individuals in the process of school improvement efforts; and in part because such efforts take place in shifting and sometimes conflicting reform contexts which tend to increase and intensify leaders' work and lives. Resilience has always been desirable in principalship but has now become an imperative. It is somewhat surprising, therefore, that there is little extant research on the nature and enactment of resilience and its relationship to successful principalship. Given the claim that principals' influence on students is second only to that of classroom teachers (Leithwood *et al.*, 2006b), this is surprising.

To lead to one's best and to teach to one's best over time require resilience. It is an essential quality and a necessary capacity to exercise both for principals and teachers. As we have established in Chapter 1, while the concept of resilience elaborated in the discipline of psychology helps clarify the personal characteristics of trait-resilient people, it fails to address how the capacity to be resilient fluctuates in different sets of positive and negative circumstances; in what ways the capacity for resilience is connected to personal or professional factors; and how capacity, can be enhanced or inhibited by the nature of the external and internal environments in which we work, the people with whom we work as well as the strength of our beliefs or aspirations (Day *et al.*, 2007b).

> Diverse demands not only challenge the breadth of knowledge and skill possessed by a leader, but also test the adaptativity and flexibility of his/her

very sense of self, how leaders conceptualise themselves in relation to the multiple social roles they must perform.

(Hanna *et al.*, 2009: 169)

It is a truism to state that head teachers in many countries over the last 20 or more years (and in the UK especially) have experienced an increase in multi-tasking and work longer and more unsocial hours in their attempts to deal with the expanding number of duties, roles and responsibilities, and accountabilities placed upon them. Such diverse and sometimes competing demands not only challenge the breadth of qualities, knowledge and skills possessed by leaders, but also test their adaptivity, flexibility and resilience.

A recent survey (Angle *et al.*, 2007) showed that, in England, only 7 per cent of secondary heads perceived that they had any time to engage in interests outside their work; it is unlikely that much will have changed in the years since then, as more recent root-and-branch reforms in the governance and curricula of schools in England and Wales demonstrate.

> I would reckon I would work 15 or 16 hours a day. The list of duties is frightening, meetings with staff, parents, builders, governors, psychologists, social workers and many others. Assemblies to run every day in two different schools, budgets and targets to set and manage, furniture to choose, caterers to handle, staff to hire, fire and reviews.
>
> (*Guardian*, 16 June, 2007, Work, p.3,
> cited in Thomson, 2009: 66)

Whilst principals in schools in different countries, and in schools experiencing different degrees of challenge, will be at different points on a continuum of working hours, available research literature points to a working life which has become less attractive in terms of working hours required to do the job well, in some countries a diminishing number of applicants for these roles and increasing evidence of stress. It is not surprising therefore, that being a head has become less attractive for many in recent years; and many schools, especially those that serve socio-economically disadvantaged communities, continue to find it difficult to attract candidates (NAHT, 2011).

If, then, responsibilities, accountabilities and the number of tasks which principals have to manage and, in many cases, lead, have increased, it follows that principals today and in the foreseeable future are likely to need to possess and apply broader sets of political, intra and inter personal and organisational qualities, strategies and skills. More importantly, in terms of achieving success, they need to be able to hold, articulate and communicate and sustain during their many daily interactions those agreed moral and ethical values, educational ideologies and purposes which drive their work and that of their colleagues.

Because leaders at all levels have clear responsibilities to ensure that staff are highly motivated, self-efficacious, committed and resilient, they themselves also need to feel a strong sense of efficacy and resilience. Ken Leithwood, a Canadian school leadership researcher of international repute, and his co-researcher Doris Jantzi have written about the connections between leaders' sense of efficacy, associations between this and their ability to contribute to improvements in student learning (Leithwood and Jantzi, 2008). Leithwood and Seashore Louis (2012), referring to the work of McCormick (2001), claim that:

> Leader confidence or self-efficacy is likely the key cognitive variable regulating leader functioning in the dynamic environment of their schools ... every major review of the leadership literature lists self-confidence as an essential characteristic for effective leadership.
>
> (Leithwood and Seashore Louis, 2012: 1)

The process of leading outside of the classroom, like the process of leading inside the classroom, requires resolute persistence and commitment which is much more than the ability to bounce back in adverse circumstances. We have shown throughout this book that resilient capacities and capabilities can be nurtured (Higgins, 1994), and can be achieved through providing relevant and practical protective factors, such as caring and attentive educational settings, positive and high expectations, positive learning environments, a strong supportive social community, and supportive peer relationships (see for example, Johnson *et al.*, 1999, Rutter *et al.*, 1979). It is thus both a product of personal and professional dispositions and values influenced by organisational and personal factors and determined by individuals' capacities to manage context-specific factors. For example, teachers may respond positively or negatively in the presence of challenging circumstances, and this will depend on the quality of organisational or colleague leadership as well as the strength of their own commitment; and extended collaborations now required by policy need to be managed in order to avoid their potential for 'collaborative inertia' (Huxham and Vangan, 2005: 13). The social construction of leadership resilience acknowledges, as the psychological construction does not, the important effects of such personal, professional and situated pressures on the capacities of heads to sustain their emotional well-being and professional commitment. The next part of this chapter will, therefore, examine three aspects of leadership resilience:

1   Resilient dispositions associated with leadership success.
2   Moral purpose.
3   Challenges to resilience: schools which serve disadvantaged communities.

Resilience dispositions associated with success

There are four dispositions, in particular, that successful principals seem to possess which build and sustain resilience in their schools:

1   A willingness to take (calculated) risks based upon clear educational values despite the vulnerability of doing so.

2   Academic optimism.
3   Trust.
4   Hope.

Vulnerability and risk

We have referred elsewhere to the work of Geert Kelchtermans and his colleagues in Belgium who have conducted small-scale, fine grained qualitative studies into the ways in which teachers' selves are constructed. Others, of a similar persuasion, have conducted parallel studies in England (Troman and Woods, 2001) and elsewhere on teacher identity (Beijaard *et al.*, 2004). They have concluded that teachers' selves are fragile and that 'vulnerability' is a feature of teaching. This may apply equally to the work of principals. We know, for example, that the creative management of ambiguities – an essential feature of leadership lives in schools – is both stimulating and stressful.

Pat Thomson, in her book *School Leadership: Heads on The Block?* (2009) characterises principalship as a risky business and cites Beck *et al.* (1994) who argue that the growth of a risk society has caused three practices to be integral to the everyday life of principals:

1   Risk assessment – the development of calculative practices which anticipate possible risks;
2   Risk avoidance – taking decisions based on the potential for adverse consequences;
3   Risk management planning – the development of rational plans to be used when risks become reality to deal with effects and prevent them spreading.

(Thomson, 2009: 4)

She juxtaposes these practices, however, with government policies in which 'an overemphasis on regurgitation of prescribed materials leads to failure to experiment, to dream of possibilities, to explore potential avenues and to face the reality of making a mistake' (Thomson, 2009: 8). Successful classrooms in successful schools are, she argues, those in which risk occurs. International research on successful principals' work has shown that among the qualities of successful principals are those associated with risk taking in the interests of challenging the boundaries of teaching and learning for the intrinsic and extrinsic moral good of the learners rather than compliance with the relatively narrow attainment targets of governments. Successful leaders embody, also, a passion for learning and an abiding sense of academic optimism (Day and Leithwood, 2007; Day *et al.*, 2011).

Academic optimism

Academic optimism in teachers has been defined as teachers' individual and collective beliefs 'that they can teach effectively, their students can learn, and parents will support them so that the teacher can press hard for learning' (Beard *et al.*, 2010). It includes 'cognitive, affective, and behavioural components of optimism merging into a single integrated construct' (2010: 1142). It is claimed to be 'one of the few organisational characteristics of schools in the United States that influences student achievement when socio-economic status and previous achievements are controlled' (2010: 1136); it 'influences student achievement directly through at least two mechanisms: motivation with high, challenging goals and co-operation among parents and teachers to improve student performance' (2010: 1143). Finally, the authors theorise from their data that 'schools and teachers with strong academic optimism have students who are highly motivated because of challenging goals, strong effort, persistence, resilience, and constructive feedback' (2010: 1143).

Academic optimism is associated, also, with relational and organisational trust (Bryk and Schneider, 2002; Louis, 2007) and nurtured, built and spread by successful principals. Thus, whilst it follows that academic optimism is a necessary constituent for success for teachers, it is not unreasonable to argue, and can be evidenced from the empirical data in this book, that academic optimism is a characteristic which is common to all successful heads too. Indeed, Beard *et al.* (2010) also associate academic optimism with 'enabling' school cultures, defined by Hoy and Miskel (2005) as hierarchies that help rather than hinder and systems of rules and regulations which guide problem solving rather than punish failure.

Leadership trust, trust in leaders

The *Oxford English Dictionary* defines trust as 'confidence in or reliance on some quality or attribute of a person or thing'. Trust is, then, associated, also, with '[t]he quality of being trustworthy; fidelity, reliability, loyalty' (www.oecd.com). In other words, trust and trustworthiness are in a reciprocal relationship. It is claimed that 'a presumption of trust rather than a presumption of mistrust helps individuals and organisations to flourish' (Seldon, 2009: Preface). 'As role models, leaders across society must meet two key criteria of trustworthiness: behave ethically and be technically proficient. The power of leaders to build or destroy trust is vast. Without honesty and competence, suspicion will grow' (Seldon, 2009: 26). In these words Seldon captures the power of school leaders to determine the moral purposes and culture (the norms of behaviour, the way we relate to each other) of the school.

Trust and its development are reciprocal, then, both in terms of:

1   People – it is the result of a two-way process and it changes as a result of people's needs.
2   The relationship of trust with actions and strategies – it both sets the environment which can determine the success of strategies (such as distributing leadership or communicating the vision) and is also a consequence of these strategies.

Thus, in order to create a culture of trust, it is not only the actions of leaders that are important but the values and virtues which they possess, articulate and communicate. In our research, we found that these included those said to be fundamental to teaching: honesty, courage, care, fairness and practical wisdom (Sockett, 1993: 62).

> Teaching necessarily demands these virtues – although many other virtues may be contingently significant. First, since teachers deal in knowledge and trade in truth, questions of honesty and deceit are part of the logic of their situation. Second, both learning and teaching involve facing difficulty and taking intellectual and psychological risks; that demands courage. Third, teachers are responsible for the development of persons, a process demanding infinite care for the individual. Fourth, fairness is necessary to the operation of rules in democratic institutions or, indeed, in one-to-one relationships. Finally, practical wisdom is essential to the complex process teaching is and, of course, may well demand the expertise of those virtues (such as patience) that are contingent to the teaching situation.
>
> (Sockett, 1993: 62–3)

Since trust relies on the values and attributes of another person, persons or group, their predispositions and reactions, it cannot be viewed as simply a characteristic. There are qualities that contribute towards the creation of trust, but these interact constantly with other variables to create an environment for improvement, making trust 'a necessary ingredient for cooperative action' (Seashore Louis 2007: 3). Trust is an individual, relational and organisational concept, and its presence and repeated enactment are as vital to successful school improvement as any expression of values, attributes and the decisions which heads may make. It cannot be fully separated from any of these elements of leadership. Indeed, recent research has suggested that 'trust in leaders both determines organisational performance and is a product of organisational performance' (Seashore Louis 2007: 4).

> The implication for administrators is that trust cannot be easily separated from expanded teacher empowerment and influence. Teachers are not passive actors in the school, but co-constructors of trust. As active professionals, teachers who feel left out of important decisions will react by withdrawing trust, which then undermines change.
>
> (Seashore Louis 2007: 18)

Teachers often recognise the difference between notional and authentic involvement in decisions, especially when the end is interpreted as a functional outcome rather than a personal one. Here we refer to the work of Fielding who distinguishes between one type of organisation where '[t]he functional is for the sake of/expressive of the personal' creating a person-centred learning community and another where '[t]he functional marginalises the personal' creating an impersonal organisation (Fielding 2003: 6, cited in Day and Leithwood 2007: 183). In the democratic 'distributed leadership' organisation, people are not merely seen as the means to an end. In employing strategies that aim to build trust in the organisation, the leader will have to place trust in others. There will thus be a difference between those heads whose trust in staff is ethically driven, aiming to develop individuals' motivation and commitment to their work and to the organisation, and those whose trust is pragmatically or functionally driven, aiming to get tasks completed on a specific timescale regardless of the cost or benefit to the individual. A person-centred approach to leadership is able to be identified by the:

> creation of an inclusive community; emphasis on relationships and ethic of care; creation of shared meanings and identities through the professional culture of the school; staff development programmes and arrangements for teaching; learning and assessment which encourage dialogue; a discourse of the personal; reciprocity of learning; encouraging new approaches to learning; remaining restless about contemporary understandings of leadership and management.
>
> (Day and Leithwood, 2007: 184)

It follows that the progressive distribution of trust is an active process which must be led and managed. To do so successfully, however, requires more than actions. It requires that the leader possesses qualities of wisdom, discernment and strategic acumen. Moreover, trust in organisations is not unconditional: 'Discerning the proper level of trust requires wisdom and discernment on the part of the educational leader. Optimal trust is prudent, measured and conditional' (Tschannen-Moran, 2004: 57)

Hope

Teaching, and thus leadership, is a values-led profession concerned at its heart with change for the betterment of pupils and, ultimately, for society as a whole. Indeed, a world without hope would be 'a world of resignation to the status quo' (Simecka, 1984: 175).

Hakanen *et al.* (2008) and Prieto *et al.* (2008) all found that variations in workers' sense of, on the one hand, exhaustion, and on the other, work engagement, were related to the interactions between their personal resources (e.g. self-efficacy, optimism, resilience), the demands of the job and the support which they received at work. Also from a psychological perspective, Peterson and Luthans (2003) found that there was an association between the expression of high levels of 'hope' by organisational leaders and job satisfaction and retention. Hope is also found to be one of four interrelated constructs of psychological capital (Luthans *et al.*, 2008), which are associated with wellbeing over time – the others being efficacy, optimism and resilience (Avey *et al.*, 2010).

Vision is an expression of hope, 'an affirmation that despite the heartbreak and trials that we face daily ... we can see that our actions can be purposeful and significant' (Sockett 1993: 85). For school principals and other leaders, vision and hope need to be revisited regularly through daily acts of aspiration and trust and not just at the end or beginning of a year staff meeting or workshop. The expression of hope through visioning is a dynamic process. It involves:

> a complex blend of evolving themes of the change programme. Visioning is a dynamic process, no more a one-time-event that has a beginning and an end than is planning. Visions are developed and reinforced from action, although they may have a seed that is based simply on hope.
>
> (Seashore Louis and Miles, 1990: 237)

Good leadership, like good teaching is, by definition, a journey of hope based upon a set of ideals. Arguably, it is our ideals that sustain us through difficult times and changing personnel and professional environments. They are an essential part of resilience:

> Having hope means that one will not give in to overwhelming anxiety ... Indeed, people who are hopeful evidence less depression than others as they maneuver through life in pursuit of their goals, are less anxious in general, and have fewer emotional distresses.
>
> (Goleman, 1995: 87)

The evidence from research is that successful leaders, especially heads, are always beacons of hope in their schools and communities.

Moral purpose

Starratt has long argued that the professional ethics of educational leadership have been a relatively neglected dimension of research (Starratt, 2012) and associated these with the promotion of authentic learning which is for the intrinsic moral good of the learner. He defines this as 'not any old kind of learning but ... a deep and broad learning that enables the child to accelerate the process of self-understanding and agency in relation to the natural, the cultural and the social worlds' (Starratt, 2012: 108); and he argues persuasively for the practice of general ethics, involving 'issues around fairness, truth telling, respect, equity, conflict, misunderstandings and loyalties' and professional ethics which promote 'the "good" involved in the practice of educating' (Starratt, 2012: 107).

It is much easier for individual teachers to express their 'moral purpose' (as Chapter 4 illustrates) when their school principals espouse and articulate a set of coherent educational values. In October 2006 a group of 100 principals from 14 different countries (the G100) at the National Academy of Education Administration (NAEA) in Beijing, China was convened to discuss the transformation of and innovation in the world's education systems. During the final session of the workshop the whole group collaborated in preparing a communiqué about their conclusions (Hopkins 2008). The final paragraphs read:

> We need to ensure that moral purpose is at the fore of all educational debates with our parents, our students, our teachers, our partners, our policy makers and our wider community.
>
> We define moral purpose as a compelling drive to do right for and by students, serving them through professional behaviours that 'raise the bar and narrow the gap' and through so doing demonstrate an intent, to learn with and from each other as we live together in this world.

It is clear from the evidence of what makes successful leaders that, whilst resilience is an essential quality, it must be understood in relation to the moral purposes and responsibility for the learning and achievement of children. Like teachers, what keeps many resilient and committed leaders going is the opportunity to make a difference – but on a greater, deeper and more systemic scale. Such strong sense of moral purpose is the heartbeat of successful leadership – which drives and inspires many outstanding and committed principals in England and in other countries to create creative, caring, inspirational and challenging environments for learning that every student and every teacher in their school deserve. In this sense, resilience without moral purpose, without a willingness to be self-reflective and learn in order to change in order to continue to improve and to serve is not enough. Resilience, also, cannot be considered in isolation from other constructs of commitment, competence, agency, vocation, individual and collective academic optimism, trust and hope. A key responsibility of every school principal is to ensure that the nature, environment and management of teachers' work is, as far as possible, designed to reduce negative experiences of stress and increase capacities for resilience. Resilient leadership, from this perspective, describes 'the potential outcome of interactions between groups of people rather than specific traits or skills of a single person' (Robinson *et al.*, 2009: 24).

Challenges to resilience: schools which serve disadvantaged communities

A growing body of research evidence suggests that whilst there are generic qualities, strategies and skills which are common to all, successful principals, those who lead schools serving disadvantaged communities, face a greater range of more persistent, intensive challenges than others and so not only need to possess these qualities to a greater degree but also need different qualities and skills which are specific to the context of their schools.

Because many of the students in these schools are at greater risk of underachieving in their personal, social and academic lives, it is particularly important to examine conditions which may help to improve this. Research into the work of school principals in England and Sweden, for example, found that principals in improving schools serving disadvantaged communities: i) face the most persistent levels of challenge; ii) apply greater combinations or clusters of strategies with greater intensity; and iii) use a broader range of personal and social skills than do those in other schools which serve more advantaged communities. Principals in these schools are often younger and less experienced than those in more advantaged schools and are responsible for leading and managing situations which are less physically and emotionally stable. For example, teacher and pupil mobility tend to be higher in disadvantaged schools and challenges of pupil and teacher motivation, pupil behaviour, engagement and attendance greater (Day and Johansson, 2008). It is not that principals in more advantaged schools work less hard or are less committed, but rather that the sets of skills and attributes used by principals in more disadvantaged schools are different, contextually related and more complex than those in more advantaged schools.

> Different leadership strategies may be effective in different circumstances and also ... the principal's purposes and the ways they act out their beliefs, values and visions in the contexts in which they work make the difference between success and failure.
>
> (Day and Leithwood, 2007: 174)

Table 7.1 below provides a number of tentative hypotheses which, together, indicate the special nature of the challenges.

Table 7.1 Characteristics and strategies of successful principals in schools serving disadvantaged communities: differences by degree

Schools serving relatively advantaged communities	Strategies and characteristics	Schools serving relatively disadvantaged communities
Important	Establish vision and set directions	Essential
Important	Understand and develop people	Essential
Important	(Re)structure and (re)culture the organisation	Essential
Challenging	Manage the teaching and learning programme	More challenging
Challenging	Values-led responsiveness to context	More challenging
Important	Delegate or distribute leadership	Important
Challenging	Build staff/pupil motivation, commitment, morale, engagement (relational trust)	More challenging

Schools serving relatively advantaged communities	Strategies and characteristics	Schools serving relatively disadvantaged communities
Challenging	Sustain staff/pupil motivation, commitment, morale, engagement (relational trust)	More challenging
Challenging	Raise teaching, learning and achievement expectations	More challenging
Challenging	Combine logic and emotion	More challenging
Important	Be responsive to and manage diverse internal and external communities	Essential
–	Manage and reduce staff and pupil mobility	Challenging
–	Manage alienation	Challenging
Important	Persistent, optimistic, resilient, leaders of hope	Essential
Important	Open minded, flexible, ready to learn from others	Essential
Important	Leadership and management of whole school change and transition	Essential

(Day and Johansson, 2008: 20–1)

Reservoirs of hope, when reservoirs run dry

Because all principals lead and manage in social arenas that are often charged with emotion, they need to be emotionally resilient, to possess inner strengths which will enable them to lead. In 2003, a secondary school principal in England published two pieces of writing arising from a 'practitioner enquiry' project supported by the National College of School Leadership. The first, '*Reservoirs of Hope*' (Flintham 2003a) was based upon interviews with 25 principals drawn from a range of school contexts, phases and regions in England and focused upon how they sustain their schools and themselves through spiritual and moral leadership based on hope. The second, '*When Reservoirs Run Dry*' (Flintham 2003b) examined through the eyes of 14 principals who had left their jobs prematurely, 'What happens when for some the pressures for action become too great, when the vision cannot be sustained, when the replenishment strategies of head teachers fail' (Flintham, 2003b: 2).

In his first, more optimistic study, Flintham found that all principals were able to articulate clearly the values which 'underpinned their approach to leadership' (2003a: 6) and to describe the strategies that enabled them to sustain themselves.

Here, Flintham's findings not only correspond closely with those of Leithwood and Jantzi (2008), Goddard *et al.* (2004), and Tschannen-Moran and Hoy (2007), but also extend them:

> Such strategies include belief networks, sustained by high levels of self-belief in the rightness of their underlying value system, support networks, sustained by families, friends and colleagues, and external networks of engagement with interests and experiences beyond the world of education.
>
> (Flintham, 2003a: 6)

We have selected below just three of the many rich texts provided by these school principals in order to illustrate what they identified as the key positive influences upon their capacity to sustain hope:

> I know I have six wells [of resilience...]: intellectual, physical, emotional, spiritual, creative and social, which need topping up and keeping in balance ... and this has to be planned rather than waiting for them to become empty.
>
> (Primary school principal: 15)

> I build in reflective time with my leadership team ... (concerned with) not 'doing' but 'why doing' ... not 'doing' but 'being'.
>
> (Secondary school principal: 30)

> Early in your headship you toe the line, you accept external professional direction rather than have the confidence to go in the direction of your beliefs ... later in headship, you have enough confidence to take risks, 'to be brave'.
>
> (Primary school principal: 27)

In the second study, Flintham (2003b) charted the reasons why 14 principals left their jobs early. Some had left in order to create other career opportunities, as education consultants, whilst others had become disillusioned with changes in the policy landscape:

> Accountability restricted my professional freedom and league tables distorted its dynamics ... I found myself out of sync with the culture of the new age.
>
> (Primary school principal: 6)

Others were losing their capacities to be resilient, experiencing:

> the intellectual tiredness and mental drain of coping with recruitment and retention issues.
>
> (Secondary school principal: 6)

One had found that being a principal had begun to encroach on the quality of relationships with family and was no longer able to tolerate that. Another, illustrating an extreme example of burnout in early principalship of a secondary school, provides an important message about the need for external support mechanisms:

> If I'd had sustainability strategies I'd have seen a way forward. The only one I had was more of the same: I enjoyed innovating which gave me satisfaction but ironically caused me to work even longer hours. I had no one professionally to turn to. I would have liked a professional listening partner (to share it all with) but (internal staff) problems meant that sort of relationship couldn't work at school and I suffered from ... professional loneliness and isolation ... My self-belief was undermined.
>
> (Secondary school principal: 10)

Whilst both of these reports are based upon small-scale, qualitative enquiry, the principals' stories provide powerful testimonies of the challenges of leading schools in contexts of on-going externally-initiated government reforms. Principals need to have the means of sustaining their own 'reservoirs of hope' if they are to lead others in doing so. Recent research by members of the International Successful School Principals Project (ISSPP) highlights the courage, determination and resilience evidenced by successful school principals across more than a dozen different countries (Moos *et al.*, 2012; Day and Gurr, 2013).

By any standards, it is clear that being a principal is a tough job, then, in cognitive, emotional and physical terms. Research in a nine-country study of 36 successful school principals in schools in urban settings (Day and Johansson, 2008) found that their success was achieved through their work in five arenas:

Arena 1: Combining demands for educational success with educational values

Here, examination results matter but relationships and social learning are as important. The ethics of care and achievement are applied equally to pupils, regardless of ability, social background, language or ethical grouping.

Arena 2: Building and sustaining an inclusive parent community

Accommodating parental needs and concerns has always been a part of the principals' work. However, in recent times more parents are organising themselves in formal and informal groups to represent and achieve their special interests. In some countries (e.g. Sweden and UK) governments are encouraging even more participation in decision making through 'free schools', thus placing principals in a competitive marketplace. In all countries, also, principals of schools in socially disadvantaged areas have to spend relatively more time negotiating with parents than their counterparts in more socially advantaged areas.

Arena 3: Building a sense of collective identity, high expectations and pride

Success requires the building and sustaining of a sense of common purpose, belonging and hope among diverse internal and external communities. This requires that principals are able to exercise high levels of emotional understandings in order to establish a collective sense of stability and 'thisness' for their school within the discontinuities of the policy and social environment.

Arena 4: Building culture – values, beliefs and ethics

Good and effective leaders are those, also, who are able to communicate values and create a common culture. What separates effective from less effective principals is not only the quality of their vision but how much they really care about (all) the people they lead and how such care is expressed through their daily words and actions. For example, successful principals' thinking and decision making about issues of social justice and equity is not a matter of following the rules. Rather, they invest much time and effort in building a shared sense of ethical norms within their schools and external communities.

Arena 5: Creating and sustaining trustful leadership

Successful principals understand that trust, obligation and solidarity work together in complementary ways, that trust in personal and organisational relations depends not only upon an assumption of the integrity of the other, but also upon the way it is expressed through, for example, the leadership distribution throughout the school; and the extent to which staff and pupils feel able to exercise discretionary judgements about the content, direction, pace and outcomes of their work.

There is no doubt that the increasingly complex and diverse social, emotional and performance-oriented demands on schools have created pressures upon heads to be more overtly successful in demonstrating a greater range of value-added achievements among all their pupils and, in particular, those that relate to measurable outcomes and those that relate to well-being, social harmony and democracy (defined differently in different countries). This has caused their work to become more demanding internally and externally in working with an increasing number of diverse communities of interest. The combinations of demands are not all new but they are certainly more intensively driven through complex policy agendas. In order to meet and mediate these demands, heads need to work successfully in a number of arenas and some – those who work in schools in especially challenging communities – need to possess more, and in some cases additional, sets of qualities and skills than those who do not work in those contexts.

Conclusions

A health warning

School leadership, like classroom teaching, is a complex process and managing complexity is, in itself, inherently stressful. It is stressful because it involves influencing others in order that they might strive to improve and thrive in different ways; and improvement involves change. Successful school leaders know that there are associations between the quality of classroom teaching and the quality of pupil learning and achievement. They know, also, that classroom teachers work to influence a range of pupils who themselves may or may not wish to learn and may or may not wish to learn in the way their teachers wish them to learn. The efforts to influence pupil learning, which teachers who are teaching to their best must make daily, are considerable, and in order for them to grow and sustain their passion, expertise and success, they themselves will need support. Like teachers, school principals may be in different phases of their professional learning lives and demonstrate different levels of competence and commitment.

Resilience is a necessary quality for leadership success. As a middle leader of a school in the UK found recently in her research:

> Absence of resilience at the most senior levels of leadership in schools can present itself as a deterioration in the general functioning of the school and can be evidenced in a variety of areas. These include loss of direction in terms of funding and budgeting; curriculum developments; teaching and learning strategies; control of discipline; staff–pupil relationships and school–community relationships.
>
> (Birkbeck, 2011: 14)

The ability of heads and teachers to sustain resilience throughout their careers will be influenced by the interaction between the strength of their own vocation, those whom they meet as part of their daily work, and the quality of the internal and external environments in which they work. Their capacities to manage unanticipated, as well as anticipated, events effectively will mediate their capacity to manage these. In times when organisational and professional change are inevitable in order to meet new social and economic challenges, it is those who are supported in managing connections between their educational values, beliefs and practices and those of their colleagues and organisations, through the exercise of individual, relation and organisational capacity for resilience, who are most likely to lead successfully.

8 The role of resilience in teachers' career-long commitment and effectiveness

Evidence from the field

Drawing upon evidence from the VITAE research (Day *et al.*, 2007a), this chapter will explore the ways in which resilience in teachers may be related to the learning and achievement of their pupils. The aims of the VITAE research were to examine variations in teachers' work, lives and effectiveness (See Chapter 1 for a brief description). In a secondary analysis of what kept 73 per cent of the 300 primary and secondary teachers in different phases of their careers committed in the profession, resilience emerged as a key factor in their quality retention (Day and Gu, 2010; Gu, in press). A total of 232 teachers' profiles were analysed under this theme. Drawing upon the experiences of these teachers, the chapter will show that for many teachers who sustain their commitment and effectiveness, three inter-related conditions – teachers' vocational selves, high quality social and professional relationships with colleagues, and leadership support and recognition – are integral in enabling them to function well in everyday teaching and learning environments as well as to weather successfully the often unpredictable, more extreme 'storms' of school and classroom life (Patterson and Kelleher, 2005) as well as the every day exigencies of teaching. In other words, their capacity for sustaining 'everyday resilience' over the course of their teaching careers is associated with their ability to manage the personal, professional and organisational contexts in which they work and live.

What our own and a range of other research reveals clearly is that teachers' sense of resilience is not only driven by their vocational commitment to make a difference to the learning of the children, but also influenced by the support and recognition of 'significant others' in their professional and personal environments. In previous chapters we have explored how a sense of vocation can provide many committed teachers with the internal drive, strength and optimism which are necessary to help every child learn on each school day. We have seen, also, the critical roles played by school leaders, particularly the head teacher, in creating and actively managing the conditions for the seeds of trust, openness, collegiality and collective responsibility to grow and flourish on their school site. In this chapter we will focus more closely on teachers' *relational resilience*, exploring how establishing connections with colleagues and pupils can create and increase the collective intellectual and emotional capital which, in turn, contributes to their sense of job fulfilment and commitment. Portraits of two resilient teachers in their early and mid-careers will be used to illustrate the impact of individual, relational and organisational factors on teachers as a means of exploring how they build, develop and draw upon their sense of resilience in the relational contexts of their work and lives, and the ways in which such resilience sustains their capacity to make a difference to the success of their pupils over time. Finally, by demonstrating the significance of associations between teachers' sense of resilience and their effectiveness, as perceived by teachers themselves as well as measured by the progress of their pupils' academic outcomes, we hope that the evidence presented in this chapter will contribute to current debates among policy makers, academics and the teaching profession about not only the retention of teachers in the profession but, more importantly, the retention of high-quality teachers.

Relationships, resilience and effectiveness

Teachers' resilience-building processes are nested in 'a web of communal relationships' (Palmer, 2007: 97) and are influenced, positively or negatively, by the quality of the relationships in which their work and lives are embedded. In our research, three sets of relationships were found to be at the heart of this web: teacher-teacher relations, teacher-principal relations and teacher-pupil relations. Individually and collectively, they shaped the social and intellectual environments of the workplace and through this, fostered or hindered teachers' sense of professionalism, commitment and control.

The former two relationships, in particular, were found to have provided the necessary structural and social conditions for teachers' collective and collaborative learning and development. Through such learning and development, many teachers were able to harness the commitments, expertise and wisdom of their colleagues for their own professional growth, whilst at the same time, enhance their capacities to connect with each other emotionally, intellectually, socially and spiritually (in terms of the sharing of values and interests). The alignment of values within 'a tight team' was perceived by many as the moral foundation for the achievement of a strong sense of collective efficacy and professional fulfilment. With regard to teacher-pupil relationships, emotional attachments between teachers and pupils were found to be closely connected with a strong sense of calling that had brought many teachers into the profession and had remained a primary source of job fulfilment over the course of their careers.

Building relational resilience with teachers

Teachers in all six professional life phases (see Chapter 5) identified in the VITAE research (Day *et al.*, 2007a; Day and Gu, 2010) reported *positive influences of collegial, emotional and intellectual connections* with colleagues on their well-being, commitment and capacity to sustain a sense of effectiveness on every working day. Between 78 and 100 per cent of teachers in different phases of their professional lives emphasised how their colleagues' passion, enthusiasm and support contributed to their sense of belonging, collective responsibility and commitment. This was especially the case for those in schools serving socio-economically challenging communities. For example, for Malcolm, a Year 9 English teacher with 26 years of experience, it was the *closeness of the relationships* with his colleagues that made him feel that his current inner-city school. His department in particular, was the 'best place' that he had ever worked:

> Personally I love working down here. It's the best place I've ever worked for – team spirit, keenness and motivation that I have and the rest of the department has ... Over here (department) I'm happy. I'm enjoying things. I'm working with people that I rate and value and I feel value me.

Related to this finding is the observation that teachers who described their workplaces as supportive and friendly communities where there was 'a good sense of "team"' among the staff were more likely to maintain their commitment and capacity to teach to their best. A total of 91 per cent of teachers who managed to sustain their sense of resilience and commitment reported *the positive influence of collegial and collaborative support* on their morale and intellectual and emotional well-being. In contrast, only 71 per cent of teachers who did not manage to sustain their resilience and commitment reported this. Results of a Chi-Square test show that the observed difference is statistically significant ($x^2=10.903$, df=1, p<0.01).

The importance of open, trusting and enduring working relationships between peers in promoting individuals' learning and growth and through this, creating creative and productive intellectual capital within the workplace, is well documented in the educational and organisational change literature (e.g. Nieto, 2003; Hargreaves and Fink, 2006; Lieberman and Miller, 2008; Hargreaves and Fullan, 2012; Louis, 2012). Evidence from the VITAE research reaffirms the main thrust of these observations. Among those who reported the positive impact of staff relationships on their work, close to one in six (16 per cent) described that working with 'really good, extremely motivated and effective staff' had the *greatest* impact on their satisfaction, morale and commitment. Central to this observation was a consistent message that being able to learn from each other, generate ideas with each other and share ideas together 'affects the effectiveness in the classroom' (Roger, 23 years in teaching).

Sustained dialogue and interaction amongst colleagues were seen by many as an effective way of building a shared repertoire of expertise and wisdom in the department and/or school. As a late entrant into the teaching profession who was now in the 'watershed' phase of her teaching career (with 8–15 years of experience), Margaret, a primary school teacher, was especially appreciative of the *strong social and intellectual bonds* in her school which enabled her to connect her own learning and her own teaching practices with those of her colleagues:

> We try and share. We discuss problem children. We discuss strategies. We share what knowledge we have, what expertise we have. We feel free to ask

people without feeling vulnerable because we don't know the answer. We feel we can ask each other.

For Kathy, who had more than 30 years of teaching experience in the primary sector, professional support from her colleagues and teaching assistants was still regarded as the most 'invaluable' and 'important' influence on her sense of efficacy, motivation and commitment. She proudly described her school as 'a very, very caring place' and attributed this to *a collegial culture of sharing* where expressing the need for help and advice was not regarded as a sign of weakness, but an entitlement to and an opportunity for learning and growth.

> I don't think anybody is afraid to hold their hands up and say, I can't do this or I don't know how to do this, help me somebody, and somebody will always help. Nobody puts themselves up as a prime example of the perfect teacher because we all know that we're not.

As Noddings (2005) argues, 'caring is a way of being in relation' (2005: 17). The ethics of care for and about the teachers has to be grounded in the belief that as they 'learn how to talk together honestly, to engage in knowledge work both as producers and critical consumers of new theories and ideas, and to make connections between their own learning, their teaching practices, and the impact these on students', they will 'begin to see themselves and act differently; they reinvent themselves as teachers and reinvigorate their careers' (Lieberman and Miller, 2008: 101). In a similar vein, Little (1990), Palmer (2007) and Hargreaves and Fullan (2012) have urged teachers themselves as well as school leaders to develop 'a more collaborative and collegial profession – not just because this is professionally supportive but because it also improves student learning and achievement' (Hargreaves and Fullan, 2012: xi–xii). Yet even today, there are many teachers who continue to teach, literally and metaphorically, behind closed doors.

The nature of connection within caring and trusting communities of learning among colleagues does not lie only in the physical communications between individuals, but also in the values and interests which they share in making a difference to the learning and achievement of every child. For Tony, a senior leader with more than 20 years' experience in the primary sector, it was the *intellectual challenges from his colleagues* within such a community that had enabled him to learn and grow:

> The biggest asset in terms of professional support is my teaching colleagues in the school. We are part of a very active bunch of monitors – we will watch each other teach and will comment on areas of strength and development and I am monitored like everybody else by curriculum co-ordinators and that's a real support to me and the quality of the learning support provision makes a huge difference in the classroom and helps to raise standards in the classroom in a large variety of ways.

Tony's experience (and that of his other 155 primary and secondary peers in our sample) provides another testimony to how such communities encourage teachers to come together to 'inquire into the need for, and then create improvements that benefit all students' (Hargreaves and Fink, 2006: 128).

As we have seen already (Chapter 3), over the past 20 years educational research has consistently reported that teaching is, by its very nature, an emotional practice (Hargreaves, 1998; Sutton and Wheatley, 2003; Kelchtermans, 2005; Zembylas, 2005, 2011; Day and Gu, 2009; Zembylas and Schutz, 2009). The inherent interconnectedness between emotion and cognition and the impact of positive emotional contexts on teachers' learning and thinking have also been acknowledged in the literature (Nias, 1996; Frijda, 2000; van Veen and Lasky, 2005). In the VITAE research, there is also an abundance of evidence which points to the importance of the relationship between strong emotional ties with colleagues and teachers' sense of motivation and commitment. For almost all the 185 teachers who reported the positive impact of close staff relationships on their work, it was the trust between colleagues and the 'pats on the back' that 'make a difference when you get up to go to work in the morning'.

Andrea, a primary school teacher with 26 years of experience in the profession, had been increasingly struggling with work-life tensions. Although her commitments to the children had remained high, her enjoyment of the job 'isn't the same as it used to be' because of 'all the pressures from outside and the pressure to do all this paperwork'. Given this, she was especially appreciative of the *social environment of her school* which she described as 'a lovely place' because the staff worked hard in an atmosphere of mutual support and good humour:

> People I work with are all very good and very supportive and I think that's one of the things in this school that keep us going. The staff in this school all get on and that is a big help when you are feeling a bit low. There is always someone to offer support and advice.

For Cherry, an early career English teacher in a challenging urban secondary school, the *'close knit team'* within her department and the wider supportive ethos in her school made a significant difference to her motivation, sense of efficacy and decision to stay in teaching:

> It's something that the school's just managed to grasp and I don't know if it's the type of people that work here or [if] it comes from above, I don't know, but the staff seem to fit and support each other. If that side wasn't there I wouldn't still be here because if you didn't have your staff members to turn to or go for a drink with on a Friday night, it is a very tough school to teach in and the problems and the workload; and if you didn't have the backup from the staff you wouldn't put up with it.

The emphasis upon the importance of collegial care, sympathy and moral support to their motivation and commitment was almost universal among the

185 teachers who reported close relations with their colleagues. The texture of care, connectedness and emotional bonds between colleagues has been found to be 'woven principally of social and interpersonal interests' (Little 1990: 513). For many teachers, those working in schools serving socio-economically challenging communities in particular, such interests often rest upon a feeling that 'we're all in the same boat and you've got to pull together; otherwise, the boat is going to sink' (Paul, 26 years of experience). In the experience of David, a primary school teacher with five years' experience, 'a good sense of community' was 'all about sharing, caring and learning'.

The mutually supportive ethos between colleagues – professionally as well as on a personal level – provides a necessary positive psychological and social environment for staff. It serves to 'bank' their positive emotions about teaching (Fredrickson, 2001, 2004), nourish their sense of subjective well-being (OECD, 2013) and keep their commitments strong. What matters most to teachers, it seems, is working in a professional school and/or departmental culture which is blended with shared values and positive emotions. This is more likely to help teachers 'transform themselves, becoming more creative, knowledgeable, resilient, socially integrated and healthy individuals' (Fredrickson, 2004: 1369). All pupils in all contexts, as Edwards (2003) argues, 'deserve to be taught by enthusiastic, motivated individuals' (2003: 11).

Building relational resilience with leaders

The need for strong leadership in creating and building a positive and collegial professional culture in schools has been consistently reported in the educational literature (e.g. Leithwood *et al.*, 2006b, 2010; Day and Leithwood, 2007; Deal and Peterson, 2009; Hargreaves and Fullan, 2012; OECD, 2012a, 2012b; Gu and Johansson, in press). There is also abundant evidence, as we have seen in Chapter 7, that trusting relationships between the head and their staff are a key feature of successful schools (e.g. Bryk *et al.*, 2010; Day *et al.*, 2011). In their work on successful urban schools, Bryk and Schneider (2002) found that 'teachers who perceive benevolent intentions on the part of their principal are more likely to feel efficacious in their jobs' (2002: 29).

In the VITAE research, we also found that teachers who reported *support and recognition from school leaders* (including principals, senior and/or middle leaders) were more likely to develop and sustain a sense of commitment and resilience in the profession ($x^2=7.155$, df=1, p<0.01). Seventy-four per cent of teachers who managed to do so, compared with 52.5 per cent who did not, reported the positive impact of school leadership on their morale, motivation and commitment. Moreover, amongst the 118 who maintained their commitment to the learning of their pupils, one in seven (14 per cent) felt that leadership support made a difference to their perceived effectiveness in the classroom. As Shirley, a primary teacher with eleven years of experience, put it: 'It [support from the head and deputy head] makes you feel better about yourself and your role, and then it makes you a more effective teacher'. In a similar vein, Kwame, a mid-career secondary school maths teacher, felt that it was the personal support and 'constructive advice on everything' from his head of department that improved his effectiveness in teaching. For Liz, a primary teacher with 25 years of experience in teaching, it was the openness and recognition from the senior leaders that made a difference to her sense of effectiveness: 'Since the change in management I've been given much more responsibility and feel a lot more valued than before; and I think that's made me a more effective teacher and a more effective leader.'

Relationships of trust and caring are the heartbeats of positive leadership. Ample examples from the VITAE research show that such relationships are founded on a *collective sense of moral purpose and responsibility* and are the culmination of mutual acceptance and recognition between the leader and the teacher of their competence, integrity and commitment. For example, Janet, a primary school teacher with more than 30 years in teaching, attributed enjoyment of the final phase of her teaching career to the leadership of her head teacher – whose trust in the commitment and integrity of the teachers, and vice versa, bound them together in a shared purpose of achievement:

> He is a very good leader but very fair. He does not bombard us with all the new initiatives. He sort of protects us in a way, I mean we all pull our weight. We had a very good Ofsted, but he doesn't bombard us and go around breathing down your neck to make sure everything is done. People are trusted to do their job and I think that works very well.

The motivation of Melanie, a secondary school maths teacher with eight years of teaching experience, increased significantly when she was treated by the new head as a 'de facto' second in command: 'That's given me more satisfaction because I feel like I've been given more responsibility. Even though I'm finding it hard work, I'm enjoying it.' Moreover, what also kept her motivation and commitment high was the collective culture of caring and appreciation that had been created by the new head:

> I think it's the sort of school we work in where you do give, and people always say the level of caring about the kids and doing things for the good of the kids is so high here in comparison to other schools ... If you take part in something, the head will thank everybody. You get a personal letter of thanks.

It was within the many reciprocal exchanges between teachers and leaders which are essential to the development of relational trust that many teachers in the VITAE research saw their motivation and commitment grow and their sense of effectiveness improve. Like many other healthy social relationships, reciprocity, trust and trustworthiness (Field, 2008) are also key features of teacher-leader relations. *Leaders are the architects of such relations.* Their personal and professional qualities and values (such as openness, fairness, respect, compassion and discernment of talent) were perceived by many VITAE teachers as being central to the creation and development of a tight sense of community in their schools. For example, Penny, a primary school teacher who had spent 25 years in teaching, believed that the leadership of her head teacher impacted on her commitment and capacity to teach to her best because '[t]he head has a vision, knows how to get there, shows us the vision rather than telling us. It makes everyone want to go with it'. For Meryl, a late-career secondary school English teacher, the visibility that the head had with the staff and his appreciation of their work had a positive effect on the motivation of her department: 'If you do something good, the head will come and thank you.'

> The head here is wonderful – he knows the students, he does bus duty and says good night to the teachers. He'll be in the staffroom at break time and doesn't hide away in his office like lots of heads do.

Bryk and Schneider (2002) describe relationships such as these as being based upon *relational trust* which is:

> appropriately viewed as an organisational property in that its constitutive elements are socially defined in the reciprocal exchanges among participants in a school community, and its presence (or absence) has important consequences for the functioning of the school and its capacity to engage fundamental change.
>
> (Bryk and Schneider 2002: 22)

By extension, *building a collective sense of commitment and resilience in a school community is also a collective endeavour and requires organisational support.* As the experiences of Claire, an early-career primary school teacher, show, it is more likely to happen if 'the leader becomes better able to open spaces in which people feel invited to create communities of mutual support' where they share the passion for teaching and learning (Palmer, 2007: 166).

Building relational resilience with pupils

Trusting teacher-pupil relationships are essential for pupil learning (Bryk and Schneider, 2002). They are also crucial for maintaining teachers' job fulfillment and commitment in teaching (see Chapter 6). Evidence from the VITAE research reaffirms this, suggesting that teachers who enjoyed positive teacher-pupil relations were more likely to report a sustained sense of resilience and commitment to making a difference to pupils' learning and growth. Eighty-nine per cent of those who demonstrated commitment and capacity to teach to their best, compared with 71 per cent who did not, enjoyed good relationships with their pupils. Results of the Chi-Square test show that the observed difference is statistically significant ($x^2=7.635$, df=1, p<0.01). Moreover, almost one in six (15 per cent) of the former group emphasised how such relationships 'produced a good dynamic in classes' (Mike, an early career maths teacher) and that 'the rapport with the children in the classroom' (Anita, a mid-career English teacher) had the greatest positive impact on their motivation and sense of effectiveness. For example:

> I have consciously worked at establishing a really good relationship with my pupils. They realised I actually value them and actually like them, and want them to achieve. We now have a lot of respect for one another.
>
> (Ruth, mid-career primary teacher)

What we also learn from these and other interviews, however, is that trusting relationships between teacher and pupil involve more than a positive, open and caring emotional connection between two parties. They also encompass *teachers' belief in pupils' endeavour to achieve.* For example, Maggie, a primary school teacher with 26 years in teaching, described her pupils as 'a lovely bunch of kids' and felt that 'I can trust them because they are good kids ... I know they will do their tasks ... and this makes me feel good'.

For Barbara, a late-career maths teacher, 'Teaching is a lot more personal now ... I get a kick out of watching them grow up'. Similarly, for Malcolm, an English teacher with 26 years' experience, his enjoyment of teaching was founded in the good relationships that he and his colleagues in the English department established with the pupils. Difficult pupils improved because of such relationships, which, in his view, had a 'massive' positive impact on good results:

> That's reflected in their behaviour, the work they produce, their results, also cross referenced to how they're performing elsewhere in the school. We don't have many problems down here in terms of attitude and behaviour, talking to the pupils. They enjoy English.

Challenges in sustaining teacher resilience: two stories from the field

For the purposes of this chapter, portraits of one beginning teacher and one mid-career teacher have been selected from teachers in the VITAE project who reported a high level of resilience over the three-year fieldwork period. These provide detailed illustrations of the ways in which personal, relational and organisational histories and current contexts impacted upon their capacity to be resilient. Their profiles are typical of the teachers who reported similar experiences of how their sense of vocation and commitment and effectiveness had been sustained as a result of support from workplace conditions (see also Chapter 6).

Portrait of a beginning teacher: schools matter

In this first example we show how the professional development and growth of a beginning teacher is perceived by her to benefit from the support of strong school leadership and the collaborative school culture which good leaders create, shape and transform. It is within such positive working environments that this teacher felt that she was able to build her resilience, efficacy and commitment, and continue to enjoy the achievement of her pupils and the advancement of her professional life.

> Pat was 26 years old, a classroom teacher and science coordinator at her first school, where she had taught for three years. Prior to this, she had run a 'parent and toddler' (small child) group.
>
> She worked in an urban primary school of 220 pupils which served an affluent, ethnically diverse community. She described herself as having reached 'the point in my life where I wanted a promotion'. After two years of teaching in her current school, Pat was promoted to membership of the senior leadership team. She was appreciated by her pupils whose progress was well beyond expectations during the lifetime of the VITAE project.

Gaining strength from the inner call to teach

Pat had always enjoyed working with the children whom she described as 'delightful'. Although she often felt 'absolutely exhausted', she continued to derive immense pleasure and rewards from the learning and growth of her pupils. Her confidence and sense of efficacy had greatly increased as a consequence of their good results.

> I just love it, just to see the smallest sign of progression, moving a child on, even just a little bit. Motivation, building confidence and independence is a big part of how I make a difference in their lives ... It just gives you a buzz to keep going, even when a lesson that has been terrifically planned goes pear shaped. It's enjoyable, but it is also exhausting. It's not having enough hours in the day, but you want it to be right.

Her love for the children did not stop at the school gate. She was planning to learn to play the piano 'or some sort of musical instrument' in her spare time, so that her pupils could 'enjoy it in the classroom'.

Connecting with pupils and colleagues

Pat's sense of resilience did not result entirely from the strong commitment which she brought to her work. It was further built and sustained as a result of a number of factors in the school environment. First among these were the good relationships which she enjoyed with her pupils. She felt that the general improvement of children across the school had enhanced her relationships with the pupils in her class. Although their socio-economic background created some challenges to her teaching in the classroom, she was pleased that the overall behaviour of children in the school was generally quite good: 'Discipline has improved and this is mainly due to raised expectations. Also, everyone deals with problem behaviour in this school, rather than any one teacher.' Over the three-year period of our contact with her, Pat also consistently described the staff at her school as extremely supportive of one another, both professionally and socially. Her teaching colleagues helped to keep her commitment and motivation strong.

Improved self-efficacy: the leadership effect

Very shortly after Pat first joined the school, Ofsted (the Office for Standards in Education, the national schools' inspection service in the UK) placed it in 'special measures' (under threat of closure because it was failing to meet basic educational standards). However, one year later, under the leadership of a new head and deputy head, it had emerged from this. This had an important influence on, for example, the school's confidence to refocus the teaching, with more freedom to develop the children's skills 'without sticking to too rigid a timetable'. Thus, over her time in the school, it had improved; and after two very difficult years, in Pat's words, 'the school is now "getting somewhere"'. Her upward commitment trajectory paralleled this.

As part of her growing self-efficacy, Pat had become more aware of not allowing herself to slip behind because 'if you let something slip, it builds up and builds up – so you don't feel good about yourself anyway'. As such, she set herself targets and was 'getting more organised'.

Support and recognition from strong leadership and the transformation of negative cultures in her school had re-ignited her long-term commitment to teaching. Not surprisingly, she had highly positive views on the school leadership: 'Everything seems to filter down really well, and everything seems to be discussed openly, and decisions then made as a whole staff. Everyone is allowed to develop.' She described the new head as 'exceptional':

> With our new head there is a lot more support for your own development in the sense of your position in the school. It's the encouragement of making decisions for the school. Also, the literacy adviser from the Local Authority (School District) is wonderful; team teaching, observations together, very good.

Although she was still 'juggling' her family life, Pat felt that her passion for teaching continued to grow. One particularly important boost to her confidence, enthusiasm and commitment was her promotion to the senior leadership team, which she saw as recognition for her potential and appreciation of her work from school management. Her perception was that this internal promotion, combined with positive external and internal professional feedback and professional and personal support from school management and her colleagues, had spurred her on even more: 'OK, I can make it even better.'

Portrait of a mid-career teacher: sustaining resilience, commitment and effectiveness against the odds

This second example illustrates how the detrimental effects of nation-wide reforms and inspections, together with age-related family commitments, may lead teachers in the key transitional phase of their professional lives to struggle with work-life tensions. It also shows that, in addition to leadership support, a sense of belonging to a collegial staff community is perceived by them to have a critical positive effect upon their commitment and intellectual and emotional development, particularly for those who strive to survive and succeed in schools serving highly deprived communities.

> Katherine, 37 years old, was head of English in an 11–16 comprehensive school. Her school was situated in an urban community of socio-economic disadvantage which had a well above average proportion (23 per cent) of pupils on the special educational needs register. She had been teaching in this school for three years, having previously worked in two others. She was eight months pregnant when she had begun the job, and inherited a department that had been without a leader for two years. Her pupils, whose progress and achievement, under her leadership, was beyond expectations, expressed affection for Katherine.

The inner sense of vocation that sustains resilience

Katherine came from a teaching family and had always loved the idea of working with children. It was not surprising that she decided to choose teaching as a life-long career because she found it stimulating and rewarding. She had a deep interest in her subject and also valued the opportunity to help children learn. Having been in teaching for 14 years, she felt that her vocation and passion for teaching had remained high.

She described herself as a career-driven person, always wanting to give her best to the learning and growth of her pupils. When she first joined her current school her motivation was very high. She enjoyed her responsibilities as head of English. However, she knew that she would not have been able to maintain her enthusiasm for the job without the understanding and support of her partner who gave her space to work at home, particularly when they were settling into their new house and their life with a second child.

Relationships count

For Katherine, her school was a social place where relationships with committed colleagues and pupils played a very large part in fulfilling her every working day with job satisfaction and joy. She described pupils in her current school, with whom she had established good relationships, as 'a breath of fresh air'. Such positive relationships and her positive attitude towards them helped create a healthy environment in the classroom. Pupils were enthusiastic about learning. Given that many parents in her school did not have 'high enough expectations' of their children, Katherine was particularly pleased with the rapport that she had achieved with her pupils and its positive effects on their learning and progress.

When she first took over the role as head of department, however, Katherine felt that there was not 'a team'. This was because prior to her arrival there had been an acting head of department and over this time there had also been curriculum changes. She was ambitious to foster team spirit through modelling and sharing good practice but wished that she had more time to 'pull everyone together'. Nevertheless, she was succeeding in establishing good relationships with her colleagues and was pleased with the outcome of her efforts. These were particularly important to her during the school inspection by Ofsted and at times when her workload volume and complexity became too intense.

The external inspection of the school, however, worked against her sense of effectiveness and confidence as a teacher. She had become exhausted and overloaded and experienced a crisis of confidence. She felt a loss of control and as a result she lamented that she did not 'really feel that good as a teacher'. Nevertheless, she remained highly motivated and committed:

> My motivation has never wavered, but my effectiveness has. Despite being totally overworked, I am now feeling positive about September. My confidence as a classroom teacher, however, is low at the moment ... I need time to consolidate and need a personal confidence boost from somewhere.

During the same period, despite the fact that she was still highly committed to her job, Katherine suffered from serious tensions that arose from managing a busy home and work life simultaneously, so much so that she even considered moving to part-time work. She realised that with two children and a full-time job, her social life had 'gone completely out the window'. Working all weekend and during holiday time had become, for her, 'a reality'. Support from her colleagues helped her to learn to use a variety of strategies to manage and maintain her sense of effectiveness at work; and, a result, her self-confidence had been restored.

School leadership matters

When Katherine first joined her current school, she had been full of enthusiasm and her sense of effectiveness rose rapidly. Her job fulfillment fluctuated over the year but she concluded that that was mainly because she was still a newcomer to the school.

Katherine felt that the structure and the senior leadership of the school made an important contribution in helping her survive and succeed, particularly during her early period in the school: 'If something is passed on through the system, it will be dealt with very quickly. So you know you've got back up.' She added that the senior leadership team (SLT) were approachable about both school and personal issues. Knowing that they would support the staff 100 per cent had helped create a 'person-centred' school culture which, in her view, brought the whole staff together as a team.

Katherine was particularly grateful for the professional and personal support she received from the principal. This helped her survive through and achieve a positive result from the school inspection. She was expecting her second child during that period and felt that '[i]f it hadn't been for the intervention of the head and his support, I think I probably would have had a nervous breakdown'.

The inspection, which had caused so much concern to Katherine, had resulted in highly commendable results in the end and this had boosted her 'confidence, pride and added motivation'. Katherine felt that she had subsequently been able to successfully rebuilt her confidence and reinforced her positive relationships with colleagues. After having recovered from a dip in her sense of effectiveness during those difficult times, then, she was now considering taking on management training to prepare for further promotion.

Connecting resilience with relative effectiveness

What the evidence in the VITAE project revealed was that different relationships within teachers' work and lives provide various conditions which nurture their learning, development and the resilience-building process and through this, promote and nourish their individual and collective efficacy and effectiveness. The research team validated the groupings of teachers' perceived career and resilience trajectories through a blind check with teachers and then explored the relationships between teachers' sense of resilience and their relative effectiveness. A statistically significant association for the two years (Cohorts 1 and 2) for which value-added data were available was found (x^2=8.320, df=2, p<0.05; x^2=9.402, df=2, p<0.01). Pupils of teachers who demonstrated a sustained sense of commitment and resilience were more likely to attain value-added results at or above the level expected. Figure 8.1 illustrates the findings for Cohort 2 (n=162). In total, 69 per cent of teachers who sustained their sense of resilience, compared with 59 per cent of those who did not, saw their pupils achieve results as expected or better than expected in our measures of pupil progress. In contrast, 18 per cent of teachers in the resilient group, compared with 41 per cent of those in the vulnerable group, saw their pupils' academic progress fall below expectations. The association is by no means perfect, however, and we do not claim a causal connection. Rather, we think that the result raises interesting avenues for further exploration of the meaning of sustaining teacher resilience for standards and improvement in other contexts and with larger samples.

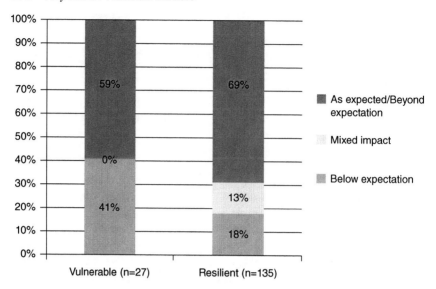

Figure 8.1 Associations between teachers' sense of resilience and relative effectiveness.

Conclusions

From these findings about teacher resilience and its associations with teacher effectiveness (both as perceived by themselves and measured by pupil attainment and progress outcomes), two key observations relating to the nature of resilience and the quality retention of teachers can be made.

First and foremost, the widely used definition of resilience as the capacity to 'bounce back' in adverse circumstances does not adequately or accurately describe the nature of resilience in teachers. This is because, at least in part, it fails to acknowledge that the ways in which teachers build their resilience are inherently embedded in their everyday professional lives. It is a complex, continuous and fluctuating process. It is influenced by a combination of workplace and personal factors and also the cognitive and emotional capacities of teachers and leaders to manage these. Resilience in teachers is about their capacity to manage the everyday challenges of the realities of teaching, whilst sustaining their sense of moral purpose and care alongside their determination to ensure, through the quality of their teaching, the progress and achievement of all their pupils. This is why we use the term 'everyday resilience'.

Second, our findings reaffirm observations of earlier studies that the nature of resilience in teachers is not innate (e.g. Gu and Day, 2007; Beltman *et al.*, 2011), but influenced by the strength of trust in the multi-layered relationships in which teachers' work and lives are embedded. Teacher resilience is a relational, multifaceted and dynamic construct. The resilience-building process is embedded in a web of interpersonal relationships which interactively influence an overall level of resilience as perceived by teachers. It is the culmination and continuation of collective and collaborative endeavours driven by a common understanding of moral purpose. It is nurtured by the social and intellectual environments in which teachers work and live, rather than determined by nature.

Evidence in our research points to the importance of three sets of relationships: with colleagues, leaders and pupils. Each plays a distinctive part in teachers' capacity to learn, develop and teach to their best:

1   Teacher–teacher relations: Collective and collaborative connections with colleagues are the culmination and continuation of a mutual endeavour. At a deeper level, strong and enduring peer connections are grounded in an ongoing shared sense of commitment, integrity and drive for the achievement of the children. They provide the necessary social capital for professional learning communities to emerge, develop and mature in schools. The OECD TALIS survey found that teachers who participate more actively in professional learning communities reported higher levels of self-efficacy (OECD, 2012b). Experiences of the VITAE teachers show that their enhanced confidence, efficacy and job fulfilment contribute to a collective sense of wisdom, expertise and empathy available in their workplace which nurtures a collective sense of efficacy and relational resilience.

2   Teacher–pupil relations: Making a difference to the lives of children draws many teachers into the profession (Hansen, 1995; OECD, 2005b; Day *et al.*, 2007a). For many teachers in different phases of their professional lives, good rapport with the pupils continues to be central to their sense of fulfilment and commitment.

3   Teacher–leader relations: School leaders are the architects of the social, emotional and intellectual organisation of the school. They 'weave' different human and material resources into a significant cultural tapestry (Deal and Peterson, 2009) which incorporates individual strengths and commitments into a collective and collaborative whole and provides a platform for collegial discourse to take shape.

9 Beyond survival

Sustaining teacher resilience and quality in times of change

Chapters 1 to 8 have shown that resilience is the result of a complex amalgam of and interaction between several forces; that these are affected by the relative strength of the influences of different personal, workplace and socio-cultural scenarios upon teachers as well as the inner strength of their educational values and their capacities to manage these; and that resilience itself is more than a capacity which enables teachers to cope or survive in adverse conditions. It is, rather, an important (but not sole) condition for sustaining good teaching on every school day. This final chapter discusses the implications of an understanding and acknowledgement of the key role played by resilience in the quality retention and continuing development of teachers for system and school leaders, teacher educators and teachers themselves.

Teacher retention: quality matters

The important role of a high quality teaching profession in raising standards and transforming educational outcomes continues to be emphasised in research and policy papers nationally and internationally. Research on teacher effectiveness consistently reports that teachers' classroom practices have the largest effects on pupil learning and achievement (Rockoff 2004; Hallinger, 2005; Rivkin *et al.*, 2005; Leithwood *et al.*, 2006a). The positive effects of high quality teaching are especially significant for pupils from socio-economically disadvantaged backgrounds. Evidence suggests that when taught by very effective teachers, pupils can gain an extra year's worth of learning (Hanushek, 1992; Sutton Trust, 2011). Internationally, comparative research evidence from the Organisation for Economic Cooperation and Development (OECD) affirms that 'teacher quality' is the single most important school variable influencing pupil achievement (OECD, 2005b). Indeed, its recent Teaching and Learning International Survey (TALIS) concluded that making teaching a more attractive and more effective profession must be the priority in all school systems if they are to secure and enhance effective learning (OECD, 2009, 2011). In a similar vein, McKinsey's reports on the experiences of the world's best performing school systems concluded that getting the right people into the teaching profession and, once in, developing them to become effective teachers, has played a central role in enabling these systems to come out on top, and more importantly, continuing to improve (Barber and Mourshed, 2007; Mourshed *et al.*, 2010).

It remains the case, however, that for diverse and complex socio-economic and political reasons, for many countries retaining and developing committed and effective teachers remains a real challenge. In many developing countries, for example, where school enrolment is on the rise, an acute shortage of primary teachers and qualified secondary school teachers represents one of the greatest hurdles to providing education for all school-age children (UNESCO, 2011). A lack of resources and financial incentive packages to attract qualified personnel into teaching has meant that quantity rather than quality – making sure someone is in the classroom – continues to be a primary concern in their efforts to provide basic education. This has meant that, unfortunately, children in countries needing teachers the most, tend to be taught by the least qualified personnel (UNESCO, 2006). In contrast, in the developed world, such as the USA, the UK and many European countries, shortage of teacher supply tends to be a particularly pressing problem for core subject areas such as maths, modern foreign languages and science (European Commission, 2012) and for schools serving socio-economically deprived communities (Ingersoll, 2001 & 2003b; Guarino *et al.*, 2006; Boyd *et al.*, 2008).

Shortage, turnover and attrition are persisting problems. Grissom (2011) found that higher teacher turnover rates in disadvantaged schools result in part from the ineffectiveness of the principal. His analysis of national school and teacher surveys showed that teacher satisfaction is likely to be lower, and the probability of teachers leaving schools significantly greater, when the leadership of the principal is weak and ineffective. Moreover, there are also troubling indicators which suggest that teacher quality also is lower in schools which serve high-need communities (Loeb *et al.*, 2005; Boyd *et al.*, 2008; Goldhaber and Hansen, 2009) where most children, who are already disadvantaged in accessing or benefiting from social capital in their early years, are then denied access to the quality education to which they are entitled when entering the formal school system.

There are other emerging and on-going problems concerning teacher supply and quality in the developed world. Recent significant falls in the proportion of graduates applying for teacher training programmes across many European countries have culminated in an urgent call to increase efforts to transform the conditions of teaching and through this, attract more suitably qualified people to the profession (Auguste *et al.*, 2010; OECD, 2011; European Commission, 2012). At the same time, the ageing population profile of the existing teaching workforce (Grissmer and Kirby, 1997; Guttman, 2001; Chevalier and Dolton, 2004; OECD, 2005b; Matheson, 2007; Aaronson, 2008; European Commission, 2012) poses pressing challenges to the nature of its composition in the future. In England, for example, close to half of the full-time teachers (46 per cent) are aged over 40, with 23 per cent of these aged over 50 (DfE, 2012). This situation is the most pronounced in primary schools in Germany, Italy and Sweden where nearly half of the full-time teachers are older than 50 (European Commission, 2012).

High rates of attrition of teachers in their first five years of teaching (Darling-Hammond, 1997; Ingersoll, 2003a; Kados and Johnson, 2007; Burghes et al., 2009; Shen and Palmer, 2009; OECD, 2005b, 2011) also remain a persistent teacher retention problem. Although some studies show that, on average, early career leavers tend to be less effective than stayers as measured by the test score gains of the pupils in their classrooms (Henry *et al.*, 2011; Goldhaber *et al.*, 2011; Boyd *et al.*, in press), others suggest that teachers with stronger qualifications and more competitive university backgrounds are more likely to exit early (Lankford *et al.*, 2002; Boyd *et al.*, 2005; Guarino *et al.*, 2006; Feng and Sass, 2011).

The reasons behind teachers' decisions to leave are complex. A common critique has, at least in part, attributed teacher attrition to a whole-sale redefinition of teacher professionalism by policy makers over time, which has been driven by 'a culture of accountability, performance, and measurability' (Luke, 2011: 370; see also Rots and Aelterman, 2008; Smith and Kovacs, 2011). Luke (2011) laments that 'the normative, the ethical, the cultural – matters of value – have quietly slipped from policy discussion (Ladwig, 2010), overridden by a focus on the measurable, the countable, and what can be said to be cost efficient and quality assured' (2011: 368). Within such a performativity culture, teacher professionalism has become more closely aligned with national educational policy which tends to define educational success in relatively narrow, instrumental terms (Furlong *et al.*, 2008). Alongside this, the power of government regulatory bodies for the setting and adjudication of standards has increased significantly over time. This has been complemented by more detailed and bureaucratic monitoring of what teachers do in their classrooms and how they do it (Luke, 2011). Thus, whether or not teachers agree with centrally prescribed policy agendas and strategies, they are expected to fulfil them in their day-to-day practices (Furlong, 2008).

It is perhaps, then, not surprising that this highly prescriptive neoliberal culture of accountability and performativity has been criticised by scholars as having contributed to and being expressive of a widely-spread lack of deep trust in teachers' professional standing, judgement and capability. Such decreased autonomy is also claimed by some to have led to high levels of professional vulnerability and stress among teachers (Hargreaves, 1994; Macdonald, 1999; Kyriacou, 2000; Lasky, 2005; Kelchtermans, 2009) and increasing levels of dissatisfaction with their working conditions (Helen, 2007; Smethem, 2007).

Although this body of research has improved our understanding of the factors which may cause some teachers to struggle and/or exit, in our view it offers a rather limited explanation as to why so many other teachers who are working with similar challenges embedded in outcomes-driven educational systems are willing, able and committed to continue to teach to their best. What tends to be absent from many of the investigations of teacher stress, attrition and job satisfaction, for example, is the integral role that teachers' professional, role and organisational identities, well-being, and sense of vocation play in enabling them to meet the daily challenges of teaching and learning; and the part played by school leaders in mediating the sometimes negative effects of educational policies and through this, shaping and influencing many, if not all, teachers' sense of job fulfilment, commitment and effectiveness. There is evidence that points to strong associations between high teacher retention rates and the positive support of school leadership (Ladd, 2009; Boyd *et al.*, 2011). The impact of strong leadership on pupil learning through building supportive school culture and creating favourable working conditions for teachers is also well documented in the teacher development, school improvement and school effectiveness literature (Hallinger, 2005; Johnson, 2004; Leithwood *et al.*, 2004, 2006b; Gu *et al.*, 2008; Day *et al.*, 2011; Sammons *et al.*, 2011). In addition, a strong sense of staff collegiality has been found to be crucial in building intellectual, emotional and social capital in schools so that teachers, and especially those working in schools serving socio-economically deprived communities, are able to maintain their integrity and commitment in times of change (Gu and Day, 2007; Allensworth *et al.*, 2009; Day *et al.*, 2011; Holme and Rangel, 2012). More importantly, we know from research that pupils of highly committed teachers are more likely to perform better academically (Day *et al.*, 2007a).

Whilst there have been many studies which have focused on particular internal and external aspects of teachers' work and lives, school systems, school leadership, national policies and their consequences, and we have referred to many of these in the pages of this book, there have been few which attempt to provide a holistic view of what constitutes the conditions for and practices of quality teachers and quality teaching. We have tried to begin to do this here. We have endeavoured to demonstrate that it would be more fruitful and educationally more meaningful if greater attention were paid to the factors that enable those who decide to stay to remain committed to the learning and achievement of our pupils. This is, in essence, a *quality retention* issue because, as Johnson and her colleagues (2005) have argued, the physical retention of teachers 'in and of itself, is not a worthy goal':

> Students are not served well when a district retains teachers without regard to quality. Little can be achieved (and much might be lost) when a district succeeds in reducing teacher turnover if some of those teachers are incompetent, mediocre, disengaged, or burnt out. Instead, student learning is the goal, and schools must seek to retain teachers who demonstrate that they are skilled and effective in the classroom, are committed to student learning, and are ready and able to contribute to the improvement of their school.
>
> (Johnson *et al.*, 2005: 2)

Beyond survival: sustaining quality in teachers and schools

Johnson and her colleagues' definition of retention brings us back to our original motivation for writing this book. Over the years, the evidence from our work with outstanding teachers and outstanding schools in changing social, cultural and political landscapes of education nationally and internationally has led us to believe that, regardless of age, experience, gender or school context, teachers and schools *can* change the worlds of their pupils and that many of them *do*! They are not simply survivors but committed and competent professionals and organisations that are proud of being at the centre of a profession which is charged with making a difference to the learning, lives and achievement of all children and young people. They have what Hargreaves and Fullan (2012: 3) call 'professional capital'. We share Nieto's (2011) respect for such teachers in her reflections on her professional work with teachers over the course of her career: 'My belief in teachers is stronger than ever because I have seen the best of them do unbelievable work in sometimes harsh circumstances' (2011: 133). These are the teachers who give witness to the essential meaning of 'everyday resilience' which we have used throughout this book.

Our definition of 'quality' in teachers should be understood in the broadest possible sense. It goes beyond the technocratic concerns for performativity and test results. In essence, the continuing aspiration for quality is driven by teachers' sense of vocation and care about and for their pupils. It is about the extra mile that the best teachers willingly travel to motivate each one of their pupils to learn and to bring about the best possible achievement in them. It is related to their passion, commitment and continuing enthusiasm for their own learning and development which is, importantly, supported by their school, and which results in an abiding sense of efficacy, hope and belief that they can and do continue to make a difference in the classroom. It is related to an individual and collective sense of moral purpose and sustained engagement with their fellow colleagues in collaborative learning and development. Finally, the improvement in the quality of teachers and teaching must be understood within the social, cultural and organisational environments of the school – which are designed, nurtured and shaped by the educational architect who lives in the principal's office.

Over the years, scholars have used different conceptual and methodological lenses to explore issues around quality in schools and schooling. We chose resilience because it enables us to probe teachers' inner and external professional worlds to explore why many are able to remain committed and passionate about making a difference and continue to do so – despite the unpredictable nature of every school day and the many physical, emotional and intellectual challenges that are associated with this. In exploring the landscapes of resilience, however, we do not seek to valorise teachers. On the contrary, we know how pressed they are, how some fall by the wayside for a variety of reasons and how not all are or remain as passionate, skilful, committed or resilient as many of those referenced in this book. However, through the lens of resilience, especially *everyday resilience* and *relational resilience*, we have tried to show throughout the book what drives teachers and school leaders to work hard, how they work, how hard their work is, and the impact that their work can have upon their pupils, colleagues and the school community. We conclude, therefore, with eight key messages.

Message 1: To teach, and to teach well over time, requires 'everyday resilience'

In reflecting on the journey of a teacher, Ayers (2010) concluded that becoming a teacher is 'a lifetime affair' (2010: 160):

> Learning to teach takes time, energy and hard work. Learning to teach well requires even more: a serious and sustained engagement with the enterprise, an intense focus on the lives of children, a passionate regard for the future – that is, for the community our students will inherit and reinvent – and for the world they are [m]arching toward.
>
> (Ayers 2010: 160)

As we have seen, the mainstream research on resilience considers adverse conditions and recurring setbacks as prerequisites for resilience and defines it as individuals' capacity to 'bounce back' in such challenging environmental circumstances (e.g. Oswald *et al.*, 2003; Tait, 2008). However, such a conceptualisation of resilience does not reveal or reflect the uncertain and unpredictable circumstances and scenarios which form the main feature of teachers' everyday professional lives. Such circumstances are an inherent part of the nature of teaching and present a constant intellectual and emotional challenge to those who strive to teach to their best on every school day. Being a resilient teacher thus means more than 'bouncing back' quickly and efficiently from unusual crises or difficulties.

We have shown in this book that teaching itself always takes place within contexts of anticipated and unanticipated changes in policy, social and workplace settings and amidst the uncertainties and vulnerabilities of classroom teaching. During their professional lives, teachers' capacity to be resilient may fluctuate, depending upon their cognitive and emotional management of the effects of different combinations of policy, socio-cultural, workplace-based and personal challenges. Such conditions demand that, regardless of differences in the degrees of challenge and change, to teach to their best all teachers need to have the capacity to be resilient; and that the endeavour to sustain quality in teaching on an everyday basis goes well beyond simply surviving.

Message 2: Resilience is closely associated with teachers' sense of identity and commitment

The truism about teaching is that it is a difficult and 'enormously complex activity' (Olsen, 2008). In his seminal work, *A Place Called School*, Goodlad (2004) concluded that:

> To reach out positively and supportively to 27 youngsters for five hours or so each day in an elementary school classroom is demanding and exhausting. To respond similarly to four to six successive classes of 25 or more students each at the secondary level may be impossible.
>
> (Goodlad 2004: 112)

Most teachers enter teaching because they want to make a difference and many of them do not leave teaching. Nieto (2003) observes that '[t]eachers who keep going in spite of everything know that teaching is more than a job' (2003: 128). Over the years, our experience of working with many committed school leaders and teachers continues to reaffirm our belief that it is the commitment to serve and the joy of being able to make a difference to the lives and achievement of children and young people that have kept them in the profession. As we noted in our Introduction to this book, we hear pupils of these leaders and teachers say to us, 'Our teachers are not here for the money. They are here because they care about us'.

Message 3: There are close associations between resilience and a strong sense of moral purpose

Resilient schools are places where teachers and pupils aspire to their own learning and development and where a clear sense of moral purpose is shared, valued and embedded in the daily life of the school. Resilience without moral purpose, without a willingness to be self-reflective and learn, and without collegial and leadership support in order to change and improve collectively and collaboratively, is not enough. For many teachers, then, teaching still essentially represents a commitment to human development:

> Knowing things and knowing how to communicate them, creating the conditions for learning to occur, being on your perceptual toes, scanning the room for opportunity – all of these aid in the growth of other human beings. Such a goal, this commitment to human development, places the teacher's work squarely in the ethical and moral domain.
>
> (Rose, 2010: 168)

For many hardworking teachers and leaders, this is perhaps the most powerful testimony of their vocation of teaching. It is also, perhaps, their most powerful emotional reward. Consistent with this, there is strong evidence from research which shows that bonuses and incentive pay do not affect teacher motivation or quality (Heneman, 1998; Kelley, 1999; Gamoran, 2012; Yuan *et al.*, 2013) because 'teachers view the receipt of a bonus as an acknowledgement of their hard work rather than an incentive to work harder' (Marsh *et al.*, 2011, cited in Yuan *et al.*, 2013: 17). A sense of moral purpose and pride in being a teacher provide many committed teachers with the inner drive, strength and optimism to help every child learn, grow and achieve. Resilient teachers, then, do not have to be extraordinary heroes. However, they can be, and often are, teachers who are striving to make an extraordinary difference in their classrooms on every ordinary school day.

Message 4: Teacher resilience-building processes are relational

We have tried to show throughout this book, through the lens of relational resilience, how establishing connections with both pupils and adults helps to produce collective intellectual, social and emotional capital for teachers' sustained job fulfilment and commitment. Teachers build and develop their sense of resilience within and through a web of trusting relationships in schools. This relational model of resilience places the capacity for mutual empowerment and growth and the importance of mutual support at the heart of the resilience-building process (Jordan, 2004). This enables us to understand teacher resilience in a situated, contextual way.

Teachers' professional worlds are made up of 'a web of communal relationships' (Palmer, 2007: 97). Three sets of relationships are at the centre of teachers' professional work and lives: teacher-pupil relations, teacher-teacher relations, and teacher-leader relations; and each of these plays a distinctive role in building and sustaining their sense of resilience over time. Trusting relationships between teachers and pupils, for example, are the heartbeat of teachers' vocational commitment. Relational trust between these two parties signals a mutual confidence in each other's endeavour to teach to their best and to learn to their best. It functions as a primary source of teachers' long-term job fulfilment – through which they feel that their hard work is rewarded and valued by the very people whose academic and individual welfare first drew them into teaching.

Collegial connections with colleagues also provide a necessary intellectual and emotional condition for collective and collaborative learning and development. Exploring the resilience-building process through the lens of collegiality has enabled us to reaffirm our earlier observation that resilience is not a quality that is reserved for the select few 'heroic' teachers. Nor is building and sustaining the capacity for resilience the sole responsibility of the individual teacher. Rather, building resilience in teachers must be both an individual and social process within school communities which are driven by a shared sense of moral purpose and in which building mutually supportive and 'growth-fostering relationships' (Jordan, 2006: 83) are shared goals:

> Social support has also been viewed as vital to resilience; it has been defined as emotional concern, instrumental aid, information, and appraisal. Most social support studies have emphasized one-way support, getting love, getting help. A relational perspective points to the importance of engaging in a relationship that contributes to all people in the relationship. The power of social support is more about mutuality than about getting for the self.
>
> (Jordan, 2006: 83)

Finally, relational trust between teachers and school leaders is essential in developing resilient teachers and building resilient schools. As Fullan (2003) has noted, relational trust 'reduces the sense of vulnerability when staff take on new tasks', and also 'creates a moral resource for school improvement' which affects teacher motivation, commitment and retention (Fullan, 2003: 42). Our research on the impact of successful school leadership on pupil outcomes (Day et al., 2011) found that such relational trust is built through the layered and cumulative application of a variety of strategic actions. The growth of organisational trust is driven by actions at all levels, but all strategic actions rely on cooperation from other members of the organisation. Communication, modelling actions, coaching and mentoring, developing staff, sharing the vision, explaining values and beliefs, making visible and viable pedagogical and curriculum decisions, appropriately restructuring organisational structures and cultures and redesigning roles and functions all contribute to the moral, intellectual, social, health and improvement capacities of schools.

Message 5: School leadership matters

> Only when participants demonstrate their commitment to engage in such work and see others doing the same can a genuine professional community grounded in relational trust emerge. Principals must take the lead and extend themselves by reaching out to others. On occasion, the principal may be called on to demonstrate trust in colleagues who may not fully reciprocate, at least initially. But they must also be prepared to use coercive power to reform a dysfunctional school community around professional norms. Interestingly, such authority may rarely need to be invoked thereafter once these new norms are firmly established.
>
> (Fullan, 2003: 64)

The quality of school leadership matters in creating, developing and broadening intellectual, social and emotional capital within and beyond the school gate and in providing optimal relational and organisational conditions for sustaining a sense of resilience, commitment and effectiveness among the staff. Supportive organisational communities do not happen by chance. They require good leadership. Knoop (2007) argues that '[c]onsidering the present pace of sociocultural change, it is difficult to imagine a time in history when good leadership was more important than it is today, and when the lack of it was more dangerous' (2007: 223).

When reviewing the relationship between power, accountability and teacher quality, Ingersoll (2012) found that '[i]n plain terms, poorly run schools can make otherwise excellent teachers not so excellent' (2012: 98). By extension, we can argue that poorly led schools can diminish rather than enrich the capacities of teachers to grow and sustain their commitment and resilience. Katherine (in Chapter 8), would probably have had a nervous breakdown and a prolonged dip in her perceived effectiveness if the senior leadership team, and the principal in particular, had not offered her the very kind of professional and personal support that she needed to boost her confidence and sense of efficacy.

Understanding the nature of the schools' internal and external contexts, how they are mediated by school leadership, especially the leadership of the principal, and through this, how the interplay between contexts may influence, positively or negatively, the fabric of every ordinary school day, is key to a deep understanding of the secrets of their success (or lack of success) over time.

Message 6: The capacity to be resilient is an important quality of successful school leaders

Henry and Milstein's (2006) work on resilience led them to conclude that '[t]eachers, students, parents, support personnel are the fabric of the school. Leaders are weavers of the fabric of resiliency initiatives' (Henry and Milstein, 2006: 8).

There is still little research that focuses upon how principals who not only successfully mediate the constantly evolving policy, social and cultural contexts of education but continue to develop their staff for the learning and achievement of their pupils, build and sustain their own capacity to be resilient. To lead a successful school through the many social and policy changes and challenges in schools in the twenty-first century requires both a strong sense of moral purpose, trustworthiness, persistence, flexible thinking, commitment to the academic progress and achievement of pupils and a passion for individual well-being and equity, and resilience. Leaders are:

> the stewards of organisational energy [resilience] ... they inspire or demoralise others, first by how effectively they manage their own energy and next by how well they manage, focus, invest and renew the collective energy [resilience] of those they lead.
>
> (Loehr and Schwartz, 2003: 5)

Like resilient teachers, resilient leaders are also driven by a strong sense of moral purpose. They care about and focus on the learning needs of pupils and the professional growth of teachers, and work hard to enhance the role of the school as an agent of social change. Leithwood *et al.* (2010) argue, for example, that there is no better reward than turning around a failing school because 'it is fundamentally about improving life chances for and opening new opportunities to the young people who learn there' (2010: 258).

Message 7: Resilience in teachers is essential, but it is not the only condition for them to be effective

We know that what teachers do in the classroom has the single, greatest effect on the quality of pupils' learning (Hattie, 2009). We also know from our work that pupils of teachers who are committed and resilient are more likely to attain results at or above the level expected. This is because, at least in part, resilience describes 'what arises in a dynamic or dialectic between person and practices that reflects the evidence that the person is acting on and reshaping challenging circumstances in their lives so that they can propel themselves forward' (Edwards, 2010).

It does not follow that every resilient teacher will be effective. A continuing dialectic between person and practices is more likely to occur in schools where there is a supportive environment for individuals' professional learning and development, and which build trusting relationships amongst staff, foster a collective sense of efficacy and resilience and, through these sustain their continuing improvement. However, until recently, this concept has been developed largely outside education. Hamel and Välikangas (2003), writing in the context of business, describe a truly resilient organisation as a workplace that is filled with excitement and argue that strategic renewal, i.e. 'creative reconstruction', 'must be the natural consequence of an organisation's innate resilience' (2003: 2–3).

Message 8: Building and sustaining the capacity for resilience is more than an individual responsibility

Over the years, we have worked with teachers also who, despite their hard work, commitment, moral purpose and dedication to the education of their pupils, struggle to improve outcomes. Those teachers who excel and whose pupils excel with them do not just do so on their own. Whilst it is clearly the responsibility of each teacher to teach to their best, it is the responsibility of each individual school, school district and national government to ensure that they are able to do so through high quality leadership and the provision of physical and other resources. *Policy makers, teacher educators and school principals need to design the means to build and sustain teachers' capacities to be resilient.* A central task for all concerned with enhancing quality and standards in schools is, therefore, not only to have a better understanding of what influences teachers' resilience over the course of a career, but also the means by which the resilience necessary for these to be sustained may be nurtured in the contexts in which they work. Promoting and cultivating healthy individual and collective learning and achievement cultures in schools is essential to how teachers feel about their work and how they think about themselves as professionals. The extent to which they are able to find continuing professional and personal fulfilment through their work, and through these, sustain their commitment to teach to their best over time, will depend to a large extent upon the opportunities they have to grow, sustain and renew their capacities to be resilient.

Bibliography

Aaronson, D. (2008) 'The impact of baby boomer retirements on teacher labor markets', *Chicago Fed Letter*, 254, September: http://www.chicagofed.org/publications/fedletter/cflseptember2008_254.pdf

Aboujaoude, E., Koran, L. M., Gamel, N., Large, M. D and Serpe, R. T. (2006) 'Potential markers for problematic internet use: a telephone survey of 2,513 adults', *CNS Spectr. 2006*; 11(10): 750–5.

Aelterman, A., Engels, N., Van Petegem, K. and Verhaeghe, J. P. (2007) 'The well-being of teachers in Flanders: the importance of a supportive school culture', *Educational Studies*, 33(3): 285–97.

Allensworth, E., Ponisciak, S. and Mazzeo, C. (2009) 'The schools teachers leave: Teacher mobility in Chicago Public Schools', Chicago: Consortium on Chicago School Research. Retrieved 1 April 2012 from http://ccsr.uchicago.edu/publications/CCSR_Teacher_Mobility.pdf

Alliance for Excellent Education (2004) *Tapping the potential: Retaining and developing high quality new teachers* (Report). Washington, DC. Retrieved 16 June, 2008, from http://www.all4ed.org/publications/TappingThePotential/TappingThePotential.pdf

Ambler, T. B. (2012) 'Autobiographical vignettes: a medium for teachers' professional learning through self-study and reflection', *Teacher Development*, 16(2): 181–97.

Andrews, D. W. (2006) *Inspiring Innovation in Learning and Living*. College of Education and Human Ecology E-News. Columbus, OH: Ohio State University.

Angle, H., Gilbrey, N. and Belcher, M. (2007) *Teachers' workload diary survey, March 2007*. London: Office of Manpower Economics, School Teachers' Review Board.

Ansell, N., Barker, J. and Smith, F. (2007) 'UNICEF Child Poverty in Perspective Report: A View from the UK', *Children's Geographies*, 5(3): 325–30.

Aspfors, J. and Bondas, L. (2013) 'Caring about Caring – Newly qualified teachers' experiences of their relationships within the school community', *Teachers and Teaching: Theory and Practice*, 19 (3): 243–59.

Auguste, B., Kihn, P. and Miller, M. (2010) *Closing the Talent Gap: Attracting and Retaining Top-Third Graduates to Careers in Teaching*. New York: McKinsey and Company.

Australian Education Union (2006) National beginning teacher survey results. http://www.acufederal.org.au?Publications?Btsurvey06.html

Avey, J. B., Luthans, F., Smith, R. M. and Palmer, N. F. (2010) 'Impact of positive psychological capital on employee well-being over time', *Journal of Occupational Health Psychology*, 15(1): 17–28.

Ayers, W. (2010) *To Teach: The Journey of a Teacher* (3rd edn). New York: Teachers College Press.

Baker, D. and LeTendre, G. (2005) *National Differences, Global Similarities: World Culture and the Future of Schooling*. California: Stanford University Press.

Ball, S. (2000) 'Performativities and fabrications in the education economy: towards the performative society', *Australian Educational Researcher*, 17(3): 1–24.

——(2003) 'The teachers' soul and the terrors of performativity', *Journal of Education Policy*, 18 (2): 215–28.

Bandura, A. (1994) 'Self-efficacy'. In V. S. Ramachaudran (ed.) *Encyclopedia of human behaviour*, 4. New York: Academic Press, pp. 71–81.

——(1997) *Self-efficacy: The Exercise of Control*. New York: Freeman.

Barbalet, J. (2002) *Emotions and Sociology*. London: Wiley.

Barber, M. and Mourshed, M. (2007) *How the World's Best Performing School Systems Come Out On Top*. New York, NY: McKinsey and Company.

Barth, R. (1976) 'A principal and his school', *The National Elementary Principal*, 56 (November/December): 9–21.

Beard, K. S, Hoy, W. K. and Hoy, A. W. (2010) 'Academic Optimism of Individual Teachers: Confirming a new construct', *Teaching and Teacher Education*, 26: 1136–44.

Beck, U., Giddens, A. and Lash, S. (1994) (eds) *Reflexive Modernization*. Cambridge: Polity Press.

Becker, H. S. (1960) 'Notes on the Concept of Commitment', *American Journal of Sociology*, 66: 32–40.

Beijaard, D. (1995) 'Teachers' Prior Experiences and Actual Perceptions of Professional Identity', *Teachers and Teaching: Theory and Practice*, 1: 281–94.

Beijaard, D., Meijer, P. C. and Verloop, N. (2004) Reconsidering research on teachers' professional identity, *Teaching and Teacher Education*, 20(2): 107–28.

Beltman, S., Mansfield, C. and Price, A. (2011) 'Thriving not just surviving: A review of research on teacher resilience', *Educational Research Review*, 6: 185–207.

Benard, B. (1991) *Fostering Resiliency in Kids: Protective Factors in the Family, School, and Community*. San Francisco: WestEd Regional Educational Laboratory.

——(1995) *Fostering Resilience in Children*, ERIC/EECE Digest, EDO-PS-99.

——(2004) *Resiliency: What we have learned*. San Francisco: West Ed.

Bernstein, B. (1996) *Pedagogy, Symbolic Control and Identity*. London: Taylor and Francis.

Birkbeck, S. (2011) *Fostering Resilience through School Leadership 2, Beyond Survival: Teachers and Resilience*. www.nottingham.ac.uk/education/.../teachersand resilience/index.aspx (retrieved 25/10/12).

Blackmore, J. (1996) 'Doing "emotional labour" in the education market place: Stories from the field of women', *Management Discourse: Studies in the Cultural Politics of Education*, 17(3): 337–49.

Borman, G. D. and Dowling, N. M. (2008) 'Teacher attrition and retention: A meta-analytic and narrative review of the research', *Review of Educational Research*, 78: 367–409.

Bowen, G. L., Ware, W. B., Rose, R. A. and Powers, J. D. (2007) 'Assessing the Functioning of Schools as Learning Organizations', *Children and Schools*, 29(4): 199–207.

Boyd, D., Lankford, H., Loeb, S. and Wyckoff, J. (2005) 'Explaining the short careers of high-achieving teachers in schools with low-performing students', *American Economic Review*, 95: 166–71.

Boyd, D., Grossman, P., Lankford, H., Loeb, S. and Wycoff, J. H. (2008) *Who Leaves? Teacher Attrition and Student Achievement*. NBER Working Paper No. W14022.

Boyd, D., Lankford, H., Loeb, S., Ronfeldt, M. and Wyckoff, J. (in press) 'The role of teacher quality in retention and hiring: Using applications-to-transfer to uncover preferences of teachers and schools', *Journal of Policy Analysis and Management*.

Bracey, G. W. (2009) *Education hell: Rhetoric vs. reality*. Alexandria, VA: Educational Research Service.

Braun, A., Maguire, M. and Ball, S. J. (2010) 'Policy enactments in UK secondary schools: examining policy, practice and school positioning', *Journal of Education Policy*, 25(4): 547–60.

Bridges, S. J. (1992) *Working in tomorrow's schools: Effects on primary teachers*. University of Canterbury Research Report No. 92–3. Canterbury: Education Department, University of Canterbury.

Bridges, S. and Searle, A. (2011) Changing workloads of primary school teachers: 'I seem to live on the edge of chaos', *School Leadership and Management*, 31(5): 413–33.

Brunetti, G. (2006) 'Resilience under fire: Perspectives on the work of experienced, inner city high school teachers in the United States', *Teaching and Teacher Education*, 22: 812–25.

Bryk, A. and Schneider, B. (2002) *Trust in Schools: A Core Resource for Improvement*. New York, NY: Russell Sage Foundation.

Bryk, A., Sebring, P., Allensworth, E., Luppescu, S. and Easton, J. (2010) *Organizing Schools for Improvement: Lessons from Chicago*. Chicago: University of Chicago Press.

Bubb, S. and Earley, P (2006) 'Induction rights and wrongs: the "educational vandalism" of new teachers' professional development', *Journal of In-service Education*, 32(1), March 2006: 5–12.

Bullough, R. V. Jnr. (2005) 'Teacher vulnerability and teachability: A case study of a mentor and two interns', *Teacher Education Quarterly*, 32(2): 23–40.

Bullough, R. V. and Hall-Keynon, K. M. (2011a) 'On Teacher Hope, Sense of Calling and Commitment to Teaching', *Teacher Education Quarterly*, 39(2): 127–40.

——(2011b) 'The call to teach and teacher hopefulness', *Teacher Development*, 15(2): 127–40.

Bullough, R. V. Jnr., Knowles, J. G. and Crow, N. A. (1991) *Emerging as a Teacher*. London: Routledge.

Burghes, D., Howson, J., Marenbon, J., O'Leary, J. and Woodhead, C. (2009) *Teachers Matter: Recruitment, Employment and Retention at Home and Abroad*. London: Politeia.

Burke, P. J. and Stets, J. E. (2009) *Identity Theory*. Oxford: Oxford University Press.

Cable, D. M. and Edwards, J. R. (2004) 'Complementary and supplementary fit: a theoretical and empirical integration', *Journal of Applied Psychology*, 89: 822–34.

Caprara, G. V., Barbarenelli, C., Steca, P. and Malone, P. S. (2006) 'Teachers' self-efficacy beliefs as determinants of job satisfaction and students' academic achievement: A study at the school level', *Journal of School Psychology*, 44: 473–90.

Carver, C. S. and Scheier, M. F. (2002) 'Optimism'. In C. R. Snyder and S. J. Lopez (eds), *Handbook of Positive Psychology*. New York: Oxford University Press.

Caspersen, J. (2013) *Professionalism Among Novice Teachers: How They Think, Act, Cope and Perceive Knowledge*. Phd thesis, Oslo and Akershus University College of Applied Sciences.

Castells, M. (1997) *The Power of Identity, The Information Age: Economy, Society and Culture Vol. II*. Cambridge, MA and Oxford, UK: Blackwell.

Castro, A., Kelly, J. and Shih, M. (2010) 'Resilience strategies for new teachers in high-needs areas', *Teaching and Teacher Education*, 26: 622–29.

Changying, W. (2007, September) 'Analysis of Teacher Attrition', *Chinese Education and Society*, 40(5): 6–10.

Chevalier, A. and Dolton, P. (2004) 'Teacher shortage: Another impending crisis?', *CentrePiece*, Winter, 15–21.

Cicchetti, D. (1993) 'Developmental psychopathology: Reactions, reflections, projections', *Developmental Review*, 13: 471–502.

Cicchetti, D. and Garmezy, N. (eds) (1993) 'Milestones in the development of resilience [Special issue]', *Development and Psychopathology*, 5(4): 497–774.

Cicchetti, D. and Valentino, K. (2006) 'An ecological–transactional perspective on child maltreatment: Failure of the average expectable environment and its influence on child development'. In D. Cicchetti and D. J. Cohen (eds), *Developmental Psychopathology: Vol. 3. Risk, disorder, and adaptation* (2nd ed., pp. 129–201). New York: Wiley.

Cohen, R. M. (2009) 'What it takes to stick it out: Two veteran inner-city teachers after 25 years', *Teachers and teaching*, 15(4): 471–91.

Cohen, S., Doyle, W. J., Turner, R. B., Alper, C. M. and Skoner, D. P. (2003) 'Emotional style and susceptibility to the common cold', *Psychosomatic Medicine*, 65: 652–7.

Collinson, V. (2008) 'Leading by Learning: new directions in the twenty-first century', *Journal of Educational Administration*, 46(4): 443–60.

Collinson, V. and Cook, T. F. (2007) *Organizational Learning: Improving Learning, Teaching in School Systems*. Thousand Oaks, CA: Sage.

Craig, C. (2007) *The potential dangers of a systematic, explicit approach to teaching social and emotional skills* (SEAL). Glasgow: Centre for Confidence and Wellbeing.

Crawford, M. (2009) 'Emotional coherence in primary school headship', *Educational Management Administration and Leadership*, 35(4): 521–34.

Csikszenthmihalyi, M. (1996) *Creativity: Flow and the Psychology of Discovery and Invention*. New York, NY: Harper Collins.

Curtis, W. J. and Cicchetti, D. (2003) 'Moving research on resilience into the 21st century: Theoretical and methodological considerations in examining the biological contributors to resilience', *Development and Psychopathology*, 15: 773–810.

Damasio, A. (2004) *Looking for Spinoza: Joy, Sorrow and the Feeling Brain*. London: Vintage.

Darling-Hammond, L. (1997) *Doing What Matters Most: Investing in Quality Teaching*. New York: National Commission on Teaching and America's Future.

——(2005) 'Policy and change: Getting beyond bureaucracy'. In A. Hargreaves (ed.), *Extending Educational Change: International Handbook of Educational Change*. Dordrecht, Netherlands: Springer, pp. 362–87.

Davidson, R. J. (2012) 'The neurobiology of compassion'. In C. K. Germer and R. D. Siegel (eds), *Wisdom and Compassion in Psychotherapy: Deepening Mindfulness in Clinical Practice* (Chapter 8). New York, NY: Guilford Press.

Davidson, R. J. and Begley, S. (2012) *The emotional life of your brain: How its unique patterns affect the way you think, feel, and live – and how you can change them.* New York, NY: Hudson Street Press.

Day, C. (1999) *Developing Teachers: The Challenges of Lifelong Learning,* Hong Kong: Falmer Press.

——(2004) *A passion for Teaching.* London: Routledge Falmer.

——(ed.) (2011) *International Handbook of Teacher and School Development.* London: Routledge.

Day, C. and Sachs, J. (2004a) *International Handbook on the Continuing Professional Development of Teachers.* Berkshire: Open University Press.

——(2004b) 'Professionalism, performativity and empowerment discourses in the politics, policies and purposes of continuing professional development'. In: C. Day and J. Sachs (eds), *International Handbook on the Continuing Professional Development of Teachers.* Maidenhead: Open University Press.

Day C. and Leithwood, K. (eds) (2007) *Successful Principal Leadership in Times of Change: An International Perspective.* Dordrecht: Springer.

Day, C. and Johansson, O. (2008) 'Leadership with a difference in Schools Serving Disadvantaged Communities: Arenas for Success'. In: K. Tirri, (ed.), *Educating Moral Sensibilities in Urban Schools.* Rotterdam, Netherlands: SENSE Publishers.

Day, C. and Kington, A. (2008) 'Identity, well-being and effectiveness: the emotional contexts of teaching', *Pedagogy, Culture and Society,* 16(1): 7–24.

Day, C. and Gu, Q. (2009) 'Teacher Emotions: Well Being and Effectiveness'. In M. Zembylas and P. Schutz (eds), *Advances in Teacher Emotion Research: The Impact on Teachers' Lives.* Dordrecht, Netherlands: Springer, pp. 15–31.

——(2010) *The New Lives of Teachers.* Abingdon, Oxon: Routledge.

Day. C. and Lee, J. C. H. (2011) *New Understandings of Teacher's Work: Emotions and Educational Change.* London: Springer.

Day, C. and Gurr, D. (2013) *Leading Schools Successfully: Stories from the Field.* London: Routledge.

Day, C., Harris, A., Hadfield, M., Tolley, H. and Beresford, J. (2000) *Leading Schools in Times of Change.* Buckingham: Open University Press.

Day, C., Harris, A. and Hadfield, M. (2001) 'Challenging the orthodoxy of effective school leadership', *International Journal of Leadership in Education,* 4(1): 39–56.

Day, C., Harris, A. and Parsons, C. (2001) *Improving Leadership: Critical Reflections on the Leadership Programme for Serving Headteachers: Room for Improvement?* British Educational Research Association Conference.

Day, C., Elliot, B. and Kington, A. (2005) 'Reforms, standards and teacher identity: Challenges of sustaining commitment', *Teaching and Teacher Education,* 21: 563–77.

Day, C., Kington, A. and Gu, Q. (2005) 'The role of identity in variations in teachers' work, lives and effectiveness'. Paper presented at ESRC Teaching and Learning Research Programme: Thematic Seminar Series, 15 March 2005.

Day, C., Kington, A., Stobart, G. and Sammons, P. (2006) 'The Personal and Professional Selves of Teachers: stable and unstable identities', *British Educational Research Journal,* 32(4): 601–16.

Day, C., Sammons, P., Stobart, G., Kington, A. and Gu, Q. (2007a) *Teachers Matter: Connecting Lives, Work and Effectiveness.* Maidenhead: Open University Press.

Day, C., Sammons, P., Hopkins, D., Harris, A., Leithwood, K., Gu, Q., Penlington, C., Mehta, P. and Kington, A. (2007b) *The Impact of Leadership on Pupil Outcomes: Interim Report,* DSCF Research Report RR018. Nottingham: Department of Children, Families and Schools/National College of School Leadership.

Day, C., Edwards, A., Griffiths, A. and Gu, Q. (2011a) *Beyond Survival: Teachers and Resilience.* Key messages from ESRC-funded Seminar series.

Day, C., Sammons, P., Leithwood, K., Hopkins, D., Gu, Q. and Brown, E., with Ahtaridou, E. (2011b) *School Leadership and Student Outcomes: Building and Sustaining Success.* Maidenhead: Open University Press.

Deal, T. E. and Peterson, K. D. (2009) *Shaping School Culture* (2nd edn). San Francisco, CA: Jossey-Bass.

Denzin, N. (1984) *On Understanding Emotion.* San Francisco: Jossey-Bass.

DfE (2012) *School Workforce in England: November, 2011.* Retrieved January 2013 from https://www.gov.uk/government/publications/school-workforce-in-england-november-2011

——(2012) *Statistical First Release: School Workforce in England: November 2011.* London: Department for Education, 25 April 2012.

DfES (Department for Education and Skills) (2005) *Primary national strategy. Excellence and enjoyment: Social and emotional aspects of learning.* London: DfES. (DfES ref: 1378_2005 G)

Dinham, S. and Scott, C. (2000) 'Moving into the third, outer domain of teacher satisfaction', *Journal of Educational Administration,* 38(4): 379–96.

——(2002) 'Pressure points: School executive and educational change', *Journal of Educational Enquiry,* 3(2): 35–52.

Dixon, J. (2001) 'Contact and boundaries: "locating" the social psychology of intergroup relations', *Theory and Psychology,* 11: 587–608.

Dokoupil, T., *The Sunday Times,* News Review, 15 July 2012, p. 2.

Ecclestone, K. and Lewis, L. (2014) 'Interventions for Resilience in Educational Settings: Challenging Policy Discourses of Risk and Vulnerability', *Journal of Educational Policy* (in press).

Edwards, A. (2007) 'Relational agency in professional practice: A CHAT analysis', *Actio: An International Journal of Human Activity Theory,* 1: 1–17.

——(2010) *Being an Expert Professional Practitioner: The Relational Turn in Expertise.* Dordrecht: Springer.

Edwards, E. A. (2003) *Retention and Motivation of Veteran Teachers: Implications for Schools.* Unpublished dissertation presented to the Faculty of the Department of Educational Leadership and Policy Analysis, East Tennessee State University.

Eilam, B. (2009) 'Learning to teach: Enhancing pre-service teachers' awareness of the complexity of teaching-learning processes', *Teachers and Teaching: Theory and Practice,* 15(1): 87–107.

Eisenhart, M. (2001) 'Educational ethnography past, present and future: Ideas to think with', *Educational Researcher,* 30(8): 16–27.

Emmet, D. (1958) *Function, Purpose, and Powers.* London: Macmillan.

Engh, A. E., Beehner, J. C., Bergman, T. J., Whitten, P. L., Hoffmeier, R. R., Seyfarth, R. M. and Cheney, D. L. (2006) 'Behavioural and hormonal responses to predation in female chacma baboons (Papio hamadryas ursinus)', *Proceedings of the Royal Society of London,* Series B, 273: 707–12.

Eraut, M., Maillardet, F., Miller, C., Steadman, S., Ali, A., Blackman, C. and Furner, J. (2004) 'Learning in the professional workplace: Relationships between learning factors and contextual factors', AERA Conference Paper, San Diego, 12 April.

Eraut, M., Steadman, S., Maillardet, F., Miller, C., Ali, A., Blackman, C., Furner, J. and Caballero, C. (2007) 'Early career learning at work: Insights into professional development during the first job', *Teaching and Learning Research Briefing*, 25 March (retrieved 1 November 2009, from www.tlrp.org/pub/documents/Eraut%20RB%2025%20FINAL.pdf).

ETUCE (2011) *Teachers' Work-related Stress: Assessing, Comparing and Evaluating the Impact of Psychosocial Hazards on Teachers at their Workplace*. Brussels: European Trade Union Committee for Education.

European Commission (2012) *Key Data on Education in Europe 2012*. Brussels: Education, Audiovisual and Culture Executive Agency.

Feng, L. and Sass, T. (2011) 'Teacher quality and teacher mobility', National Center for Analysis of Longitudinal Data in Education, Research Working Paper 57.

Field, J. (2008) *Social Capital* (2nd edn). London and New York: Routledge.

Fielding, M. (2000) 'Community, philosophy and education policy: Against effectiveness ideology and the immiseration of contemporary schooling', *Journal of Education Policy*, 15(4): 397–415.

Flintham, A. J. (2003a) *Reservoirs of Hope: Spiritual and Moral Leadership in Headteachers*. Nottingham: National College for School Leadership.

——(2003b) *When Reservoirs Run Dry: Why Some Headteachers Leave Headship Early*. Full Practitioner Enquiry Report. Nottingham: National College for School Leadership.

Flores, M. A. (2004) 'The impact of school culture and leadership on new teachers' learning in the workplace', *International Journal of Leadership in Education*, 7(4): 297–318.

Flores, M. A. and Day, C. (2006) 'Contexts which shape and reshape new teachers' identities: A multi-perspective study', *Teaching and Teacher Education*, 22: 219–32.

Foresight Mental Capital and Wellbeing Project (2008) *Final Project Report*. London: The Government Office for Science.

Fredrickson, B. L. (2001) 'The role of positive emotions in positive psychology: the broaden-and-build theory of positive emotions', *American Psychologist*, 56(3): 218–26.

——(2004) 'The broaden-and-build theory of positive emotions', *Philosophical Transactions of the Royal Society B: Biological Sciences*, 359: 1367–77.

Fried, R. (2001) *The Passionate Teacher: A Practical Guide* (2nd edn). Boston: Beacon Press.

Frijda, N. H. (2000) 'The psychologists' point of view'. In M. Lewis and J. M. Haviland-Jones (eds), *Handbook of Emotions* (2nd edn). New York/London: The Guilford Press, pp. 59–74.

Fullan, M. (1999) *Change Forces: The Sequel*. Philadelphia, PA: Falmer Press.

——(2003) *The Moral Imperatives of School Leadership*. Thousand Oaks, CA: Corwin Press.

Fuller, F. and Brown, O. (1975) 'Becoming a teacher'. In: K. Ryan (ed.), *Teacher Education: Seventy-fourth Yearbook of the National Society for the Study of Education*. Chicago: University of Chicago Press.

Furlong, J. (2008) 'Making teaching a 21st-century profession: Tony Blair's big prize', *Oxford Review of Education*, 34(6): 727–39.

Furlong, J., McNamara, O., Campbell, A., Howson, J. and Lewis, S. (2008) 'Partnership, policy and politics: initial teacher education in England under New Labour', Special issue of *Teachers and Teaching: Theory and Practice*: 'Research and Policy in Teacher Education: International Perspectives', 14(4): 307–18.

Furu, E. M. (2007) 'Emotional aspects of action learning'. In: E. M. Furu, T. Lud and T. Tiller (eds), *Action Research. A Nordic Perspective*. HoyskoleForlaget: Norwegian Academic Press, pp. 185–202.

Gamoran, A. (2012) 'Improving teacher quality'. In S. Kelly (ed.), *Assessing Teacher Quality: Understanding Teacher Effects on Instruction and Achievement*. New York, NY: Teachers College Press, pp. 201–14.

Glaser-Zikuda, M. and Fuss, S. (2008) 'Impact of Teacher Competencies on Student Emotions: A Multi-Method Approach', *International Journal of Educational Research*, 47(2): 136–47.

Glasser, W. (1965) *Schools Without Failure*. New York: Harper & Row.

Goddard, R. (2002) 'Collective efficacy and school organisation: A multilevel analysis of teacher influence in schools', *Theory and Research in Educational Administration*, 1: 169–84.

Goddard, R., Hoy, W. K. and Hoy, A. W. (2004) 'Collective efficacy beliefs: Theoretical developments, empirical evidence, and future directions', *Educational Researcher*, 33(3): 1–13.

Goldhaber, D. and Hansen, M. (2009) 'National board certification and teachers' career paths: Does NBPTS certification influence how long teachers remain in the profession and where they teach?', *Education Finance and Policy*, 4(3): 229–62.

Goldhaber, D., Gross, B. and Player, D. (2011) 'Teacher career paths, teacher quality and persistence in the classroom: Are public schools keeping their best?', *Journal of Policy Analysis and Management*, 30(1): 57–87.

Goleman, D. (1995) *Emotional Intelligence*. New York: Bantam.

——(2006) *Social Intelligence: The New Science of Human Relationships*. New York, NY: Bantam Dell.

Gonzalez, N., Moll, L. C. and Amanti, C. (2005) *Funds of Knowledge: Theorizing Practices in Households, Communities, and Classrooms*. London: Routledge.

Goodlad, J. (2004) *A Place Called School*. New York, NY: McGraw-Hill.

Goodwin, R. (2005) 'Why I Study Relationships and Culture', *The Psychologist*, 18(10): 614–15.

Gordon, K. A. (1995) 'The self-concept and motivational patterns of resilient African American high school students', *Journal of Black Psychology*, 21: 239–55.

Gordon, K. A., Longo, M. and Trickett, M. (2000) 'Fostering Resilience in Children', *The Ohio State University Bulletin*, 875–99: http://ohioline.osu.edu/b875.

Gore, S. and Eckenrode, J. (1994) 'Context and process in research on risk and resilience'. In: R. Haggerty, L. R. Sherrod, N. Garmezy and M. Rutter (eds) *Stress, Risk and Resilience in Children and Adolescents: Process, Mechanisms and Interventions*. New York: Cambridge University Press, pp. 19–63.

Gorman, C. (2005, January 17) 'The importance of resilience', *Time*, 165(3): A52-A55.

Gray, J. (2012) 'Wellbeing Matters Too', *Research Intelligence*, 117: Spring, 2012: 30.

Gray, J., Galton, M., McLaughlin, C., Clarke, B. and Symonds, J. (2011) *The Supportive School: Wellbeing and the Young Adolescent*. Newcastle upon Tyne: Cambridge Scholars Publishing.

Greenberg, M. (2006) 'Promoting resilience in children and youth: Preventive interventions and their interface with neuroscience', *Annals of the New York Academy of Sciences*, 1094: 139–50.

Grissmer, D. and Kirby, S. N. (1997) 'Teacher turnover and teacher quality', *Teachers College Record*, 99(1): 57–61.

Grissom, J. A. (2011) 'Can good principals keep teachers in disadvantaged schools? Linking principal effectiveness to teacher satisfaction and turnover in hard-to-staff environments', *Teachers College Record*, 113(11): 2552–85.

Grubb, N. W. (2007) 'The elusiveness of educational equity: From revenues to resources to results'. In: S. H. Fuhrman, D. K. Cohen and F. Mosher (eds), *The State of Education Policy Research*. New York, NY: Routledge, pp. 157–78.

Gu, Q. (in press) 'The role of resilience in teachers' career long commitment and effectiveness', *Teachers and Teaching: Theory and Practice*.

Gu, Q. and Day, C. (2007) 'Teachers' resilience: A necessary condition for effectiveness', *Teaching and Teacher Education*, 23: 1302–16.

——(2013) 'Challenges to teacher resilience: Conditions count', *British Educational Research Journal*, 39(1): 22–44.

——(forthcoming) 'Understanding teacher resilience in times of change', *Teachers and Teaching: Theory and Practice*.

Gu, Q. and Li, Q. (2013) 'Sustaining resilience in times of change: stories from Chinese teachers', Special Issue of *Asia-Pacific Journal of Teacher Education*, 41(3): 288–303.

Gu, Q. and Johansson, O. (in press) 'Sustaining school performance: school contexts matter', *International Journal of Leadership in Education*. DOI: http://www.tandfonline.com/doi/abs/10.1080/13603124.2012.732242

Gu, Q., Sammons, P. and Mehta, P. (2008) 'Leadership characteristics and practices in schools with different effectiveness and improvement profiles', *School Leadership and Management*, 28(1): 43–63.

Guardian, Saturday 16 June, 2007, Work, p. 3.

Guarino, C. M., Santibanez, L. and Daley, G. A. (2006) 'Teacher recruitment and retention: A review of the recent empirical literature', *Review of Educational Research*, 76(2): 173–208.

Guttman, C. (2001) 'A hard sell for teaching'. *The Courier UNSCO*, October.

Hakanen, J. J., Schaufeli, W. B. and Ahola, K. (2008) 'The Job Demands-Resources model: A three year cross-lagged study of burnout, depression, commitment, and work engagement', *Work and Stress*, 22: 224–41.

Hall, D. T. (1996) 'Long live the career'. In: D. T. Hall and Associates (eds) *The Career is Dead – Long Live the Career*. San Francisco, CA: Jossey-Bass.

Hallinger, P. (2005) 'Instructional leadership and the school principal: A passing fancy that refuses to fade away', *Leadership and Policy in Schools*, 4(3): 1–20.

Hamel, G. and Välikangas, L. (2003) 'The quest for resilience', *Harvard Business Review*, September: 1–13.

Hamon, H. and Rotman, P. (1984) *Tant qu'il y aura des profs*. Paris: Editions du Seuil.

Hansen, D. T. (1995) *The Call to Teach*. New York: Teachers College Press.

Hanushek, E. A. (1992) 'The trade-off between child quantity and quality', *Journal of Political Economy*, 100(1) (February): 84–117.

Hargreaves, A. (1994) *Changing teachers, changing times: Teachers' work and culture in the postmodern age*. London: Cassell.

——(1998) 'The emotional practice of teaching', *Teaching and Teacher Education*, 14(8): 835–54.

——(2000) 'Mixed emotions: teachers' perceptions of their interactions with students', *Teaching and Teacher Education*, 16: 811–26.

——(2011) 'System redesign for system capacity building', *Journal of Educational Administration*, 49(6): 685–700.

Hargreaves, A. and Fullan, M. (1999) 'Mentoring in the new millennium', *Professionally Speaking*, December 1999, pp. 19–23.

Hargreaves, A. and Fink, D. (2006) *Sustainable Leadership*. San Francisco, CA: Jossey-Bass.

Hargreaves, A. and Fullan, M. (2012) *Professional Capital: Transforming Teaching in Every School*. New York, NY: Teachers College Press.

Harré, R. and Van Langenhove, L. (eds) (1999) *Positioning Theory: Moral Contexts of Intentional Action*. Malden: Blackwell.

Harris, P. L. (2005) 'Conversation, pretense, and theory of mind'. In: J. W. Astington and J. A. Baird (eds), *Why Language Matters for Theory of Mind*. New York: Oxford University Press, pp. 70–83.

Hastings, R. P. and Bham, M. S. (2003) 'The relationship between student behaviour patterns and teacher burnout', *School Psychology International*, 24: 115–27.

Hattie, J. (2009) *Visible Learning: Synthesis of over 800 Meta-analyses Relating to Achievement*. London: Routledge.

Heck, R. H. and Hallinger, P. (2005) 'The study of educational leadership and management: Where does the field stand today?', *Educational Management Administration and Leadership*, 33(2): 229–44.

Heck, R. and Hallinger, P. (2009) 'Assessing the contribution of principal and teacher leadership to school improvement', *American Educational Research Journal*, 46: 659–89.

Helen, G. (2007) 'Remodelling the school workforce in England: A study in tyranny', *Journal for Critical Education Policy Studies*, 5. Retrieved from http://www.jceps.com/ index.php?pageID=article&articleID=84

Henderson, N. and Milstein, M. (2003) *Resiliency in Schools: Making it Happen for Students and Educators*. Thousand Oaks, CA: Corwin Press.

Heneman, H. G. (1998) 'Assessment of the motivational reactions of teachers to a school-based performance award programme', *Journal of Personnel Evaluation in Education*, 12: 43–59.

Henry, D. A. and Milstein, M. (2006) 'Building leadership capacity through resiliency', Paper presented at the Commonwealth Council for Educational Administration and Management, Lefcosia, Cyprus.

Henry, G. T., Bastian, K. C. and Fortner, C. K. (2011) 'Stayers and leavers: early career teacher effectivness and attrition', *Educational Researcher*, 40(6): 271–80.

Herzberg, F. (1966) *Work and the Nature of Man*. Cleveland, OH: World Publishing Company.

Higgins, G. O. (1994) *Resilient Adults: Overcoming a Cruel Past*. San Francisco: Jossey-Bass.

Hobson, A. and Ashby, P. (2010) 'Scaffolding or reality aftershock: second year teachers' experiences of post-induction support', draft paper, University of Nottingham.

Hochschild, A. (1983) *The Managed Heart: Commercialization of Human Feeling*. Berkeley: University of California Press.

Holme, J. and Rangel, V. (2012) 'Putting school reform in its place: Social geography, organizational social capital, and school performance', *American Educational Research Journal*, 49(2): 257–83.

Hong, J. (2010) 'Pre-service and beginning teachers' professional identity and its relation to dropping out of the profession', *Teaching and Teacher Education*, 26(8): 1530–43.

——(2012) 'Why do some beginning teachers leave the school, and others stay? Understanding teacher resilience through psychological lenses', *Teachers and Teaching: Theory and Practice*, 18(4): 417–40.

Hopkins, D. (2008) 'Realising the potential of system leadership'. In: B. Pont, D. Nusche and D. Hopkins (eds), *Improving School Leadership Volume 2: Case Studies on System Leadership*. Retrieved from OECD website: http://www.oecd-ilibrary. org (pp. 21–35).

——(2009) *The Emergency of System Leadership. A report*. Nottingham: National College for School Leadership.

Howard, S., Dryden, J. and Johnson, B. (1999) 'Childhood resilience: review and critique of literature', *Oxford Review of Education*, 25(3): 307–23.

Hoy, W. K. and Tschannen-Moran, M. (1999) 'Five faces of trust: An empirical confirmation in urban elementary schools', *Journal of School Leadership*, 9(4): 184–208.

Hoy, W. K. and Sweetland, S. (2001) 'Designing better schools: The meaning and measure of enabling school structures', *Educational Administration Quarterly*, 39(3): 296–321.

Hoy, W. K. and Miskel, C. G. (2005) *Educational Administration: Theory, Research and Practice* (7th edn). New York: McGraw Hill.

HSE (Health and Safety Executive) (2000) *The Scale of Occupational Stress: A Further Analysis of the Impact of Demographic Factors and Type of Job*. Retrieved 9 July 2011 from http://www.hse.gov.uk/research/crr_pdf/2000/crr00311.pdf

——(2011) *Stress-related and Psychological Disorders: Occupation and Industry (2007/8-2009/10)*. Retrieved 9 July 2011 from http://www.hse.gov.uk/ statistics/causdis/stress/occupation.htm

Huberman, M. (1989) 'The professional life cycle of teachers', *Teachers College Record*, 91(1), Fall, 31–57.

——(1993) *The Lives of Teachers*. London: Cassell.

Huisman, S., Singer, N. R. and Catapano, S. (2010) 'Resiliency to success: supporting novice urban teachers', *Teacher Development*, 14(4): 483–99.

Huxham, C. and Vangen, S. (2005) *Managing to Collaborate: The Theory and Practice of Collaborative Advantage*. Abingdon, Oxon: Routledge.

Ingersoll, R. M. (2001) 'Teacher turnover and teacher shortages: An organizational analysis', *American Educational Research Journal*, 38(3): 499–534.

Ingersoll, R. (2003a) 'Is there really a teacher shortage?' Philadelphia, PA: Consortium for Policy Research in Education, University of Pennsylvania. Retrieved from http://www.gse.upenn.edu/pdf/rmi/Shortage-RMI-09-2003.pdf

——(2003b) *Who Controls Teachers' Work?* Cambridge, MA: Harvard University Press.

——(2012) 'Power, accountability and the teacher quality problem'. In: S. Kelly (ed.) *Assessing Teacher Quality: Understanding Teacher Effects on instruction and Achievement.* New York: Teachers College Press, pp. 97–109.

Ingersoll, R. M. and Smith, T. M. (2003) 'The wrong solution to teacher shortages', *Educational Leadership,* 60(8): 30–3.

Ingersoll, R. and Perda, D. (2011) 'How high is teacher turnover and is it a problem?' Philadelphia: University of Pennsylvania, Consortium for Policy Research in Education.

Isen, A. M. (1990) 'The influence of positive and negative affect on cognitive organization: some implications for development'. In: N. Stein, B. Leventhal and T. Trabasso (eds), *Psychological and Biological Approaches to Emotion.* Hillsdale, NJ: Erlbaum, pp. 75–94.

Isenberger, L. and Zembylas, M. (2006) 'The emotional labour of caring in teaching', *Teaching and Teacher Education,* 22(1): 120–34.

Jesus, S. N. and Lens, W. (2005) 'An integrated model for the study of teacher motivation', *Applied Psychology: An International Review,* 54(1): 119–34.

Johnson, B. and Down, B. (2012) 'Reconceptualising early career teacher resilience: A critical alternative'. Paper presented at the Annual European Conference on Education, Vienna.

Johnson, B., Howard, S. and Oswald, M. (1999) 'Quantifying and prioritising resilience-promoting factors: teachers' views'. Paper presented at the Australian Association for Research in Education and New Zealand Association for Research in Education conference, Melbourne, 29 November–2 December.

Johnson, B., Down, B., Le Cornu, R., Peters, J., Sullivan, A., Pearce, J. and Hunter, J. (2010) 'Conditions that support early career teacher resilience'. Paper presented at the Annual Conference of the Australian Teacher Education, Townsville.

Johnson, B., Down, B., Le Cornu, R., Peters, J., Sullivan, A. M., Pearce, J. and Hunter, J. (2012) *Early Career Teachers: Stories of Resilience. Report from an ARC Linkage Project (2008–2012): 'Addressing the Teacher Exodus: Enhancing Early Career Teacher Resilience and Retention in Changing Times'.* Adelaide, South Australia: University of South Australia.

Johnson, N. (2003) *Perspectives on Education. Working in Teams.* Melbourne: Department of Education and Training (Victoria).

Johnson, S. M. (2004) *Finders and Keepers.* San Francisco, CA: Jossey-Bass.

Johnson, S. M., Berg, J. H. and Donaldson, M. L. (2005a) *A Review of the Literature on Teacher Retention.* Cambridge, MA: Harvard Graduate School of Education.

Johnson, S., Cooper, C., Cartwright, S., Donald, I., Taylor, P. and Millet, C. (2005b) 'The experience of work-related stress across occupations', *Journal of Managerial Psychology,* 20(2): 178-87.

Jones, N. (2002) 'The Tandem Project: inspiring the teacher – South West regional pilot programme 2001', *Education Review,* 15: 29–34.

Jordan, J. (1992) 'Relational resilience'. Paper presented on 1 April 1992 as part of the Stone Centre Colloquium Series.

——(2004) 'Relational resilience'. In: J. Jordan and M. Walker (eds) *The Complexity of Connection: Writings from the Stone Center's Jean Baker Miller Training Institute.* New York: Guildford Press, pp. 28–46.

——(2006) 'Relational resilience in girls'. In: S. Goldstein and R. B. Brooks (eds) *Handbook of Resilience in Children*. New York, NY: Springer, pp. 79–90.

——(2010) *Relational-cultural Therapy*. Washington, DC: American Psychological Association.

——(2012) 'Relational resilience in girls'. In: S. Goldstein and R. B. Brooks (eds) *Handbook of Resilience in Children* (2nd edn). New York, NY: Springer, pp. 73–86.

Kanter, R. M. (1972) *Commitment and Community: Communes and Utopias in Sociological Perspective*. Cambridge, MA: Harvard University Press.

Karasek, R. A. (1979) 'Job demands, job decision latitude, and mental strain: implications for job redesign', *Administrative Science Quarterly*, 24(2): 285–308.

Karasek, R. and Theorell, T. (1990) *Healthy Work: Stress, Productivity, and the Reconstruction of Working Life*. New York: Basic Books.

Kelchtermans, G. (1993) Getting the stories, understanding the lives: From careers stories to teachers' professional development. *Teaching and Teacher Education*, [9 (5/6): 443–456].

——(2005) 'Teachers' emotions in educational reforms: self-understanding, vulnerable commitment and micropolitical literacy', *Teaching and Teacher Education*, 21: 995–1006.

——(2009) 'Who I am in how I teach is the message: self-understanding, vulnerabilty and reflection', *Teachers and Teaching: Theory and Practice*, 15(2): 257–72.

——(2010) 'Narratives and biography in teacher education'. In: P. Penelope, B. Eva and M. Barry (eds), *International Encyclopedia of Education*. Oxford: Elsevier, pp. 610–14.

Kelchtermans, G. and Ballet, K. (2002) 'The micropolitics of teacher induction: A narrative biographical study on teacher socialisation', *Teaching and Teacher Education*, 18: 105–20.

Kelley, C. (1999) 'The motivational impact of school-based performance awards', *Journal of Personnel Evaluation in Education*, 12: 309–26.

Kennedy, A. (2005) 'Models of continuing professional development: a framework for analysis', *Journal of Inservice Education*, 31(2): 221–7.

Kennedy, M. M. (2008) 'Sorting out Teacher Quality', *Phi Delta Kappa International Inc*, 90(01), Sept 2008: 60.

——(2010) 'Attribution Error and the Quest for Teacher Quality', *Educational Researcher*, 39(8): 591–8.

King, B. and Newman, F. (2001) 'Building school capacity through professional development: conceptual and empirical considerations', *International Journal of Educational Management*, 15(2): 86–94.

Kirk, J. and Wall, C. (2010) 'Resilience and loss in work identities: a narrative analysis of some retired teachers' work-life histories', *British Educational Research Journal*, 36(4): 627–41.

Kitching, K., Morgan, M. and O'Leary, M. (2009) 'It's the little things: Exploring the importance of commonplace events for early-career teachers' motivation', *Teachers and Teaching: Theory and Practice*, 15(1): 43–58.

Klassen, R. M. and Anderson, C. J. K. (2009) 'How times change: Secondary teachers' job satisfaction and dissatisfaction in 1962 and 2007', *British Educational Research Journal*, 35(5): 745–59.

Klassen, R., Usher, E. and Bong, M. (2010) 'Teachers' collective efficacy, job satisfaction, and job stress in cross-cultural context', *The Journal of Experimental Education*, 78: 464–86.

Knoop, H. H. (2007) 'Control and responsibility'. In H. Gardener (ed.) *Responsibility at Work*. San Francisco, CA: Jossey-Bass.

Kyriacou, C. (2000) *Stress Busting for Teachers*. Cheltenham: Stanley Thornes Ltd.

Ladd, H. (2009) 'Teachers' perceptions of their working conditions: How predictive of policy-relevant outcomes', National Center for Analysis of Longitudinal Data in Education, Research Working Paper No. 33. Washington, DC: Calder.

Ladwig, J. G. (2010) 'Beyond academic outcomes', *Review of Research in Education*, 34: 113–41.

Lankford, M., Loeb, S. and Wyckoff, J. (2002) 'Teacher sorting and the plight of urban schools: a descriptive analysis', *Educational Evalution and Policy Analysis*, 13(3): 256–68.

Lasky, S. (2003) 'Teacher professional vulnerability in a context of standards based reforms'. Paper presented at the annual meeting of the American Educational Research Association, Chicago.

——(2005) 'A sociocultural approach to understanding teacher identity, agency and professional vulnerability in a context of seconary school reform', *Teaching and Teacher Education*, 21: 899–916.

Lazarus, R. S. (1991) *Emotion and Adaptation*. New York: Oxford University Press.

Leana, C. (2011) 'The Missing Link in School Reform', *Stanford Social Innovation Review*, Fall. Leland Stanford Jr. University. Retrieved on 1 April 2012 from http://www.ssireview.org/articles/entry/the_missing_link_in_school_reform

Leitch, R. (2010) 'Masks as self study. Challenging and sustaining teachers' personal and professional personae in early–mid career life phases', *Teachers and Teaching: Theory and Practice*, 16(3): 329–52.

Leithwood, K. (2012) *The Ontario Leadership Framework with a Discussion of the Research Foundations*, March, 2012. Ontario, Canada: The Institute of Educational Leadership.

Leithwood, K. and Jantzi, D. (2008) 'Linking leadership to student learning: The contributions of leader efficacy', *Educational Administration Quarterly*, 44: 496–528.

Leithwood, K. and Seashore Louis, K. (2012) *Linking Leadership to Student Learning*. San Francisco, Jossey-Bass.

Leithwood, K., Seashore Louis, K., Anderson, S. and Wahlstrom, K. (2004) *How Leadership Influences Student Learning*. St. Paul, MN: Center for Applied Research and Educational Improvement.

Leithwood, K., Day, C., Sammons, P., Harris, A. and Hopkins, D. (2006a) *Successful School Leadership: What it is and how it influences pupil learning*. London, UK: DfES. Available at http://www.dfes.gov.uk/research/data/uploadfiles/RR800.pdf

Leithwood, K., Day, C., Sammons, P., Harris, A. and Hopkins, D. (2006b) *Seven Strong Claims about Successful School Leadership*. Nottingham: National College for School Leadership.

Leithwood, K., Harris, A. and Strauss, T. (2010) *Leading School Turnaround*. San Francisco, CA: Jossey-Bass.

Lieberman, A. and Miller, L. (1992) *Teachers – Their World and Their Work: Implications for School Improvement*. New York: Teachers College Press.

Lieberman, A. and Miller, L. (eds) (2008) *Teachers in Professional Communities*. New York and London: Teachers College Press.

Little, J. W. (1990) 'The persistence of privacy: Autonomy and initiative in teachers' professional relations', *Teachers College Record*, 91: 509–36.

Loeb, S., Darling-Hammond, L. and Luczak, J. (2005) 'How teaching conditions predict teacher turnover in California schools', *Peabody Journal of Education*, 80(3): 44–70.

Loehr, J. and Schwartz, T. (2003) *The Power of Full Engagement*. New York: Free Press.

Louis, K. S. (2007) 'Trust and improvement in schools', *Journal of Educational Change*, 8: 1–24.

——(2012) 'Learning communities in learning schools: Developing the social capacity for change'. In: C. Day (ed.) *The Routledge International Handbook of Teacher and School Development*. London and New York: Routledge, pp. 477–92.

Lovett, S. and Cameron, M. (2014) 'The impact of working conditions on teacher job satisfaction, retention and career decisions: Findings from the Teachers of Promise Study 9 years on', in *Teachers and Teaching: Theory and Practice* (in press).

Luke, A. (2011) 'Generalizing across borders: policy and the limits of educational science', *Educational Researcher*, 40(8): 367–77.

Luthans, F., Avolio, B. J., Avey, J. B. and Norman, S. M. (2007) 'Positive psychological capital: Measurement and relationship with performance and satisfaction', *Personnel Psychology*, 60: 541–72.

Luthans, F., Avey, J. and Patera, J. (2008) 'Experimental analysis of web-based training intervention to develop positive psychological capital', *Academy of Management, Learning and Education*, 7(2): 209–21.

Luthar, S. (1996) *Resilience: A Construct of Value?* Paper presented at the 104th Annual Convention of the American Psychological Association, Toronto.

——(2006) 'Resilience in development: A synthesis of research across five decades'. In: D. Cicchetti and D. J. Cohen (eds) *Developmental Psychopathology: Risk, Disorder, and Adaptation* (2nd edn). New York: Wiley, pp. 739–95.

Luthar, S. and Brown, P. (2007) 'Maximizing resilience through diverse levels of inquiry: Prevailing paradigms, possibilities, and priorities for the future', *Development and Psychopathology*, 19: 931–55.

Luthar, S. S., Cicchetti, D. and Becker, B. (2000) 'The construct of resilience: A critical evaluation and guidelines for future work', *Child Development*, 71: 543–62.

McCormack, A. and Thomas, K. (2003) 'Is survival enough? Induction experiences of beginning teachers within a New South Wales context', *Asia-Pacific Journal of Teacher Education*, 31(2): 125–38.

Macdonald, D. (1999) 'Teacher attrition: a review of literature', *Teaching and Teacher Education*, 15: 835–48.

McIntyre, F. (2003) *Transition to Teaching: New Teachers of 2001 and 2002. Report of their first two years of teaching in Ontario*. Toronto, ON: Ontario College of Teachers. Retrieved 12 June, 2003, from www.oct.ca

McLaughlin, C. (2008) 'Emotional well-being and its relationships to schools and classrooms: a critical reflection', *British Journal of Guidance and Counselling*, 36(4): 353–66.

MacLure, M. (1993) 'Arguing for yourself: identity as an organising principle in teachers' jobs and lives', *British Educational Research Journal*, 19(4): 311–22.

Maddi, S. R. (2002) 'The story of hardiness: Twenty years of theorizing, research, and practice', *Consulting Psychology Journal*, 54: 173–85.

——(2006) 'Hardiness: The courage to grow from stresses', *The Journal of Positive Psychology*, 1: 1–9.

Mansfield, C. F., Beltman, S., Price, A. and McConney, A. (2012) '"Don't sweat the small stuff": Understanding teacher resilience at the chalkface', *Teaching and Teacher Education*, 28: 357–67.

Manuel, J. (2003) '"Such are the ambitions of youth": Exploring issues of retention and attrition of early career teachers in New South Wales', *Asia-Pacific Journal of Teacher Education*, 31(2): 140–51.

Markow, D. and Martin, S. (2005) *The MetLife Survey of the American Teacher: Transitions and the Role of Supportive Relationships*. New York: MetLife.

Marsh, J. A., Springer, M. G., McCaffrey, D. F., Yuan, K., Epstein, S., Koppich, J. E., Kalra, N., DiMartino, C. and Peng, A. (2011) *A Big Apple for Educators: New York City's Experiment with Schoolwide Performance Bonuses*. Santa Monica, CA: RAND Corporation.

Marzano, R. J. (2000) *A New Era of School Reform: Going Where the Research Takes Us*. Aurora, CO: Mid-Continent Research for Education and Learning.

Masten, A. (1994) 'Resilience in individual development: successful adaptation despite risk and adversity'. In: M. C. Wang and E. W. Gordon (eds) *Educational Resilience in Inner-City America: Challenges and Prospects*. Hillsdale, NJ: Erlbaum, pp. 3–25.

Masten, A. S. (2001) 'Ordinary magic: resilience process in development', *American Psychologist*, 56: 227–39.

Masten, A. and Garmezy, N. (1985) 'Risk, vulnerability, and protective factors in developmental psychopathology'. In: B. Lahey and A. Kazdin (eds), *Advances in Clinical Child Psychology*, 8: 1–52. New York: Plenum Press.

Masten, A. S., Hubbard, J. J., Gest, S. D., Tellegen, A., Garmezy, N. and Ramirez, M. (1999) 'Adaptation in the context of adversity: Pathways to resilience and maladaptation from childhood to late adolescence', *Development and Psychopathology*, 11: 143–69.

Matheson, I. (2007) 'Current demographics in the school teacher population in Scotland', Paper presented at the Scottish Educational Research Association conference.

Mawhinney, H., Hass, J. and Wood, C. (2005) 'Teachers' collective efficacy beliefs in professional learning communities', *Leading and Managing*, 11(2): 12–45.

Mayer, J. D., Salovey, P. and Caruso, D. R. (2004) 'Emotional intelligence: Theory findings and implications', *Psychological Inquiry*, 15: 197–215.

Meister, D. G. and Ahrens, P. (2011) 'Resisting plateauing: Four veteran teachers' stories', *Teaching and Teacher Education*, 27: 770–8.

Melucci, A. (1996) *Challenging Codes: Collective Action in the Information Age*. New York: Press Syndicate of the University of Cambridge.

Miller, R. (2008) 'Tales of Teacher Absence: New Research Yields Patterns that Speak to Policymakers', *Center for American Progress*, October, 2008. Retrieved from http://www.americanprogress.org/wp-content/uploads/issues/2008/10/pdf/teacher_absence.pdf

Ministerial Council on Education (2003) *Employment, Training and Youth Affairs*. Retrieved 1 March 2013 from http://www.mceecdya.edu.au/mceecdya/teacher-demand-and-supply-200311940.html

Mitchell, C. and Sackney, L. (2000) *Profound Improvement: Building Capacity for a Learning Community*. Lisse, Netherlands: Swets & Zeitlinger.

Moe, A., Pazzaglia, F. and Ronconi, L. (2010) 'When being able is not enough. The combined value of positive effect and self efficacy for job satisfaction in teaching', *Teacher and Teacher Education*, 26: 1145–53.

Moore-Johnson, S. with the Project on the Next Generation of Teachers (2004) *Finders and Keepers: Helping New Teachers Survive and Thrive in Our Schools*. San Francisco, CA: John Wiley & Sons.

Moos, L., Johansson, O. and Day, C. (eds) (2012) *How School Principals Sustain Success over Time: International Perspectives*. Dordrecht: Springer.

Morgan, M., Ludlow, L., Kitching, K., O'Leary, M. and Clarke, A. (2010) 'What makes teachers tick? Sustaining events in new teachers' lives', *British Educational Research Journal*, 36(2): 191–208.

Mourshed, M., Chijioke, C. and Barber, M. (2010) *How the World's Most Improved School Systems Keep Getting Better*. New York, NY: McKinsey and Company.

Müller, K., Alliata, R. and Benninghoff, F. (2009) 'Attracting and retaining teachers: A question of motivation', *Educational Management Administration and Leadership*, 37(5): 574–99.

NAHT (National Association of Headteachers) (2011) *Annual Report of the State of the Labour Market for Senior Staff in Schools in England & Wales*. Haywards Heath, West Sussex: NAHT.

Nash, P. (2005) Speech to Worklife Support Conference. London Well Being Conference, London, 21 April 2005.

NCSL (National College for School Leadership) (2003) *School Leadership 2003*. Nottingham: National College for School Leadership.

Neenan, M. (2009) *Developing Resilience*. Hove, East Sussex: Routledge.

NEF (New Economics Foundation) (2007) *National Accounts of Well-being: Bringing real wealth onto the balance sheet*. London: NEF.

——(2009) *National Accounts of Well-being: Bringing real wealth onto the balance sheet*. London: NEF.

Nias, J. (1981) 'Commitment and motivation in primary school teachers', *Educational Review*, 33(3): 181–90.

——(1989) *Primary Teachers Talking*. London: Routledge.

——(1996) 'Thinking about feeling: The emotions in teaching', *Cambridge Journal of Education*, 26(3): 293–306.

——(1999) 'Teachers' moral purposes: Stress, vulnerability, and strength'. In: R. Vandenberghe and A. M. Huberman (eds), *Understanding and Preventing Teacher Burnout: A Sourcebook of International Research and Practice*. Cambridge: Cambridge University Press, pp. 223–37.

Nieto, S. (2003) *What Keeps Teachers Going?* New York: Teachers College Press.

——(2010) 'Foreword'. In: W. Ayers, *To Teach: The Journey of A Teacher* (3rd edn). New York, NY: Teachers College Press, pp. ix–x.

——(2011) 'Critical hope, in spite of it all'. In: R. F. Elmore (ed.) *I Used to Think … and Now I Think*. Cambridge, MA: Harvard Education Press, pp. 127–33.

Noddings, N. (2005) *The Challenge to Care in Schools*. New York and London: Teachers College Press.

——(2010) *The Maternal Factor: Two Paths to Morality*. Berkeley and Los Angeles, CA: University of California Press

O'Connor, K. E. (2008) '"You choose to care": Teachers, emotions and professional identity', *Teachers and Teacher Education*, 24(1): 117–26.

O'Connell Higgins, G. (2004) *Resilient Adults: Overcoming a Cruel Past*. San Francisco, CA: Jossey-Bass.

OECD (2005a) *Education at a Glance*. Paris: OECD.

——(2005b) *Teachers Matter: Attracting, Developing and Retaining Effective Teachers*. Paris: OECD.

——(2008) *Improving School Leadership*. Paris: OECD.

——(2009) *Creating Effective Teaching and Learning Environments: First Results from TALIS*. Paris: OECD.

——(2010) *Education Today: The OECD Perspective*. Paris: OECD.

——(2011) *Building a High-Quality Teaching Profession: Lessons from Around the World*. Paris: OECD.

——(2012a) *Preparing Teachers and Developing School Leaders for the 21st Century*. Paris: OECD.

——(2012b) *Education Today 2013*. Paris: OECD.

——(2013) *OECD Guidelines on Measuring Subjective Well-being*. Paris: OECD.

Olsen, B. (2008) *Teaching What They Learn, Learning What They Live*. Boulder, CO: Paradigm Publishers.

Olsen, B. and Sexton, D. (2009) 'Threat rigidity, school reform, and how teachers view their work inside current education policy contexts', *American Educational Research Journal*, 46(1): 9–44.

Oswald, M., Johnson, B. and Howard, S. (2003) 'Quantifying and evaluating resilience-promoting factors – teachers' beliefs and perceived roles', *Research in Education*, 70: 50–64.

Palmer, P. J. (1998) *The Courage to Teach: Exploring the Inner Landscape of a Teacher's Life*. San Francisco, CA: Jossey-Bass.

——(2007) *The Courage to Teach: Exploring the Inner Landscape of a Teacher's Life* (10th Anniversary edition). San Francisco: Jossey-Bass.

Patterson, J. and Kelleher, P. (2005) *Resilient School Leaders: Strategies for Turning Adversity into Achievement*. Alexandria, VA: Association for Supervision and Curriculum Development.

Pence, A. R. (ed.) (1998) *Ecological Research with Children and Families: From Concepts to Methodology*. New York: Teachers' College Press.

Peters, J. and Pearce, J. (2012) 'Relationships and early career teacher resilience: a role for school principals', *Teachers and Teaching: Theory and Practice*, 18(2): 249–62.

Peterson, C. (2006) *A Primer in Positive Psychology*. New York: Oxford University Press.

Peterson, S. J. and Luthans, F. (2003) 'The positive impact and development of hopeful leaders', *Leadership and Organization Development Journal*, 24: 26–31.

Pillen, M., Beijaard, D. and van Brok, P. (2012) 'Tensions in learning to teach: accommodation and the development of teacher identity', *European Journal of Teacher Education*, 55(1): 8–24.

PricewaterhouseCoopers (2001) *Teacher Workload Study*. London: DfES.

Prieto, L. L., Soria, M. S., Martinez, I. M. and Schaufeli, W. (2008) 'Extension of the Job Demands-Resources model in the prediction of burnout and engagement among teachers over time', *Psicothema*, 70: 354–60.

Putnam, R. D. (1993) 'The prosperous community: Social capital and public life', *The American Prospect*, 4(13): 11–18.

Pyhältö, K., Pietarinen, J. and Salmeha-Aro, K. (2011) 'Teacher-working environment fit as a framework for burnout experienced by Finnish teachers', *Teaching and Teacher Education*, 27(7): 1101–1110.

Rhodes, C., Nevill, A. and Allan, J. (2004) 'Valuing and supporting teachers: A survey of teacher satisfaction, dissatisfaction, morale and retention in an English local education authority', *Research in Education*, 71: 67–80.

Richardson, G. E., Neiger, B. L., Jenson, S. and Kumpfer, K. L. (1990) 'The resiliency model', *Health Education*, 21(6): 33–9.

Rinke, C. (2008) 'Understanding teachers' careers: Linking professional life to professional path', *Educational Research Review*, 3: 1–13.

Rivkin, S. G., Hanushek, E. A. and Kain, J. F. (2005) 'Teachers, schools and academic achievement', *Econometrica*, 73(2): 417–58.

Robinson, V., Hohepa, M. and Lloyd, C. (2009) *School Leadership and Student Outcomes: Identifying What Works and Why. Best Evidence Syntheses Iteration (BES)*, Ministry of Education, New Zealand. Available from http://educationcounts.govt.nz/goto/BES

Rockoff, J. E. (2004) 'The impact of individual teachers on student achievement: evidence from panel data', *American Economic Review Papers and Proceedings*, 94(2): 247–52.

Ronfeldt, M., Loeb, S. and Wykckoff, J. (2013) 'How Teacher Turnover Harms Student Achievement', *American Educational Research Journal*, 50(1): 4–36.

Roosmarijn, M. C., Zwetsloot, G. I. J. M., Bos, E. H. and Wiezer, N. M. (in press) 'Exploring teacher and school resilience as a new perspective to solve persistent problems in the educational sector', *Teachers and Teaching: Theory and Practice*.

Rose, M. (2010) 'Afterward'. In: W. Ayers, *To Teach: The Journey of a Teacher*. New York, NY: Teachers College Press, pp. 167–9.

Rots, I. and Aelterman, A. (2008) 'Two profiles of teacher education graduates: A discriminant analysis of teaching commitment', *European Educational Research Journal*, 7: 523–34.

Rutter, M. (1990) 'Psychosocial resilience and protective mechanisms'. In: J. Rolf, A. S. Masten, D. Cicchetti, K. H. Nuechterlein and S. Weintraub (eds), *Risk and Protective Factors in the Development of Psychopathology*. New York: Cambridge University Press, pp. 181–214.

——(2006) *Genes and Behavior: Nature–nurture Interplay Explained*. Malden, MA: Blackwell.

Rutter, M., Maughan, B., Mortimore, P., Ouston, J. and Smith, A. (1979) *Fifteen Thousand Hours: Schools and Their Effects on Children*. Cambridge, MA: Harvard University Press.

Ryan, R. M. and Deci, E. I. (2000a) 'Intrinsic and Extrinsic Motivations: Classic Definitions and New Directions', *Contemporary Educational Psychology*, 25: 54–67.

——(2000b) 'Self-Determination Theory and the Facilitation of Intrinsic Motivation, Social Development and Well-Being', *American Psychologist*, 55: 68–78.

Sachs, J. (2001) 'Teacher professional identity: competing discourses, competing outcomes', *Journal of Education Policy*, 16(2): 149–61.

——(2003a) *The Activist Teaching Profession*. Buckingham: Open University Press.

——(2003b) 'The activist professional', *Journal of Educational Change*, 1: 77–95.

——(2011) 'Skilling or Emancipating? Metaphors for Continuing Teacher Professional Development'. In: N. Mockler and J. Sachs (eds), *Rethinking Educational Practice Through Reflexive Inquiry*. Dordrecht: Springer, pp. 153–68.

Salovey, P. and Mayer, J. D. (1989) 'Emotional Intelligence', *Imagination, Cognition, and Personality*, 9: 185–211.

Sammons, P., Day, C., Kington, A., Gu, Q., Stobart, G. and Smees, R. (2007) 'Exploring variations in teachers' work, lives and their effects on pupils: key findings and implications from a longitudinal mixed-method study', *British Educational Research Journal*, 33(5): 681–701.

Sammons, P., Gu, Q., Day, C. and Ko, J. (2011) 'Exploring the impact of school leadership on pupil outcomes', *International Journal of Educational Management*, 25(1): 83–101.

Schaufeli, W. B. and Buunk, B. P. (2003) 'Burnout: An overview of 25 years of research in theorizing'. In: M. J. Schabracq, J. A. M. Winnubst and C. L. Cooper (eds) *The Handbook of Work and Health Psychology*. Chichester: Wiley, pp. 383–425.

Scheopner, A. J. (2010) 'Irreconcilable differences: Teacher attrition in public and catholic schools', *Educational Research Review*, 5(3): 261–77.

Schlichte, J., Yssel, N. and Merbler, J. (2005) 'Pathways to burnout: Case studies in teacher isolation and alienation', *Preventing School Failure*, 50(1): 35–40.

Schutz, P. A. and Zembylas, M. (eds) (2009) *Advances in Teacher Emotion Research: The Impact on Teachers' Lives*. New York: Springer.

Scott, C., Stone, B. and Dinham, S. (2001) '"I love teaching but…" International patterns of teacher discontent', *Educational Policy Analysis Archives*, 9(28): 1–16.

Scott, C. and Dinham, S. (2002) 'The beatings will continue until quality improves: carrots and sticks in the search for educational improvement', *Teacher Development*, 6(1): 15–31.

Seashore Louis, K. (2007) 'Trust and Improvement in Schools', *Journal of Educational Change*, 8: 1–24.

Seashore Louis, K. and Miles, M. B. (1990) *Improving the Urban High School: What Works and Why?* New York, NY: Teachers College Press.

Seldon, A. (2009) *Trust: How we lost it and how to get it back*. London: Biteback Publishing.

Seligman, M. (1998) *Learned Optimism: How to change your mind and your life*. New York: Pocket Books.

Sharp, P. (2001) *Nurturing Emotional Literacy*. London: David Fulton.

Shen, J. and Palmer, L. B. (2009) 'Inadequate preparation does impact teacher attrition'. In: J. Shen (ed.), *School Leaders: Professional and Demographic Characteristics*. New York: Peter Lang, pp. 125–40.

Shulman, L. (1998) 'Theory, practice, and the education of professionals', *The Elementary School Journal*, 98(5): 511–26.

Simecka, M. (1984) 'A world with utopias or without them?' In: P. Alexander and R. Gill (eds), *Utopias*, London: Duchworth.

Smethem, L. (2007) 'Retention and intention in teaching careers: Will the new generation stay?', *Teachers and Teaching: Theory and Practice*, 13: 465–80.

Smith, M. K. (2004) 'Nel Noddings, the ethics of care and education'. Retrieved from: www.infed.org/thinkers/noddings.htm

Smith, T. and Ingersoll, R. (2004) 'What are the effects of induction and mentoring on beginning teacher turnover?', *American Educational Research Journal*, 41(3): 681–714.

Smith, J. M. and Kovacs, P. E. (2011) 'The impact of standards-based reform on teachers: the case of "No Child Left Behind"', *Teachers and Teaching: Theory and Practice*, 7(2): 201–225.

Smithers, A. and Robinson, P. (2003) *Factors affecting teachers' decisions to leave the profession. Research report 430.* London: Department for Education and Skills.

Snyder, C. R., Irving, L. and Anderson, J. R. (1991) 'Hope and health: Measuring the will and the ways'. In: C. R. Snyder and D. R. Forsyth (eds), *Handbook of Social and Clinical Psychology: The Health Perspective.* Elmsford, New York: Pergamon Press, pp. 285–305, cited in C. R. Snyder (2000) 'Hypothesis: There is Hope'. In: C. R. Snyder (ed), *Handbook of Hope Theory, Measures and Applications.* San Diego: Academic Press, pp. 3–21.

Sockett, H. (1993) The Moral Base for Teacher Professionalism. New York: Teachers College Press.

Solomon, R. C. and Flores, F. (2001) *Building Trust in Business, Politics, Relationships and Life.* New York: Oxford University Press.

Stanley, J. (2012) 'How Can Teachers Be Stressed?', 10 September 2012: Huffington Post. http://www.huffingtonpost.co.uk/julian-stanley/teachers-how-can-they-be-stressed_b_1864160.html

Starratt, R. J. (2012) *Cultivating the Ethical School.* Abingdon, Oxon: Routledge.

Steptoe, A., Wardle. J. and Marmot, M. (2005) 'Positive affect and health-related neuroendocrine, cardiovascular, and inflammatory processes', *Proceedings of the National Academy of Sciences*, USA.

Sternberg, R. J. (ed.) (2000) *Handbook of Intelligence.* Cambridge: Cambridge University Press.

Stets, J. E. and Burke, P. J. (2000) 'Identity theory and social identity theory', *Social Psychology Quarterly*, 63(3): 224–37.

Stoll, L. (2009) 'Capacity building for school improvement or creating capacity for learning? A changing landscape', *Journal of Educational Change*, 10: 115–27.

Stronach, I., Corbin, B., McNamara, O., Stark, S. and Warne, T. (2002) 'Towards an uncertain politics of professionalism: Teacher and nurse identities in flux', *Journal of Educational Policy*, 17(1): 109–38.

Sutton, R. and Wheatley, K. F. (2003) 'Teachers' emotions and teaching: A review of the literature and directors for future research', *Educational Psychology Review*, 15(4): 327–58.

Sutton Trust (2011) *Improving the Impact of Teachers on Pupil Achievement in the UK – Interim Findings.* London: The Sutton Trust.

Swann, M., McIntyre, D., Pell, T., Hargreaves. L. and Cunningham, M. (2010) 'Teachers' conceptions of teacher professionalism in England in 2003 and 2006', *British Educational Research Journal*, 36(4): 549–71.

Tait, M. (2008) 'Resilience as a contributor to novice teacher success, commitment, and retention', *Teacher Education Quarterly*, 35(4): 57–75.

Talbert, J. E. and McLaughlin, M. W. (2006) *Building School-Based Teacher Learning Communities: Professional Strategies to Improve Student Achievement.* New York: Teachers College Press.

Taris, T. W., Kompier, M. A., De Lange, A. H., Schaufeli, W. B. and Schreurs, P.J.G. (2003) 'Learning new behaviour patterns: a longitudinal test of Karasek's active learning hypothesis among Dutch teachers', *Work and Stress*, 17(1): 1–20.

Taylor, S. (2007) 'Social support'. In: H. S. Friedman and R. C. Silver (eds), *Foundations of Health Psychology*. New York: Oxford University Press, pp. 145–71.

Thomson, P. (2009) *School Leadership – Heads on the Block?* London: Routledge.

Torres, A. S. (2012) '"Hello, goodbye": Exploring the phenomenon of leaving teaching early', *Journal of Educational Change*, 13: 117–54.

Tricarico, K. M., Jacobs, J. and Yendol-Hoppey, D. (2012) Reflection on their first five years of teaching: understanding staying and impact power. Paper presented at AERA, Vancouver, Canada, April 2012.

Troman, G. and Woods, P. (2001) *Primary Teachers' Stress*. London: Routledge.

Tschannen-Moran, M. (2004) *Trust Matters: Leadership for Successful Schools*. San Francisco, CA: Jossey-Bass.

Tschannen-Moran, M. and Hoy, A. W. (2001) 'Teacher efficacy: Capturing an elusive construct', *Teacher and Teacher Education*, 17: 783–805.

——(2007) 'The differential antecedents of self-efficacy beliefs of novice and experienced teachers', *Teaching and Teacher Education*, 23: 944–56.

Tschannen-Moran, M. and Barr, M. (2004) 'Fostering student learning: The relationship of collective teacher efficacy and student achievement', *Leadership and Policy in Schools*, 3(3): 189–209.

Tucker, M. (2011) *Surpassing Shanghai*. Harvard: Harvard Educational Publishing Group.

UNESCO (2006) *Teachers and Educational Quality: Monitoring Global Needs for 2015*. Paris: UNESCO.

——(2011) *The Global Demand for Primary Teachers – 2011 Update*. Paris: UNESCO.

Ungar, M. (2004) 'A constructionist discourse on resilience: multiple contexts, multiple realities among at-risk children and youth', *Youth and Society*, 35: 341–65.

UNICEF (2007) *Child Poverty in Perspective: Overview of Child Well-Being in Rich Countries: A Comprehensive Assessment of the Lives and Well-Being of Children and Adolescents in the Economically Advanced Nations*. Florence: UNICEF, Innocenti Research Centre.

Van den Berg, R. (2002) 'Teachers' meanings regarding educational practice', *Review of Educational Research*, 72(4): 577–625.

van Veen, K. and Lasky, S. (2005) 'Editorial: Emotions as a lens to explore teacher identity and change: different theoretical approaches', *Teaching and Teacher Education*, 21: 895–8.

van Veen, K. and Sleegers, P. (2006) 'How does it feel? Teachers' emotions in a context of change', *Journal of Curriculum Studies*, 38(1), 85–111.

Wallace Foundation (2013) *The School Principal as Leader: Guiding Schools to Better Teaching and Learning*, Jan 2013. New York, NY: The Wallace Foundation.

Waller, M. (2001) 'Resilience in ecosystemic context: Evolution of the concept', *American Journal of Orthopsychiatry*, 7(3): 290–7.

Walsh, F. (1998) *Strengthening Family Resilience*. New York: Guildford Press.

Wang, J. L. (2004) 'Rural–urban differences in the prevalence of major depression and associated impairment', *Social Psychiatry and Psychiatric Epidemiology*, 39(1): 19–25.

Wang, M. (1997) 'Next steps in inner city education: focusing on resilience development and learning success', *Education and Urban Society*, 29(3): 255–76.

Watson, C. (2006) 'Narratives of practice and the construction of identity in teaching', *Teachers and Teaching*, 12: 509–26.

Webb, R., Vulliamy, G., Hämäläinen, S., Sarja, A., Kimonen, E. and Nevalainen, R. (2004) 'Pressures, rewards and teacher retention: a comparative study of primary teaching in England and Finland', *Scandinavian Journal of Educational Research*, 48(2): 169–88.

Weiss, E. M. (1999) 'Perceived workplace conditions and first-year teachers' morale, career choice commitment, and planned retention: A secondary analysis', *Teaching and Teacher Education*, 15: 861–79.

Wenger, E. (1998) *Communities of Practice: Learning, Meaning, and Identity.* Cambridge: Cambridge University Press.

Werner, E. and Smith, R. (1988) *Vulnerable but Invincible: A Longitudinal Study of Resilient Children and Youth.* New York: Adams Bannister & Cox.

Wilshaw, M. (2012) 'The Good Teacher', *Journal of the Royal Society of Arts*, Summer 2012: 16–17.

Wood, A. (2005) 'The importance of principals: Site administrators' roles in novice teacher induction', *American Secondary Education*, 33(2): 39–62.

Wright Mills, C. (1959) *The Sociological Imagination.* New York: Oxford University Press.

Wriqi, C. (2008) 'The structure of secondary school teacher job satisfaction and its relationship with attrition and work enthusiasm', *Chinese Education and Society*, 40(5): 17–31.

Yendol-Hoppey, D., Dana, N. and Jacobs, J. (2009) Critical concepts of mentoring in an urban setting. *The New Educator*, 5, 22–44

Yuan, K., Le, V., McCaffrey, D., Marsh, J., Hamilton, L., Stecher, B. and Springer, M. (2013) 'Incentive pay programs do not affect teacher motivation or reported practices: results from three randomized studies', *Educational Evaluation and Policy Analysis*, 35(1): 3–22.

Zembylas, M. (2005) 'Discursive practices, genealogies, and emotional rules: A poststructuralist view on emotion and identity in teaching', *Teaching and Teacher Education*, 21(8): 935–48.

——(2011) 'Teaching and teacher emotions: A post-structural perspective'. In: C. Day and J. Chi-Kin Lee (eds), *New Understandings of Teachers' Work.* Dordrecht, Netherlands: Springer, pp. 31–43.

Zembylas, M. and Schutz, P. (eds) (2009) *Teachers' Emotions in the Age of School Reform and the Demands for Performativity.* Dordrecht: Springer.

Zucker, R. A. (2006) 'Alcohol use and the alcohol use disorders: A developmental-biopsychosocial systems formulation covering the life course'. In: D. Cicchetti and D. Cohen (eds), *Developmental Psychopathology: Vol. 3. Risk, disorder, and adaptation* (2nd edn), pp. 620–56. New York: Wiley.

Index

Page references containing 't' refer to tabulated information. Those containing 'f' refer to figures. Italicised entries refer to titles of documents.